Monatshefte Occasional Volume Number 1

German Studies in the United States
Assessment and Outlook

Edited by

Walter F. W. Lohnes
Valters Nollendorfs

Published for *Monatshefte*

The University of Wisconsin Press

Cosponsored by the Institute of German Studies,
Indiana University

Published 1976

The University of Wisconsin Press
Box 1379, Madison, Wisconsin 53701

The University of Wisconsin Press, Ltd.
70 Great Russell Street, London

First printing

Printed in the United States of America

For LC CIP information see page 264

ISBN 0-299-97009-4 cloth, 0-299-97010-8 paper

ACKNOWLEDGMENTS

The financial support of the following organizations is gratefully acknowledged:

- The National Teachers' Seminary Fund, University of Wisconsin-Madison: initial publication subsidy.

- The Institute of German Studies, Indiana University: matching publication subsidy through a grant from Stiftung Volkswagenwerk.

- The Goethe House New York: hosting of editorial conference in New York, May 1975.

- The Anonymous Fund, University of Wisconsin-Madison: support of editorial conference in Madison, Wisconsin, October 1975.

We also thank a number of other organizations and individuals who gave their time and support to the project, particularly the Modern Language Association and the Association of the Departments of Foreign Languages through their joint staff members Richard I. Brod and Kathryn Buck; the American Association of Teachers of German and its past president Reinhold Grimm; the *Unterrichtspraxis* and its editors Gerhard Weiss and William Petig; and all those who participated with valuable advice in our meetings and conferences, particularly James Marchand and Egon Schwarz.

CONTENTS

INTRODUCTION

The more this volume has neared its completion, the more it seems to have moved away from completeness. Its contribution probably does not lie as much in the conclusions it has reached as in the thinking it has engendered. As you are now about to read what the contributors have wrought, we would like you to consider this only the end of the beginning in a continuing process of professional self-assessment.

We cannot lay claim to being the first who started the process. As the fat 1960's were turning into the lean 1970's, many members of the German-teaching profession in the United States started searching for theoretical and practical solutions to the problems that seemed to descend upon us with unexpected suddenness. The fact that our—primarily practical—problems coincided with the—primarily ideological—self-assessments of *Germanistik* in Germany and the developing trend toward a broader interdisciplinary concept of German culture studies both compounded and simplified our own attempts at problem-solving. It was difficult to separate the specifically American aspects of the crisis from those facing the profession in Germany and internationally. At the same time— the critical thinking processes elsewhere helped us avoid a sense of isolation and provided useful *Denkmodelle* for our own self-evaluation.

But as long as this self-evaluation occurred haphazardly and without a clear focus, it was bound to have haphazard effects. As a 1974 survey in the Personalia of the *Monatshefte* showed, the response to the problems was not only theoretical but practical as well: 25% of the departments responding indicated curricular changes in the previous five years, 16% indicated program changes, and 62% indicated a wide variety of new courses outside existing programs, the majority being literature in translation and culture. Yet this survey also indicated that there was no well-reflected reform movement in action as was revealed by terminological confusion, especially in the area of culture studies. Therefore a coordinated collection of essays by a cross-section of concerned members of the profession seemed to be a natural first step toward a tentative consensus.

To avoid the possibility that individual contributions might stand all alone in splendid isolation, several meetings and editorial conferences were held to outline the basic problems, to determine areas of agreement, and to avoid unnecessary duplication. The first informal meeting took place during the 1973 MLA Conference in Chicago, attended by Charlotte Brancaforte, Joe Fugate, Diether Haenicke, Victor Lange, James Marchand, David Miles, Kenneth Northcott, Lucy Price, Egon Schwarz, and the editors. The discussion centered on some of the problems the profession was facing and ways to overcome them: the economic situation, decreasing enrollments, and some of the inherent weaknesses in traditional programs; the vanishing language requirements; the need for professional interaction on all levels of instruction as a prerequisite for finding viable solutions; and the need to define the specific situation, characteristics, and goals of the German-teaching profession in the United States as compared to *Germanistik* in Germany. It was decided to seek federal funding for a week-long workshop to present position papers and coordinate views.

Our attempts to obtain funds for a workshop were unsuccessful, and we decided instead to seek financial support for more modest regional conferences. Another informal meeting at the 1974 MLA Convention in New York drew additional members of the profession whom we had enlisted, and we established a tentative timetable for completing the project. Through the generosity of the Goethe House in New York an editorial conference took place there on 9 and 10 May 1975 with William Crossgrove, Barbara Elling, Eva and Jere Fleck, Sol Gittleman, Louis Helbig, Valters Nollendorfs, Jeffrey Sammons, and Volkmar Sander participating and with several members of the Goethe House staff and the MLA headquarters in attendance. The Anonymous Fund at the University of Wisconsin-Madison enabled us to assemble the following participants in Madison, Wisconsin on 10 and 11 October 1975: Jürgen Eichhoff, Frank Grittner, Louis Helbig, Peter Heller, Walter Lohnes, Valters Nollendorfs, Kenneth Northcott, Eberhard Reichmann, Henry Remak, Frank Ryder, Guy Stern, and Freeman Twaddell. The conference drew a good attendance, particularly from the local Department of German.

During the conference it became clear that many potentially fruitful areas of investigation had as yet been left unexplored and that to a great extent we still were on the way toward rather than at a consensus, even though we were close to the end and publication deadlines were approaching with undue haste. It also became more and more apparent that the volume—despite, but perhaps even more because of, coordination—was not going to avoid a certain amount of repetition.

And yet—whatever repetition there is, it seems, on second thought, to fulfill at least two important functions. First of all, it reinforces some commonly held insights and ideas and thus constitutes a basis for a consensus. Secondly, occurring as it does in various contexts and perspectives, it points toward some unity in the diversity of opinions and real conditions in which we function. As a matter of fact, in the context of the American educational scene and the way it functions, only a continuing discussion and no final conclusions may be possible.

Therefore it was decided to continue the discussion of professional concerns even after the publication of this volume—at MLA and AATG conventions, at special conferences similar to the editorial conferences in 1975, at professional seminars, and in professional journals. The *Monatshefte* has indicated that henceforth the entire Personalia issue will be devoted to professional matters and that an annual group meeting will take place at the MLA convention to present and discuss contributions to these issues.

Such is the future course as we perceive it. Returning to the present and specifically to this volume you are about to read, we want to point out two potential areas of misunderstanding.

The first has to do with the term German Studies. We have sought to apply it in the broadest possible sense to encompass all instructional and research activities of the profession: both the established ones and the ones now being developed. These include recent endeavors to define new methodologies and programs for interdisciplinary German culture studies. Since these endeavors generally involve both the addition of new substantial components to traditional curricula and a reorientation toward a broader view of our entire mission, the term German Studies has usually been applied more narrowly to mean this addition and reorientation. We prefer the broader conception, which allows for the coexistence of various conceptual and program models ranging from the traditional where still viable to the innovative where feasible, and including various intermediate models where necessary.

In this broader sense, the term German Studies seems also more appropriate to describe the specific characteristics of what we are or should be doing in the United States as compared to the German-speaking countries. German Studies, we think, are not and should not be *Germanistik*, even the *künftige Germanistik* discussed in the two pioneering Reihe Hanser volumes, which assess the situation in Germany. Some of the differences may be philosophic, but most are of a more basic practical, not to say existential, nature:

1. Our *Auseinandersetzung* with old-school *Germanistik* neither had to be nor could be as vehement or central as in Germany. American scholarship never really participated in mainstream developments of *Germanistik*, especially during its less glorious moments during Hitler's reign and the period of post-war readjustment.

2. Our social and educational functions and responsibilities in the United States differ radically from those of our counterparts in the German-speaking countries. What they do is much more central to their entire society and the educational system than what we do to ours.

3. We have to create our own clientele through our language programs, whereas our counterparts in German-speaking countries have a self-renewing inexhaustible supply of pupils and students.

4. Our counterparts in German-speaking countries are primarily interpreters of the *native* language, literature, and culture; we are primarily the teachers and mediators of a *foreign* language, literature, and culture.

5. Specialization is possible to a much greater extent among our colleagues in German-speaking countries than it is in the United States. Our specific situation demands that most of us should be generalists.

6. American education—both on the secondary and higher education levels—is much more diversified and much less centralized than the educational systems in Europe. While our colleagues in the Federal Republic can think in terms of and develop *Denkmodelle* generally applicable to all or at least most educational situations or institutions, we have to contend with a multitude of situations and jurisdictions that preclude instantaneous and uniform reforms even under the most advantageous circumstances.

The second potential misunderstanding has to do with the nature of the contributions. This is not a collection of papers on teaching methodology or subject matter for German Studies in the United States. While some of these items inevitably enter into discussion, they do not form the primary focus of the volume.

The primary focus is twofold: (1) To assess the German-teaching profession in the United States in its full context—from primary to graduate school: its *raison d'*être in the present academic, social, and cultural situation; its structures, programs, and aims; and the people through whom and for whom it functions. (2) To offer strategies for survival and suggestions for self-improvement during the lean years ahead when our well-being and growth will not be able to rely on the benevolence of others but only on our own ingenuity, perseverance, and self-sufficiency.

We hope that the volume will help us all to respond to the future difficulties with perspicuity, wisdom, and self-confidence. We also hope that it will engender a continued dialogue which will help us all to stay in touch with each other and with the times ahead.

W.F.W.L.
V.N.

THOUGHTS IN SEASON

VICTOR LANGE
Princeton University

Interest in the study of languages, ancient or modern, has diminished in the past decade, not only in the United States but in every Western society, to the point where the sturdiest convictions of seasoned teachers and the most fervent pleas of the defenders of humane values seem to have gone unheeded. In Italy the teaching of German is in danger of disappearing altogether from school and university curricula; French and English are, in many German schools, offered merely as electives; in the United States even a level of interest that has for a generation been far below the impressive support given to language study in the Soviet Union seems seriously threatened by the apathy or wrong-headedness of curriculum planners, of counsellors and of those who articulate our educational vision. The teaching of German has, in our schools and colleges, passed through hectic fluctuations between proud enthusiasm and the melancholy acceptance of a steadily declining percentage of its share in the totality of humanistic offerings. We need no statistics to realize how often in the past century the popularity and vitality of the American study of German has been sapped by disaster or folly.

It may be useful and may contribute to the sort of level-headed self-scrutiny without which foreign language study cannot hope to flourish within an increasingly technological-minded educational system, if we take a look at some of the central convictions and impulses that seem over the years to have motivated and sustained the interest of our schools and colleges in the study of German, of the language itself, its literature and, altogether, the social life of which that language and literature are a telling reflection.

We may regard it as an historical axiom which for many generations determined the study of foreign languages, that its ultimate target and its self-evident justification was not merely the acquisition of a practical skill but the prospect of exploring the impressive realization of the "genius" of that language in its social, historical and literary documents. The effective use of a foreign language in situations of personal exchange is, at any rate, a goal that has only recently been offered (or demanded) as a sufficient justification of language learning. Reading and writing have traditionally been the competences that were expected from the relatively scant hours allotted to the study of a modern language. By whatever logic it is urged, this is a perfectly appropriate aim which may or may not be thought to be preferable to a proficiency in the current spoken language. Indeed, I have known intelligent, perceptive and resolute defenders of German or Italian in English schools and colleges who have urged that these be taught as "dead" languages, much like Latin or ancient Greek. Few in this country would seriously argue such a view, even though the advocacy of what is sometimes envisioned as a "reading knowledge" seems (if it is to mean more than a mere decoding competence) to come close to that interesting if eccentric notion. Whether language study is pursued by traditional methods or by the more attractive and, with a sufficient allocation of time, perhaps more rewarding techniques of language instruction that were developed by distinguished American linguists during and after the Second World War, the professed target has been the achievement of an ability to read, understand and reflect upon texts, both literary and casual, that are written in the foreign language, perhaps available only in that language, and conveying something of the energies—aesthetic, social, political or scientific—that are embodied in it.

To offer such a broad definition is not to ignore the wide range of expectations and the scale of proficiency, from the most modest to the near-native, that it may well contain. But if the experience of a foreign language is to result in more than a superficial acquaintance with grammatical rules and exercises, it must be directed towards a close understanding of the texts in which it becomes specific and telling. Literature has, therefore, traditionally been the ultimate object of language teaching—literature in the widest sense of the term and not, certainly, only in its most sophisticated or rarefied mode.

The effort to approach that literature as a linguistic object is only the first in a succession of attempts at understanding its "literacy," the particular ways of its functioning within the web of culture. Literature and culture are inextricably interrelated; yet for an understanding of the forms in which each offers itself to our attention, we must employ methods of approach and of judgment that require specific criteria and a particular range of knowledge. The reading of literature and the reading of culture are, of course, not the same thing: whatever it may be that makes one depend upon the other, each demands certain well-defined and appropriate presuppositions. This is tantamount to saying that teachers of foreign languages, literatures, and cultures can be effective only if they are explicitly aware of these presuppositions, make them the principles and criteria of their work as interpreters and convey them as significant and rewarding to students and future teachers. It need hardly be said that this is a condition for the comprehension of all aggregates of culture: teachers of English or American language or literature must be concerned no less than those of Greek, French or German with the difficult, and challenging, task of operating within a system of critical judgment that will relate the intentions and forms of their subject matter to the avowed aspirations and predilections of their own society.

II

The interpretation of literature, whether of our own tradition and its documents, or, once removed from this elementary condition, as the object of an intercultural sort of curiosity, must proceed from social and individual assumptions and beliefs held by artists and critics alike. A certain coincidence between the experienced social world as it emerges in the native literary texts and in the critical act is to a decisive degree determined by the instrument of the language common to both that provides something like a consensus of the premises and postulates sustaining the totality of literary creation and reception.

If this totality, or homogeneity, seems more or less definable within a single field of linguistic experience, it represents a matter of considerable difficulty in a critical procedure that involves two systems of language and their divergent cultural implications. To read a Chinese document with full awareness of its Chinese ambience should be feasible and rewarding not only for native speakers of Chinese, but, we should like to think, to a significant extent and with due regard for the differences in historical and social assumptions, also for non-Chinese readers. What may be achieved within a closed circle of understanding cannot naively be performed when we move to the far less easily defined procedure of *interpreting* the documents of one given linguistic key to readers thoroughly conditioned in another. To convey, analyze, and relate Wordsworth to English or, with certain modifications, American readers, is one thing; to make "The Prelude" intelligible, palpable and ultimately resonant and effective to French or German readers is quite another. Even if we were to assume that it is the purpose of interpretation to lay bare and make meaningful those social and intellectual elements by which a given work is conditioned, if we thought it possible to articulate to a reader, whether native or foreign, the objectively "English" characteristics, the "English" tradition of feeling, judgment and form within which the Wordsworth poem should be read and understood, we cannot (and perhaps should not) perform this critical act without bringing impulses of opinion or taste to bear upon the text that are imbedded in the cultural matrix of our own linguistic preconceptions.

This, it seems to me, is an issue to which, as interpreters of German literature vis-à-vis American students and readers we have seldom paid sufficient attention. The reading of German literary works by American readers cannot be satisfactorily performed without regard to their own distinctly non-German presumptions; it cannot be made rewarding, that is to say, if we suspend or disregard American cultural sensibilities in favor of historical, philosophical and aesthetic propositions offered in an uncritical spirit either of blind enthusiasm or a relativistic obtuseness.

What I have formulated as a somewhat simplified issue represents the indispensable premise for a critical view at the topography and the mode of operation of what is summarily understood to be *Germanistik* in America. Whatever that term has historically meant within the German education system, it has, in America, for long referred to two distinct areas and modes of teaching and research. In its broadest sense *Germanistik* has, in America, meant the transmission and presentation of German cultural attitudes and institutions, both social and literary, to a fairly disparate and heterogeneous, chiefly academic, audience. It has addressed itself to undergraduates motivated by an interest in the language and civilization of one of the major European societies or, with more specific aims, to more advanced students who tended to specialize in German in hopes of continuing and enlarging their interests on the graduate level. The goals and targets of the two levels, undergraduate and graduate, have traditionally been differentiated in quantitative, seldom however, in methodological terms. For both "tracks," the contents as well as the critical procedures have, almost without exception, been determined by the principles and practices of the German academic establishment.

There can be no doubt that the eminence of German *Germanistik* has for long offered enviable models of scholarly achievement and of intellectual vitality. And in a general sense, that example is properly granted unconditional admiration. Yet, in several critical respects, the conditions under which American *Germanistik* has traditionally operated have differed from those that have given meaning to German Studies within the German educational system. One of these differences has been—until recently—the nearly unshakeable American faith in the "liberalizing" effect which the study of foreign languages and literatures (quite apart from the possible advantage of professional graduate training) has within a carefully designed program of education.

In the classical structure of the German university, both the general educational concerns and the explicit focus of German Studies upon the needs of future teachers were by tradition subordinated to more scholarly aspirations. It is only within the present decade that teacher-oriented "didactics," as a field of *Germanistik*, has become an integral and accepted part of university instruction. For a definition of *Germanistik* in its contemporary practice, this extension represents far more than a mere addition to previously offered subject matter: it reflects the increasingly central conviction that the university study of German literature must not be pursued "for its own sake" but be embedded in a broadly pedagogical or even "political" purpose.

In this respect, then, German and American views of the aims and procedures of *Germanistik* seem to begin to coincide. But the two continue to differ dramatically in at least one respect: if in Germany much of the curriculum planning and of the contents and methods of instruction in German (or similarly English or French) studies presupposes a vital impact upon the subsequent teaching in the schools and upon the social and cultural behavior of students and future teachers, this is, either in scope or intention, scarcely the case in America. The idea, basic to the present German educational philosophy, that the study of any university subject, but especially that of the humanistic and social sciences, should in one way or another contribute to the critical awareness of a citizen who is to be decisively formed by his university studies, this is, we must admit, as yet barely articulated in the curricula of American university or college departments of foreign languages.

Modern linguistic theory has, in Germany as well as in America, to a remarkable degree affected the manner of approach not merely to language study but, more importantly, to the interpretation of literature. Instead of the traditional access to language and literature, whether German or foreign, by way of a philological (that is to say, historical) understanding of speech, contemporary linguistics has impressively pointed to the behavioral nature of language and, consequently, of the documents in which that language is tellingly employed. It has sharpened the awareness of the particular conditions under which the speaker (and writer) of a language develops strategies of communication. To identify these strategies has become one of the most intriguing pursuits of modern literary criticism. Instead of isolating the presumed objective ideas and values contained in a text, its interpretation is now directed at the far more elusive system of obliquely presented intentions, at the recognition of attitudes, of individual and collective beliefs and aspirations.

III

The assertion that we should know a foreign language in order to "understand" the literature in that language is trivial only to those who do not bother to ask the questions that are implied in that presumed platitude. We understand, of course, only what can be related to concepts that are already familiar to us. An understanding of a foreign literature therefore requires the application of critical notions that are extrapolated from a study of our own native tradition and that are subsequently brought to bear upon materials, however strange, that will in some degree respond to the critical questions we bring to them. This elementary consideration seems to me to be the very premise of all forms of cultural confrontation; it applies to anthropological enquiries no less than to critical efforts at understanding literary works written in a foreign language. If we look at the history of the teaching of German literature in the United States, we cannot escape the fact of its almost total dependence upon the impulses and perspectives of *German* literary and historical scholarship.

The superb quality of that scholarship is beyond dispute, and the importance of acquainting American students with its ethos and its individual accomplishments cannot be sufficiently urged. But there is an aspect of American interest in German literature which reaches from an early view of it in undergraduate teaching to the questions and answers that should give meaning to scholarship on a more advanced level: it is the proposition that this study must be nourished by the sensibilities we bring, as American readers, to the understanding and interpretation of texts argued, written and shaped in the foreign language. To insist upon the belief that the foreign work must be judged "on its own terms" would disqualify most of us from a truly rewarding reading not only of the great classics of Russian and Chinese literature but, above all, of the Bible, which we seldom approach "on its own terms" and which, I suspect, few are able adequately to discuss in Hebrew or Greek. I am not here concerned with the possibility or advisability, much underrated by some, of reading and teaching foreign works in English translation; what matters at this time is a more general point: the mode of approach to German texts which is in all too many cases eagerly derived from patterns predefined in the context of German experiences and pedagogical aims, rather than developed from the sources of American reflection and imagination.

We can put it differently and say that German literature, as commonly interpreted in our schools and colleges, has all too often been studied in splendid isolation; students are seldom introduced to major or minor German poetry by encouraging them to consider a given piece, beyond its linguistic curiosity, as a poetic document that requires for its adequate exploration more than naive sentiment and a worshipful respect for its German ambience. We need only consider how seldom (Fairley and Enright are notable exceptions) Goethe's *Faust* has been taught without recourse, grateful or helpless, to meanings and readings that were found pre-digested in half a dozen German commentaries. The courage to draw for the interpretation of a masterpiece written in a foreign language upon native American resources of feeling and judgment, upon issues and experiences articulated in the American context, is a procedure that is rarely practiced by our teachers of German. They prefer instead to unravel German critical concepts before students who might well be led, by their experience of a foreign work, to galvanize their own perceptions.

On the level of exacting textual and historical scholarship, the excellence of individual American contributions to *Germanistik* has for long been readily recognized. If these studies have, often enough, depended upon pre-suppositions derived from German academic practice, this should be no cause for disappointment or for surprise. Recent French critical theory, or Heidegger's categories, have been of obvious benefit for American criticism. Such models have been productive as they have stimulated American sensibilities. For nearly a century American *Germanistik* has drawn for its methods and approaches upon the awesome tradition of German philological preeminence; its objects, its topics, its vocabulary have, until recently, been suggested by attitudes and values pre-shaped by German scholarship and criticism. The most conspicuous of the founding fathers of *Germanistik* in America—Kuno Francke, von Jagemann, Hohlfeld, Fife, Faust, Goebel, Nordmeyer, Roedder, Feise, Kurrelmeyer, Schütze, Morgan—were, if not German natives transplanted after their academic training at German universities, certainly dependent in the direction of their scholarship and their teaching, on German academic ideals. Whatever the depth of their attachment to American life, the justification of their scholarly efforts was derived from an unshakeable faith in the exemplary model of German idealism, both social and cultural. Kuno Francke's celebrated volumes *Die Kulturwerte der deutschen Literatur* (1910, 1923) as well as A.B. Faust's *The*

German Element in the United States (1909) are sustained equally by an unconditional admiration for German values in their most absolute sense and a fervent conviction of their civilizing effect upon American ways of life.

If we cast a glance at the volumes of *Monatshefte* prior to the First World War, we shall be struck by the curious mixture in almost every issue, of labored pedantry and the unquestioned assumption that the teaching of German should be motivated by a passionate and unswerving attachment to the values—political, philosophical and literary—that were then held in Germany: pride in the German imperial power, reverence for the idealism which German artists and thinkers appeared to defend against all corrosion of public and private life by the alien forces of materialism and, most emphatically, the example which this sum of superior aspiration offered for the missionary work of American teachers of German. That this zealous attitude expressed itself in countless contributions whose hortatory passion strikes us today as astonishingly simple-minded is not as surprising as the appearance in the January 1917 issue, of a dithyrambic poem composed by such a distinguished Germanist as Kuno Francke, whose apostrophe to *Deutsches Volk*, we must suspect, fell altogether upon the receptive ears of the profession:

> Wie du jauchzend kämpfest und jauchzend leidest!
> Wie du jauchzend dich an Hingabe weidest!
> Wie du jauchzend zerschleuderst den Ansturm der Welt,
> Ganz auf die innere Kraft nur gestellt! etc.

It is superfluous to point to the pervasive nationalistic tone in much German teaching in America before the First World War: similar jingoism can be found in the journals devoted to the teaching of French or Spanish. What is more important is the consistent reverberation of German concepts that are pronounced in a magisterial tone without regard for their entirely problematical meaning in an American context: "Die Zivilisation," we read in an article published in 1918, "ist etwas was zu vermeiden ist. Die Kultur etwas was bejaht werden muß." It is true that the difference in the level and the quality of scholarly and pedagogical contributions before 1918 and after 1928 when *Monatshefte* resumed publication after a decade of suspension, is remarkable: almost at once readers are now given detailed surveys of the changed intellectual climate in Germany, of the work of Troeltsch, Max Weber, Kahler, and Gundolf. The new historical and critical approaches that had emerged from German scholars such as Walzel, Korff, Strich, or Nadler begin to color and enliven the professional debates among American Germanists and to determine the directions of their more advanced research.

If a residue of admiration for the German philological tradition remained, with changed ingredients, to give self-confidence to American studies of German, this can hardly be deplored. What appears problematical is the indifference of much of that teaching to the receptivity which American students brought to this body of German material, to German methodological notions, and to the German view of their possible uses beyond the classroom. It is necessary not merely to recognize the remarkable quality and usefulness of much of that German-oriented, philologically directed scholarship but, above all, to understand the reason for its continuing claim to legitimacy within the American system of higher education.

The eminent example of German philology, classical as well as modern, was, of course, until the First World War compelling for all literary and textual research, whether English, French, German, or Latin. The three tenets of this faith were, first, the assumption that a maximum of historical documentation and knowledge offered the most rewarding means of access to an understanding of a text; second, that the historical scheme within which a text could and should be given its place and resonance, tended to coincide with a strong nationalistic reading of that history by German political or cultural historians, (not only Treitschke, but more persuasively and less shrilly, Dilthey and K. Lamprecht); such a reading inevitably attached "redemptive" values to such movements as German mysticism and idealism, the "Storm and Stress" rebellion against French classicism, the romantic assertion of distinctly national energies, altogether and repeatedly the triumph of feeling over reason, the resistance to technology and the emerging economic order among German novelists of the mid-nineteeth century or, more recently, the proud assumption of specifically German spiritual energies in the assessment of expressionist literature and art. The third reason for the uncritical projection of a German tradition was the disarming belief that no other canon of literature had, since Lessing, Herder, Goethe, and Schiller, so impressively offered instances of an idealistic view of the human condition—a view that rested on a generalized understanding of man, rather than on the more cautious, more specific modern interest in the particularity of his nature and of his social and cultural setting. Even before the turn of the century, and strikingly so after the First World War, the idealistic and historical bases of the German philological tradition, however eroded by critical theories and methods, were still essentially tied to German forms of thinking and therefore not immediately transferable to non-German subject matter.

At the same time, during the early decades of the century, American life and literature developed a remarkable sense of self-reliance, a pride in the specificity of its own historical experience, a palpable resolve to emancipate itself from European precepts and to resist what James Russell Lowell had considered "a certain condescension in foreigners" towards the American experience. Two distinguished, though in some respects eccentric, works by American scholars, Irving Babbitt's *The New Laocoon* (1910) and Santayana's *Three Philosophical Poets* (1910) suggest the degree to which points of view resolutely un-European and altogether free of the terminology of the pervasive German scholarship could be advanced.

Little of this independence of judgment can be found in American academic studies of German; indeed, it was the more journalistic interest in contemporary and classical German literature with which men like James Huneker and H.L. Mencken proposed to nourish the growing American self-awareness. Academic Germanists, on the contrary, stubbornly asserted the preeminence of the methodology of their German peers. To examine the twenty volumes of the formidable set of *German Classics* (1913 ff.) is to recognize the undiminished respect of American teachers of German for the still powerful ideological model of German critical opinion and, altogether, of German *Germanistik*: the long Introduction to the *German Classics* was written not by an American scholar, but by R.M. Meyer, the most prolific among German academic critics. This sort of dependence is, of course, a complex issue which the political and cultural historians must analyze. But what matters for our present argument, because it determined German Studies in the United States until the Second World War, is the palpable discrepancy between the procedures of literary scholars and critics and those pursued by academic teachers (and students) of German.

Modern language studies in America depended for their appeal in large measure upon an assumption that was compelling in the nineteenth century but that has become increasingly dubious in our time: the assumption that these studies offer nearly absolute models of thought, behavior and artistry which American students could only be urged to emulate. This conviction, whether applied to Italian art, French civilization, or German literature to some degree continued effective until well into the present. But as it ceased to be unequivocally persuasive, the function of these subjects in American schools and colleges had to be reconsidered. In this complex of respect and admiration, German philological models had seemed a central ingredient for the pursuit of literary scholarship: as this tradition ceased to be unquestioningly compelling, the bond of common purpose and approach that had previously joined the study of *all* foreign literatures began to loosen. What had been a universal faith in the methods of German philology was henceforth replaced by impulses drawn from the critical practices of French, English or German, but which were, in turn, seldom explicitly related to native American sensibilities.

It is this discrepancy and this lack of interest among American teachers of foreign literatures in bringing American curiosity and American intellectual and literary experiences into the treatment and interpretation of European letters that has in large measure contributed to the diminished relevance of German, or French, studies in America. It is well to remember that German, English or French scholars, critics and readers have never failed to read the great works of the European tradition in terms concretely appropriate to their own self-awareness. It is, of course, a deliberate exaggeration, but not without its truth, if we say that the best English scholars of Italian have been wont to read Dante (in the original) as though he were an English poet, Germans as though Shakespeare or Shaw were, in a special sense, German writers, the French as though Wagner had written his libretti as well as his music preeminently for them. This "natural" reading of foreign literature qua literature is, among American experts in foreign literatures a rare skill and one only recently declared legitimate.

It was not the echo of the methodology of Wölfflin or Strich, of Petersen or Korff, of Boeckmann or Emrich that brought German literature into a lively relationship with the sensibilities of American students, not the preoccupation in the nineteen-thirties of American *Germanistik* with the German interpretation of *historical* concepts of stylistic topologies. It was rather the striking effectiveness which some German refugee scholars evolved in an academic setting in which they had to make every effort to be heard and recognized. With few exceptions (such as, it seems to me, Karl Viëtor) a considerable number of exiled German scholars and critics of literature, history and philosophy (Sommerfeld, Schirokauer, Seidlin, Bergsträsser, Cassirer, Tillich, Holborn, etc.) moved to examine and broaden the range of their interest and their methodology in order to become partners in that far-reaching critical discourse which so strikingly enlivened American humanistic scholarship in the years after the Second World War. What German refugee scholars contributed to the American study of art history and musicology, or psychology and anthropology, is paralleled by the indelible effect on literary scholarship of René Wellek, Erich Auerbach or Leo Spitzer.

This inestimable enrichment of American academic life accomplished, beyond any detailed scholarly contributions, a shift in the view of the functioning of "foreign" models and perspectives of thinking, of the "uses" of a variety of cultural materials and forms, within the American experience.

It is thus not surprising that American students of the modern languages should in the past decade have sought increasingly to see the foreign culture and its literature in "comparative" terms and no longer in the light of the apodictic claims to its superior efficacy. This shift in perspective is altogether splendid and of considerable consequence for the future concerns of our profession. It need not, indeed should not, result in an indifference to the importance of reading the German or French texts in the original language. To read Hölderlin or works of the German Expressionists, of Benn or Brecht or Celan should, among other perhaps over-riding benefits, lead to an understanding of the role which the language and literature of a given linguistic group can play, for better or worse, at a particular historical moment and in a particular social context. This totality of significance we must analyze with an incorruptible eye for the specific circumstance as well as its exemplary implications.

IV

We are today facing not merely a temporary decline in interest in some of the modern languages but the emergence of vehicles and media of universality— whether the mathematical language of the computer or the new language of rock music—which counteract the traditional reverence for an available range and hierarchy of contents and symbols; among these threatened vehicles of civilization is language shaped and illuminated in literature. Unless we offer in our work as teachers and scholars constant reminders of the creative resources of language and of its differentiated power in an interplay of native and foreign speech, we shall not stem the ominous drift towards a "sound-culture" and a further weakening of the verbal order.

However ready we may be to enlarge the range of our concerns beyond literature in its preeminent status, however obvious the need for making the terrain of our work as broad and rich as possible, we must not forget, as interpreters of the foreign culture, that our ultimate task is the articulation of issues and problems that must be related to questions that arise here and now. The ideal of impartiality and objectivity can be easily misapplied to serve lethargy and self-satisfaction. We are, for instance, rightly, asked to speak about life and letters not merely in one part of Germany but in the DDR as well; but the presentation and study of that literature will be meaningless if it is undertaken as though it were merely a body of experience and writing that happens, like Austrian or Swiss literature, to be written and published in an adjoining geographical area. We must make clear, with due critical respect for its legitimacy and its merits, that that literature depends upon a social vision which is only in its most abstract consequences seriously shared by the West German establishment and which, if properly understood, is barely compatible with the political faith professed by a large number of Americans and, by inference, of American teachers and students of German. It is a peculiarly comforting notion held by many of those charged with interpreting the whole canon of German culture to American students and readers that these differences, radical and ineluctible as they are in their consequences, can be presented with protestations either of objectivity or of urbanity, as though they were, in some vague sense, interesting or curious, but ultimately without much serious force upon the thinking of our students.

Ever since foreign social and cultural patterns have ceased to serve as admirable and superior models of behavior, ever since the social scientist has urged a judicious detachment and offered contrastive principles instead of the hortatory and even adulatory attitudes that determined foreign language teaching for nearly a century prior to World War II, we have had no alternative except to embrace the modest, if more sensible, goal of comparative approaches. As scholars and teachers of German, we cannot underrate the importance of making the broadest possible range of information on German life available to students on all levels of interest. But what seems to me of equal or even greater urgency is the resolution that is required to find means of relating our material to the receptive expectations and the individual and social predispositions and potentials of those who are willing to work with us. It is not enough to proclaim, however vigorously and persuasively, the excellence of German literature or the charms of German customs and antiquities or the pathos of much recent German history; as interpreters we must at all times ask ourselves how this body of behavior, knowledge, achievement or failure can become alive in the minds who bring to the study of a foreign culture not a *tabula rasa*, and who are not, as Locke put it, "void of all characters, without any ideas." We cannot hope to make our knowledge truly significant and effective without relating it to the experiences by which students grow into citizens. All teaching, especially of so complex and fascinating a subject as the understanding of a foreign culture, must ultimately contribute to the shaping of minds in a society which cannot flourish by abstract projections of an earthly paradise but only by the resolution of its teachers and learners to move critically towards richer perception, clearer definitions and humane decisions.

To live within the hypotheses and practices of one single culture is not merely a deplorable sign of provincialism, but an admission of unpreparedness for the social and political demands that contemporary society makes upon us. Not to have read the great literary documents of our time—Joyce, Mann, Beckett—not to have enquired into the impulses and formal solutions that have produced Schönberg or Pollock and Henry Moore, not to be familiar with Max Weber or Piaget or Wittgenstein is to be incapable of meeting the benumbing, or intoxicating, onslaught of the political and social platitudes that seek to win our acquiescence.

What is needed in order to return the teaching of modern languages and literatures to a position of general effectiveness (as against its value as mere entertainment or as a tourist facility) is the conviction that only a comparative or contrastive approach will elicit the sort of questions and produce the sort of answers that are likely to affect the lives of our students as members of a mature society. We shall be quickly and justly eliminated as participants in a productive system of education if we cannot persuade our peers as well as our students that what we teach goes to the heart of our vision of an intelligent and creative society, that it must ultimately be concerned with opening minds to the challenges that come to us from the great writers whose voice we cannot afford to disregard. This is the gist of that memorable passage in a letter which in 1904 the twenty-year-old Kafka wrote to a friend:

> If the book we are reading does not awaken us like a fist hammering on our skull, why do we read it? So that it should make us happy? Good God, we would be quite happy if we had no books, and, if need be, we could ourselves write such books as make us happy. But what we need are books that come upon us like a great misfortune and that distress us like the death of a friend whom we loved better than we love ourselves; as though we had been driven deep into the woods, far away from all other human beings; like suicide. A book must be an ice-axe to break the frozen sea within us.

SOME CONSIDERATIONS ON OUR INVISIBILITY

JEFFREY L. SAMMONS
Yale University

It has become customary in our agony of self-examination to identify practices and habits in our profession that ought promptly to be changed; usually less explicit is the implication that there are actual persons responsible for these practices and habits who ought to be induced to change themselves, or, failing that, be made to disappear, if that can be arranged. I have made such arguments and proposals myself on occasion, but my remarks here are not of this kind. Rather, I wish to point to a worrisome aspect of our situation that is truly nobody's fault and, in a sense, is the reverse side of a great strength in our profession. The problem I have in mind is, in fact, not subject to immediate correction, though I think it would be well to become more conscious of it, and perhaps there are ways we can begin to mitigate its effects.

The point of my remarks can be verified by anyone with a little private experiment. Make a list of the twenty outstanding Germanists in North America in regard to their creativity, their productivity, and their accomplishments on the forward edge of scholarship in our field. Now ask yourself how many of these habitually write in German, publish abroad, and consequently have much larger reputations in the German-speaking countries than in the American academic community. I should be surprised if many lists showed fewer than twelve persons of this description. My own (which will not be produced even under subpoena) came up with fourteen, of whom two are borderline cases. When, in full awareness of the dubiousness of such rankings, I tried to halve the list, the proportion shot up to eight out of ten. My list, although it will differ from those of others, is not, I think, eccentric, and I believe it illustrates a condition that has some ramifications for our welfare generally.

There is no need to go at any length into the historical reasons for this. We all know that, up until around the First World War, German language and literature throve in American universities, so that our subject was well integrated into the educated consciousness. A pretty piece of evidence of this among many is the course of elegant and amiable lectures on *The Spirit of Modern Philosophy* given by the eminent idealist Josiah Royce to a general audience at Harvard in 1890, in which the philosopher was able to allude easily to Goethe and Schiller, Novalis, the Schlegels, and Jean Paul, Heine and Hoffmann, with obvious assurance that the audience would understand whereof he spoke. The subsequent deplorable deterioration in the standing of our field was relieved only in the 1930's by the influx of immigrants and exiles who contributed vastly to its recovery. A new generation of scholars from abroad after World War II made possible the great expansion whose end we have recently experienced. Therefore it is not surprising that much of the intellectual leadership in our field should be rooted abroad, and we can easily calculate where we would be if this were not the case. We certainly have every reason to be proud of the contributions of American Germanists to scholarship abroad, to criticism and theory, and to every sort of learned task from book reviewing and bibliography to participation in major editing projects. We can be confident that, from this point of view, American *Germanistik* is not negligible. But, with all the gratitude and gratification that these circumstances must arouse in us, we may still observe that certain problems have emerged in consequence. The question is whether there really is an American *Germanistik* participating in the fullness of its strength in American scholarly life, whether some substantial portion of our scholarship has not become a province of the German university and therefore a great deal more visible there than here, as well as more preoccupied with its concerns than with ours. A further question is whether the bad situation we face at the bottom of the academic pyramid, with declining enrollments and the constriction of opportunity for younger scholars, may not have something to do with our relative absence from the general American community of the educated and from the consciousness and respect of our fellows.

It is at the interface between scholarship and the larger educated public that this absence is perhaps most evident. The names of our leading scholars, some of which are household words abroad, do not seem to come to mind to editors when contributions are solicited to the major vehicles of general informed discussion. Our appearances within recent recall in the *New York Times Book Review* have been, to put the best possible word on it, infrequent. I have not looked again at the whole run of the *New York Review of Books,* but I have read it religiously since its first issue and I can only recall one occasion on which an American Germanist contributed a review article; certainly the overall tendency of that important publication has been to turn to Britain or to scholars in other fields when topics of German literature and the culture come up. I have, however, made a count in what seems to me a fair example of a challenging and prestigious interdisciplinary publication relevant to our interests, *New Literary History.* Of the 204 articles that have appeared in its first six years, not a single one has been contributed by an American Germanist, although it is hardly an insular journal, having featured Hans Robert Jauss, Robert Weimann, Wolfgang Iser, J.P. Stern, and even Wilhelm Girnus. Surely this record is out of proportion to the intellectual strength of American *Germanistik* and reflects a fairly thorough condition of incognito that begins in the university community itself.

One of my eminent colleagues occasionally mutters about the sort of person who appears to know more about the latest quarrel over parity at the University of Bremen than he does about the operation of his own undergraduate institution. I don't suppose that this is a generalizable complaint, although it is possible that some of our colleagues have not wholly grasped that the undergraduate college is the heart of the American university, upon whose health the health of the whole institution depends, and that, especially now, the undergraduate program in our field is a much more important responsibility than our over-extended graduate programs. It does seem to me that there are certain disadvantages in an American *Germanistik* that uncritically accepts models for its renovation from the abrasive discussion abroad about a *künftige Germanistik*. We have a different task to accomplish and we are in a very different kind of situation.

German *Germanistik* is a mass subject with a crucial social function. Much of the radicalism in contemporary discussion emerges from the recognition that the primary function of German *Germanistik* is the training of schoolteachers. Naturally didactic and pedagogical issues, questions of ideology and historical understanding, all kinds of bitter reckonings with the weight of the past have shaped the debate. Here, however, our subject is one that contains a potential for enrichment and the widening of horizons that is not self-evident to the culture in which we live. We have to compete for attention and show our public that we have in our keeping matters worthy of interest. In this respect the current German iconoclasm toward the canon is of little help, for our canon is not established in our public to begin with. Surely we cannot approach students who know Wordsworth and Keats, Jane Austen and Henry James, with Gutzkow, Freiligrath, or Georg Weerth as examples of the strength we have to offer. Our colleagues in the English departments are happy to take charge of Goethe and the Romantics, Kafka and Mann; are we to leave these to them and preoccupy ourselves with *poetae minores* and *querelles allemandes* about subliterature, reception history, and the giving of ideological grades to literary texts? Several years ago, upon the completion of a pedestrian tunnel at my university, the first graffito to appear on its now rather—uh—colorful walls advised: "Read Kleist." I expect that, in this country, we shall be better off reading Kleist than reading Gervinus.

The question reaches into scholarly practice as well. Some years ago this was less of an issue, as German literary study passed through what turned out to be a brief episode of textual criticism, so that for a time there was the appearance of a shared community of scholarship. In retrospect it may appear that *werkimmanente Interpretation* and the New Criticism were less identical than they first seemed to be, especially in regard to the New Criticism's democratizing origins and rational foundations. In any case, literary criticism and *Literaturwissenschaft* have again bifurcated—the intellectual worlds, say, of Murray Krieger and Jürgen Habermas are wholly non-contiguous—and it would seem to be the appropriate task of an American *Germanistik* to achieve a double optic upon this development: on the one hand seeking a thoughtful and sympathetic transmission of current German preoccupations for their value in enriching and renovating literary study; on the other hand engaging it critically by the standards of what is after all a very great tradition of literary criticism and theory that is our native patrimony. Should it not trouble us that of the two major American books that have endeavored to meet the first responsibility, the author of one, Fredric Jameson's *Marxism and Form,* is a Romanist, and of the other, Martin Jay's *The Dialectical Imagination,* a historian? The recently founded journal, *New German Critique,* is an instructive and, within limits, valuable contribution to this purpose, but its rigorous sectarian allegiance is likely to inhibit its resonance. The most pressing need is not for a deeper German-centered parochialism, but for bringing a more cosmopolitan experience to bear upon the new dogmatics of *Literaturwissenschaft.*

This appears to me to be a task that we are discharging hardly at all, neither in a mediating nor in a critical fashion. Would it not seem to the advantage of an American *Germanistik,* as it has been regularly to German studies in Great Britain, to avail itself of the intellectual resources nearest at hand, not only to make itself intelligible and useful to its own public, but also to contribute something to *Germanistik* as an international discipline? It troubles me sometimes to see American-based Germanists occasionally sharing the wild misconceptions and poorly informed dismissals of Anglo-American criticism that are customary in German dissertations. The closest most of us seem to get to a poetics in any way resembling that taken for granted in the institutions in which we are housed is Ingarden. Surely this is an unwise limitation to impose upon ourselves, especially insofar as the center of gravity of literary criticism, and of literary theory and aesthetics generally, was for some fifty years located in the English-speaking countries, a hegemony that has only recently been challenged by European developments. It is my observation—and it is a curious one—that this task of assimilation and informed confrontation is now predominantly being carried out, not by West Germans or Americans, but by Eastern Europeans—besides Robert Weimann in East Germany, we encounter such names as Viktor Žmegač and Zdenko Škreb, Vladimír Karbusický and Zoran Konstantinović, and that of the brilliant Polish theoretician Stefan Morawski. If an American scholar could produce a treatise from a non-Marxist point of view of the stature of Morawski's *Inquiries into the Fundamentals of Aesthetics* (Cambridge, Mass.: MIT Press, 1974), that would be an achievement redounding to our credit and standing. It might be mentioned in passing that Morawski has not only heard of John Dewey, but actually composed his book in contact with the greatest of American aestheticians, Monroe Beardsley. I have not seen much heedfulness of this kind among our colleagues. Even a subject like literary sociology, now an inextricable component of *Literaturwissenschaft,* ought to be pursued by us with some involvement, even if a critical one, with, say, Kenneth Burke and Hugh Dalziel Duncan, Richard Altick and William Charvat, César Graña and George Dickie, not to speak of British contributors like Bruford, Watt, Hoggart, and Williams. In functioning as an outer annex of German *Germanistik,* only accidentally located in North America, we are failing our public, which understandably ignores us, and failing as well to provide the critical foil from which *Literaturwissenschaft* could well profit.

On similar grounds, I think we need to be a little careful that our efforts to protect and improve our situation do not become so fixated on problems of curriculum and student numbers that they carry us altogether out of the scholarly community. The development of strategies for the diversification of the German field and for impressing our public within and without the university with the significance of German life and culture is certainly very necessary. But suggestions that our difficulties can be relieved by articulating an animus against literature or by calling for an end to scholarly productivity have little merit. The one can only reinforce the readiness of some of our colleagues in the humanities to suspect that we do not have in our keeping a corpus of value commensurate with their own, while the other would not only soon leave us with nothing to teach that was not wholly dependent on foreign scholarship, but would deepen our isolation and accelerate our demise. It is futile to think that a discipline can maintain itself for very long in the academic community without scholarly standing, and it will be risky to allow our justified and needful concerns about pedagogy and practicality to submerge that consideration. Conscientious teaching is grounded in scholarship. (By scholarship I mean, of course, study, not necessarily the quantity of journal articles.) It requires long, living immersion in the areas of learning. Consequently I doubt that retraining ourselves in allegedly relevant topics by means of self-inflicted crash courses will be a healthy long-term solution. Students have a right to more and they know the difference; furthermore, the students are not our only constituency, and our welfare may well turn more in the long run on the regard of our peers. I worry that our field is developing a crisis-management ingenuity devised to make a public show of our usefulness rather than considering the ends to which our present and available strengths are being applied.

Furthermore, we tend to increase our isolation by a curious, I think sometimes rather fussy, allergy to the English language. We give German titles to one of our scholarly journals and to the pedagogical organ of our profession, even though much of their contents are written in English. I do not mean to suggest that anybody but ourselves would read them if their titles were in English, but we ought in principle to take cognizance of the fact that German is at present a semi-exotic language in the United States and employing it is rather like dropping a *Tarnkappe* over a publication. In recent years several conferences and workshop meetings have been held that have been truly encouraging displays of excellence in our field, but they might as well have been held in Klagenfurt, for, almost without exception, the contributions and discussions have been in German, so that the valuable volumes they have generated have had to be published abroad. It has all been very edifying for internal use, but we could hardly make ourselves more invisible to our environment if we were trying to be a conspiracy. Such a policy is not likely to engage the enthusiastic attention of sponsoring institutions, and the consequence is likely to be unstable support. The overwhelming bulk of our major work is written in German and published abroad. I believe that I purchase nearly every book published by an American university press on a subject of German literature; I do not find that this outlay weighs heavily on my budget. In this connection I often think of the *Yale French Review,* which has established a considerable esteem and rolls along regularly on a modest subsidy. I take it that its success is due not only to its worthwhile topics, but also to its policy of accepting contributions in English only, a considerable concession for Romanists, who used to think that cultural matters could only be discussed in French.

It is not clear to me how much we can do about all this, although an articulate recognition of our situation ought to be of some use; it would doubtless be worthwhile if the ongoing struggle to improve our standing at the curricular level were to be accompanied by some introspection on the heights of our professional work. Probably the future holds some changes. It is evident that the combination of constricted employment opportunities and current immigration regulations will greatly diminish the influx of foreign scholars into our universities. This is a misfortune in some respects that will cause us trouble before long, but one consequence is likely to be a gradual Americanization of our field, which may prove desirable if it does not go too far. We must always be bilingual and multicultural in our departments; we must always maintain a productive interdependence with the cultures we study; and it would be dreadfully regressive if we were to reach a point where our understanding and judgment of those cultures were to rest solely on the common sense of our own; at the same time I think we should seek a way back into the shared life of the American academic community.

In the meantime, there are two things we might mull over. It is my observation that in some of our best institutions, when senior positions become available, there is a tendency to try to move the acknowledged stars of our profession back and forth across the map. This practice is not peculiar to our discipline; under the circumstances, however, a greater readiness to promote middle-rank people, many of whom do have a greater symbiosis with the academic environment, would be desirable as a policy. In the present hard times this doubtless means constant squabbling with administrations about promotion and tenure, but that is an obligation we have to the integrity of our profession and it needs to be pursued not only in individual cases, but as an issue of national policy for all professional organizations. Secondly, some of our more resourceful colleagues should put their heads together to see if there is anything that can be done to relieve the dearth of publishing opportunities in this country. University presses are growing increasingly inhospitable, and many were never very forthcoming to us anyway, having little idea of who we are or what we do. Our journals grow thinner while the backlog of submissions and book reviews grows fatter. Younger scholars have to dig deeply into shallow pockets for publication subsidies, especially for publication abroad. I wish we were not obliged to do so much of this. Publication abroad is all right for internal communication and for establishing the scholar's own credentials, but, so far as visibility in the academic community is concerned, even an English-language book published in Germany or Switzerland or Holland might as well have been dropped into the Atlantic. We need at least a holding action on publishing opportunities, so that they do not gradually vanish altogether like the Cheshire cat.

Our problem, however, is more than one of strategic behavior in our academic and social environment. I think it would be a mistake for our upcoming generation to become wholly assimilated to the current *furor teutonicus.* There have been important developments in *Literaturwissenschaft,* and American colleagues have been making splendid contributions to it. But, on the whole, what German literary study may have gained in intensity of purpose has been purchased with an increasing impoverishment of vision and sensibility. Nowhere is this more evident than in my own subject, Heine, where the gain in understanding is sadly out of proportion to the quantity of verbiage and commotion that has been generated. I am afraid that much of what is solemnly or vociferously debated in our field would seem comic and archaic, perhaps occasionally somewhat ominous, to many of our colleagues in our own institutions. At the same time we tend to put ourselves out of the control of interdisciplinary dialogue by an inward turning, our tendency to speak only to one another in codes that only we recognize. This is not to say that the most significant impulses of contemporary *Literaturwissenschaft* are irrelevant to American scholarship; indeed, American literary criticism is badly in need of a confrontation with them, so that we might be relieved of such spectacles as the mighty Northrop Frye disposing of literary sociology by jousting with a paper tiger like Marshall McLuhan. But we can only participate in this necessary reciprocal enrichment if we remember where we live and for whose benefit we are supported.

THE PROFESSION: FIGURES AND TRENDS

VOLKMAR SANDER
New York University

Futurology is a risky undertaking, and planning the future of education seems to be no exception. On both sides of the Atlantic, and regardless of political and social systems, all nations have been caught unprepared first for the expansion due to the postwar population explosion and then again for the anticipated shrinkage in student enrollment or spiraling cost during a recession. The alternative to poor planning, on the other hand, is obviously not to stop anticipating the future but to try harder to make correct projections and to prepare accordingly.[1]

General Enrollment

Although the spectacular growth in enrollment that we became accustomed to in the sixties is slowing down, overall enrollment in institutions of higher education will continue to increase, if on a much smaller scale:

Total enrollment

1972 (actual):   9,215,000
1976 (projected):   10,034,000
1982 (projected):   10,416,000 (plus 13% over 1972)

This overall figure is deceptive, however. For if broken down into 4-year and 2-year institutions it becomes apparent that the lion's share of the expected growth (62.5%) will take place in the 2-year institutions in non degree-credit enrollment, whereas the 4-year institutions will grow hardly at all after 1976, and actually decline after 1980:

---

[1] Besides reports published by the U.S. Department of Health, Education and Welfare/ Education Division, I am particularly indebted to Richard I. Brod, Director of MLA Foreign Language Programs and Coordinator of ADFL, for the following data.

	1972 actual	1982 projected	percent change
4-year institutions			
degree-credit enrollment	6,473,000	6,684,000	+ 3.3%
non-degree credit enrmt.	76,000	69,000	− 9.2%
Total 4-year	6,549,000	6,753,000	+ 3.1%
2-year institutions			
degree-credit enrollment	1,792,000	2,243,000	+25.2%
non-degree credit enrmt.	874,000	1,420,000	+62.5%
Total 2-year	2,666,000	3,663,000	+37.4%

More crucial are the numbers of actual and future high school students, both for their immediate impact on the demand for certified teachers now and in the near future as well as the reserve pool of future college students. The total number of 14–17 year-olds will decline by about 15% by 1983:

Age:	14–17	18–21
1972:	16,522,000	15,362,000
1978:	16,254,000	16,900,000
1983:	13,996,000	15,955,000

According to one report, the 18–21 age group will have shrunk to 14 million by 1988.[2] Enrollment in grades 9–12 by 1982 will have decreased by 11% in public, 14% in private schools over 1972. This shrinking number of high school students accounts for a predicted loss of 3% of classroom teachers' positions between now and 1982, practically limiting job opportunities to the relatively small number of natural attrition through retirement. In absolute numbers, the demand for additional certified teachers in all fields, which between 1968 and 1972 was about 200,000 annually, is expected to drop to about 170,000 annually for the five year span 1973–77, and to 150,000 annually for 1978–82.

Foreign Languages

Even during the period of overall growth during the sixties, the share of foreign languages in high school, although increasing in absolute numbers, did not grow very much when compared with the general growth in enrollment. It did, however, grow in higher education, especially on the graduate level.

The figures for high school foreign languages enrollment for three key years were:

[2] Allan Cartter, "The Academic Labor Market," in: Margaret Gordon, ed., *Higher Education and the Labor Market* (Carnegie Commission on Higher Education, 1974).

	1960	*1965*	*1970*
Public HS	8,649,495 (100%)	11,611,197 (100%)	13,301,883 (100%)
All MFL's	1,867,358 (21.7%)	3,067,613 (26.4%)	3,514,053 (26.4%)
Spanish	933,409 (10.8%)	1,426,822 (12.3%)	1,810,775 (13.6%)
French	744,404 (8.6%)	1,252,373 (10.8%)	1,230,686 (9.3%)
German	150,764 (1.7%)	328,028 (2.8%)	410,535 (3.1%)
Latin	654,670 (7.6%)	591,445 (5.1%)	265,293 (2.0%)

By 1972–73 the percentage of enrollment in all foreign languages combined had again dropped to 24.4% (for comparison: home economics: 24.8%; industrial arts: 30.4%; music: 32.7%).

On the college level, an MLA survey taken in the fall of 1974 shows the following trends[3]:

	1970 over 1968	*1972 over 1970*	*1974 over 1972*	*1974 over 1968*
French	−7.4%	−18.4%	−13.6%	−34.8%
German	−6.3%	−12.8%	−14.1%	−29.6%
Italian	12.8%	−2.7%	−0.9%	8.7%
Russian	−11.1%	0.6%	−10.7%	−20.1%
Spanish	6.7%	−6.3%	−0.7%	−0.7%
Total	−1.8%	−11.5%	−7.9%	−19.9%

One of the major reasons for the decline in foreign language enrollment is, of course, the lack of pressure provided by college entrance and degree requirements. Although there is no proof of increased student hostility toward foreign language study in particular, the decline in foreign language enrollment can be linked directly to student resistance and rejection of requirements in general. A decade ago only one in ten colleges required no knowledge of a foreign language at all, fully 90% required some knowledge either for entering or for the degree. By 1975 the statistic had changed to roughly 4:6. The breakdown is as follows:

	1965	*1970*	*1975*
Institutions with entrance requirements:	33.6%	27.4%	18.6%
Institutions with degree requirements:	88.9%	76.7%	54.0%
Institutions with entrance but no degree req'ts	2.0%	5.0%	7.6%
Institutions with degree but no entrance req'ts	57.3%	54.3%	43.2%
Total with entrance and/or degree requirements	90.9%	81.7%	61.8%
Total with neither entrance nor degree req'ts	9.1%	18.3%	38.2%

[3]*ADFL Bulletin*, 7:2 (November 1975).

German

Growth in the area of German in the sixties was even more spectacular than that of foreign languages in general, and the impending decline will be even harsher. The number of institutions teaching German were:

1965: 1,358   1970: 1,649   1972: 1,433

The 1975 *Peterson's Annual Guide to Graduate Study* lists 180 programs giving advanced degrees in German, of which 164 are in the U.S., 16 in Canada. The *Monatshefte* Personalia 1974–75 lists a total of 212 departments offering German with the following breakdown as to levels:

	U.S.	Canada	Total
Offering no degree:	4	0	4
Up to B.A. degree:	64	10	74
Up to M.A. degree:	54	9	63
Up to Ph.D. degree:	62	9	71
Total:	184	28	212

The graduate expansion rate was far too rapid in view of the diminishing role foreign languages now play in the undergraduate curriculum. This becomes even more evident when looking at the various levels of higher degrees (USOE figures):

Degrees awarded in German	B.A.	M.A.	Ph.D.
1960	659	126	21
1961	847	153	37
1962	1,075	212	44
1963	1,317	274	30
1964	1,591	344	75
1965	1,798	414	63
1966	2,061	514	93
1967	2,193	637	93
1968	2,368	771	117
1969	2,718	762	126
1970	2,652	669	118
1971	2,601	690	144
1972	2,477	608	167

Thus the number of B.A.'s awarded grew by roughly 370%, that of M.A.'s by 480%, and of Ph.D.'s by 800%. The most disturbing conclusion emerging from these figures, however, is that whereas the number of B.A.'s and M.A.'s had started to decline by 1971 and had reached again about the level of 1967 by 1972, the number of Ph.D.'s continued to rise (see the next table). The steep rise in Ph.D. production in German during the late 1960's and early 1970's is partly due to enlarged programs of older institutions but also to the addition of a number of new ones instituted during the last decade, as the following list, compiled from the *Monatshefte,* shows:

	1965	66	67	68	69	70	71	72	73	74	Total
U. of Alberta	–	–	–	–	–	1	3	–	1	–	5
Boston College	–	–	–	–	–	–	–	4	2	1	7
Boston Univ.	–	1	–	–	–	–	1	–	–	–	2
Brigham Young	–	–	–	–	–	–	1	–	1	–	2
U. of Brit. Col.	–	–	–	1	–	1	–	–	3	3	8
Brown	–	–	2	1	1	2	–	1	1	3	11
Bryn Mawr	–	–	1	–	–	1	–	1	3	–	6
U. of Calif											
Berkeley	2	2	–	4	10	4	4	3	6	1	36
Davis	–	–	–	–	–	–	–	–	4	2	6
Los Angeles	3	2	3	2	3	3	7	7	6	3	39
Riverside	–	–	–	–	–	–	–	2	2	1	5
Santa Barbara	–	–	–	1	–	–	1	1	1	–	4
Santa Cruz	–	–	–	–	–	–	–	1	–	1	2
Case Western Res.	–	–	–	1	–	–	2	2	1	1	7
Catholic U.	–	1	–	–	–	–	–	–	–	–	1
U. of Chicago	1	1	3	1	3	2	–	3	3	6	23
Cincinnati	–	3	–	2	2	1	1	–	2	1	12
U. of Colorado	–	5	3	2	1	4	4	4	4	4	31
Columbia	3	1	–	7	4	2	5	3	1	3	29
U. of Conn.	–	4	1	2	–	1	1	3	4	3	19
Cornell	1	2	–	–	1	11	3	2	7	1	28
CUNY	–	–	–	–	–	–	–	2	2	–	4
Florida	–	–	–	–	–	–	–	–	1	–	1
Geo. Wash. U.	–	1	–	–	–	–	2	2	–	–	5
Harvard	1	6	4	4	4	10	3	5	8	6	51
Illinois	4	1	4	–	3	3	7	2	7	7	38
Ill. Chicago	–	–	–	–	–	–	–	–	1	–	1
Indiana	5	3	3	–	4	4	9	12	6	6	52
Iowa U.	–	1	5	–	–	–	–	–	–	–	6
U. of Iowa	1	–	–	–	–	–	2	–	2	5	10
Johns Hopkins	2	1	1	2	4	3	5	5	5	2	30
U. of Kansas	2	2	–	1	4	2	2	4	3	4	24
U. of Kentucky	–	–	–	–	–	–	1	2	1	–	4

Continued

	1965	66	67	68	69	70	71	72	73	74	Total
Louisiana State	–	–	–	–	3	–	2	1	4	–	10
U. of Maryland	1	1	–	–	1	1	–	3	3	–	10
U. of Mass.	–	–	–	1	2	1	2	1	1	–	8
McGill U.	3	2	2	3	1	–	1	6	3	–	21
Mich. State	1	–	2	3	1	2	6	4	5	1	25
U. of Mich.	2	2	7	–	5	5	6	6	6	5	44
U. of Minn.	–	4	1	3	4	3	2	2	1	4	24
Monash U.	–	–	–	1	–	–	–	–	–	–	1
U. of Nebraska	–	–	–	–	1	–	1	–	3	3	8
New York Univ.	4	6	2	7	8	6	4	4	9	5	55
U. of North Carol.	–	–	3	5	–	2	2	1	2	6	21
Northwestern	6	–	3	2	6	1	3	1	4	3	29
Ohio State	1	4	4	2	7	1	6	4	5	–	34
U. of Ontario	–	–	–	–	–	–	–	1	–	–	1
U. of Western Ont.	–	–	–	–	–	–	–	–	1	–	1
Oregon	–	–	–	2	1	1	3	2	3	4	16
Penn State	1	2	–	–	–	–	–	1	1	–	5
U. of Penna.	1	3	2	4	4	1	4	7	4	3	33
Pittsburgh	–	–	–	1	–	–	1	2	2	2	8
Princeton	4	2	5	7	1	3	3	1	4	4	34
Queens	–	–	–	–	–	–	1	1	2	1	5
Rice	–	3	–	4	5	2	3	4	1	3	25
Rochester	–	–	–	–	–	–	–	–	1	–	1
Rutgers	2	1	3	1	4	1	2	4	5	3	26
U. of South. Calif.	–	2	4	6	3	5	4	3	2	–	29
Stanford	4	4	9	8	5	11	5	9	13	4	72
SUNY											
Binghamton	–	–	–	–	–	–	–	–	1	1	2
Buffalo	–	–	1	–	–	1	–	1	–	–	3
Stony Brook	–	–	–	–	–	–	–	1	–	–	1
Syracuse	1	–	–	–	1	–	–	1	1	–	4
U. of Tennessee	–	–	–	–	–	–	1	1	–	–	2
Texas	1	8	2	7	6	4	3	6	–	7	44
Toronto	–	2	–	2	1	2	2	2	1	5	17
Tufts	–	–	–	–	–	–	–	1	–	–	1
Tulane	1	–	–	4	4	3	2	2	3	4	23
Utah	1	1	–	–	–	1	–	5	2	–	10
Vanderbilt	1	4	2	4	2	3	3	1	–	–	20
U. of Virginia	–	–	–	–	–	–	1	1	–	–	2
U. of Washington	5	4	3	9	5	3	9	6	6	4	54
Washington U.	1	–	1	2	2	2	3	2	5	3	21
U. of Waterloo	–	–	–	–	2	2	1	1	1	–	7
Wayne State	–	–	1	–	–	–	–	1	2	1	5
U. of Wisconsin	–	2	4	2	4	5	3	6	7	6	39
Yale	3	5	1	4	9	6	6	3	2	3	42
Total	69	99	92	125	142	133	159	180	204	149	1,352

Thus about one half (53.9%) of all Ph.D.'s in German during the last ten years graduated from 17 institutions which awarded at least three per year:

1.	Stanford	72
2.	New York University	55
3.	U. of Washington	54
4.	Indiana	52
5.	Harvard	51
6.	Texas	44
6.	Univ. of Michigan	44
8.	Yale	42
9.	U. of Wisconsin-Madison	39
9.	UC Los Angeles	39
11.	U. of Illinois-Urbana	38
12.	Berkeley	36
13.	Princeton	34
13.	Ohio State	34
15.	U. of Pennsylvania	33
16.	Colorado	31
17.	Johns Hopkins	30
	Total	728

Another 15 institutions, granting at least 2 on the average per year, awarded 368 degrees, or 27.2%, whereas the remaining 256 degrees (18.9%) were distributed among 45 institutions granting fewer than one degree per year over the last decade.

Projection

Apart from the anticipated shrinking in the number of first high school and eventually college students later in the seventies, a further restriction in potential position openings can be seen in the age breakdown of current faculty members. "As a result of the tighter job market for potential new faculty the present (1972–73) teaching faculty in American colleges and universities is, on average, older than the 1968–69 faculty had been. Currently, almost three-fifths are over age 40.—Consistent with the 'aging' of the faculty, more faculty members today hold senior ranks and are tenured. Fully half hold the rank of either associate or full professor, and two-thirds have tenure."[4] In 1973 this was the age distribution of all university and college faculty:

[4]*ACE Research Reports,* 8:2 (1973)

60+	55–60	50–55	45–50	40–45	Total 40+
7.7%	8.4%	12.1%	14.8%	15.7%	58.7%

By 1978 the percentage of faculty members over 40 will have risen to 66.7%, by 1983 to almost 70%.

In addition to lower enrollment and locked-in (and hence expensive) faculty, there is the projection of accelerated cost. College costs are not only going up—they are going up faster than most other things. The projected figure for tuition, room, and board in 1982–83 is given by the USOE as $1,948 for public, $4,297 for private universities. The same source reported that the cost of higher education during the last decade rose 15% faster than the Cost-of-Living Index. According to the *New York Times* (23 April 1975) one private university (Stanford) reported "that from 1966–74 its cost had risen at 1.4 times the general rate of inflation." Since education is a labor-intensive industry with as much as 80% of most college budgets going into salaries, we can expect more pressure to increase student-teacher ratios and faculty course loads, and to eliminate courses that are considered marginal because of underenrollment.

For many years we trained too few, now we are clearly training too many professionals for an ever more restricted job market with all the disappointment and human misery involved for those of our younger colleagues who, highly trained and highly motivated and led on by our uncritical (if only tacit) promises, will now have to find jobs elsewhere. Faced with these bleak statistics, it seems high time for the profession to take stock and to rethink the role we want to play and are best trained to play in a changing pattern of education. The overproduction in institutions of higher education, especially on the graduate level, is alarming but will probably take care of itself under mounting pressure. I should also think that the field of German is probably here to stay, "Literatur ist immer ein Angebot zur Diskussion" (K.O. Conrady), but it seems equally apparent that other ways will have to be found in which our special knowledge can be of use if we want to avoid the total elimination of departments of German on many campuses.

No longer protected by foreign language requirements or unquestioned traditional structures of our discipline and the humanities in general, we have to fend for ourselves in the open marketplace. Although our tasks here are very different from those of *Germanistik* in Germany, it seems to me that ours, too, is not so much a crisis of methods or organization, of what to teach and to whom, but a crisis of the function and role of the humanities within society. Role-expectation and the struggle for fellow-travellers: apart from all the things we shall have to do in the future necessary for survival, I should hope we can also find the time to get together with our colleagues in the other languages and humanities to discuss the long-range effects of these changes. We do not have to accept the role society tries to impose on us, which reduces us to meaningless insignificance on the fringe of academia and society; or if we do, it will have to be a society very different from the one we know. More immediate considerations for survival must come first, but I do not think it is too early to start thinking about the implications of these changes, not just for ourselves in this particular field, but for all.

GERMAN STUDIES:
A PRAGMATIC LOOK AHEAD

VALTERS NOLLENDORFS
University of Wisconsin-Madison

The only ones who can indulge in uncompromising idealism are those who have everything and those who have nothing. Others have to compromise their idealism to a greater or lesser degree with pragmatism because they have either too much to lose or too little to gain by being uncompromising.

I do not intend to denigrate idealism. We as a profession thrive on it. All humanistic disciplines thrive on it as they strive toward their utterly impractical ultimate goals which do not lend themselves to quantification and enumeration. Yet as we practice idealism, a certain sense of self-survival must assert itself in this altogether too pragmatic world of ours—both without and within academia. To be able to carry out our idealistic mission we first have to assure ourselves of a strong enough basis of existence. And that means being practical, being adaptable if need be, having a Schweykian soul as well as a Faustian one.

There are many good reasons why this need to be pragmatic applies particularly to the German-teaching profession in the United States and why it is particularly acute at this time. Let me mention only the two basic ones:
1. Our functional value in American academic and extraacademic society is relatively low.
2. Recent and anticipated educational realities and trends threaten to erode the bases of our existence.

This may sound harsh after the public support and growth we—among other languages and the sciences—enjoyed in the 1960's, but only by being harsh can we hope to regain a sense of our real situation not tainted by the unreal euphoria of the last decade. In those years—aided and abetted by the post-war baby boom and post-sputnik push to keep up with the Ivanoviches—we either failed or did not care to see that we were dealing with an exceptional and to a great extent artificial situation. The least we can do now is to realize that the situation was unreal and artificial. If we dare do more—we will also have to realize that our present and future problems have been compounded by our failure to cope adequately with it.

If we discount the 1960's as an aberration—at least as far as unsolicited public support is concerned—and ponder our normal social situation, we have to realize that we are a minority discipline and a "foreign" one at that. Which means: we neither have a potentially unlimited number of students whose native language and literature is our business, nor do we fulfill a socially indispensable social function within the United States. We are not what *Germanistik* is to the Germans and English to Americans. Before we can teach our students *about* the German language, we have to teach them the language first; before we can talk about German literature, we have to teach them a lot about the language in which it is written. And—we have to supply the missing German cultural environment however we can as we go along. The bulk of our profession's effort and time is spent in *preparatory* work. It also means that there are relatively few people outside our profession in the United States who would feel severely deprived if we stopped or were forced to stop functioning altogether—didn't that almost happen some sixty years ago?—as compared to, let us say, the concern that would be caused by all our English-teaching colleagues going on interminable strike no matter how suspicious we are about the job they are doing. All by ourselves, we have relatively little social weight; our weight depends to a great extent on the social weight we possess as part of the entire humanistic learning tradition in this country.

What I want to show is simply this: we are tremendously dependent on each other and on others when it comes to the bases of our very existence. We are dependent on each other as members of a profession; we are dependent on other humanistic disciplines in the educational setting; and we are dependent on the society within which and for which we function. Our ability to become aware of these interdependencies and our ability to develop them to mutual advantage are going to determine to a great extent how well we survive the times when our social value is being questioned either directly—by cutting language requirements and programs in the face of fiscal austerity and changing educational values—or indirectly—by a growing emphasis on professional and vocational education even as the few professional and vocational opportunities offered by our field are becoming fewer and fewer.

That brings me to the second point—the present and future educational trends and realities. In my opinion, these are the most important factors to be considered when we weigh our own situation now and in the next decade:

1. Population trends indicate a leveling off and a decline. These trends are making themselves felt in the educational system and will affect the number of students in schools, colleges, and universities for some time to come. Even if there were a sudden increase in birth rate now, colleges would not be affected until the late 1990's.[1]

2. Educational trends indicate a growing emphasis on vocational, career-oriented, and adult training. These trends are reflected in the growth of community and two-year colleges which right now is far ahead of the

[1]Volkmar Sander (p. 25 of this volume) cites projections indicating a 15% decline of 14–17 year olds, from ca. 16,500,000 in 1972 to ca. 14,000,000 in 1983.

growth of traditional liberal arts and graduate institutions.[2] To what extent these trends reflect short term concerns and to what extent they portend long term shifts in attitudes is hard to predict, but the late 1970's and the early 1980's certainly will be governed by them.

3.   There will be relatively little demand for additional teachers and professors not only because of enrollment trends but also because the educational boom years resulted in the employment of many young educators, most of whom have attained tenure in their jobs.[3] Until the 1990's the largest demand for teachers will be in growing areas *within* the educational system. Twenty years hence we may be faced with a teacher shortage again—when large numbers hired in the 1960's start retiring.

Not only the locked-in faculties but also some additional factors are our inheritance from the 1960's. Statistics compiled by Volkmar Sander (pp. 27–28) show that, as our enrollments are decreasing, we are turning out the largest crop of Ph.D.'s in our history, who are automatically faced with unemployment. It does not really help them or our consciences to note that the situation is just as bad in other disciplines. Though we will not be able to create jobs for them all, it should at least be incumbent upon us to alleviate the situation as much as possible.[4]

What hinders us, I feel, is an even worse, though unmeasurable, inheritance

---

[2] The statistics cited by Volkmar Sander in this volume indicate, for the decade 1972–1982, an enrollment growth of 37.4% for two-year colleges versus only 3.1% for four-year institutions. Even more significant is the anticipated growth of non-degree credit enrollments at two-year colleges: 62.5%.

[3] Volkmar Sander cites the following figures for 1973: only 16.1% of all college faculties were over 55; 42.6% were between 40 and 55—with retirement ages in the late 1980's and in the 1990's. Most of those are tenured in, while most of the remaining 40% of younger faculty members probably are not. As we proceed, faculties will grow older, with few younger replacements being hired and probably many non-tenured faculty members being dismissed. The percentage of faculty members over 40 will have increased to 66.7 by 1978 and to almost 70 by 1983.

[4] I cannot quite agree with the radical cure proposed by Jeffrey Sammons in his article "Fewer but Better Russians: An Argument and a Proposal Concerning the Job Market and Graduate Student Teaching," *Unterrichtspraxis*, 7:2 (Fall 1974), 14–21: to do away with the institution of teaching assistants and thus relieve simultaneously the job market (by hiring young Ph.D.s instead of TAs) and the graduate programs (by reduced support levels for graduate students). It is clear that our Ph.D. programs are too productive for the demand and that there are some programs, particularly among the ones created in the 1960's, which are marginal at best (see Volkmar Sander's statistics compiled from the *Monatshefte* Personalia issues and Frank Ryder's assessment of graduate programs elsewhere in this volume); but even the healthier programs might have difficulty if their traditional means of support were cut as much as Sammons suggests. Prudent pruning is, however, an absolute must and should be best achieved by raising and tightening standards—both academic and pedagogic—in our graduate programs to assure that only the best scholars and teachers, those really competitive, reach the Ph.D. job market. Relaxation of standards, I am afraid, was one of the by-products of the preceding era.

from the 1960's: our attitudes that are still feeding on the—shortsighted if not false—assumptions of that decade. Some of us have weathered the first storm relatively unscathed and feel no need to worry; others, though worse off, are wishfully thinking that not the 1960's but the 1970's are an exception. Both of these attitudes are dangerous. Any individual feelings of superiority in times of general adversity are shortsighted: what befalls any of us will eventually have repercussions even for the best of us. And a refusal to face reality will result in reality sneaking up on us—from behind.

What do these trends and attitudes bode for us? Assuming for a moment that we cannot or prefer not to devise strategies to counter the trends, the future looks particularly bleak. First of all, we have traditionally been dependent on a large number of students in our beginning language courses. A decreasing student population will mean a smaller pool from which we can draw our own students. The pool available to us will be furthermore drained by continued emphasis on career-oriented goals because we, as a humanistic discipline, may seem dispensable and because our traditional career goal, the teaching profession, is in a depressed state.

Assuming, however, that we do not simply want to expect the inevitable from behind—what do we have to do to face the problem head on? There is a fourfold answer:

1. We will have to become more competitive for our students at the input stage.
2. We will have to keep the students who have started German longer than we traditionally have in the past.
3. We will have to provide our students with alternative goals.
4. We will have to obtain a broader base of support in the society and in academia.

I consider the third point to be the key to solve the first two: our ability to attract and keep students will depend on our ability to articulate our programs and motivate our students in very practical ways. And since most of our students will not—they never have—or will not be able to go into teaching, that means providing them with other attainable goals or at least articulating those goals clearly. Luckily—what we need to do is also sound educational practice. We realize, or should realize, that a smattering of a year or two of high school or a few semesters of college German courses—oftentimes under the duress of a requirement—is not really very purposeful; and we also realize, or should realize, that even the non-German major can legitimately expect that his German studies will not only "broaden" him in some vague way but fulfill some definable practical goals as well.

The fact that we have not paid or have not had to pay attention to some of these considerations in the past is really no excuse. Before the 1960's both our own resources, our educational philosophy, and our students' educational expectations were different; the 1960's changed all of that. They left us with a problem but also with a means at least to try to overcome it—in the form of surplus personnel. I think we would be remiss if we did not accept the challenge.

Let me take my own advice and attempt to detail some of the problem areas and possible solutions for the late 1970's and early 1980's under three broad headings: (1) Society and Public Relations; (2) Students and Programs; (3) Professional Interdependence.

Society and Public Relations

As the available supply of potential German students grows smaller—because of decreasing numbers and the increasing appeal of vocational programs—we will have to become more effective and aggressive in our efforts to convince the society at large, and especially those segments of the society controlling educational policies, that we indeed fulfill a socially useful function.

Compared to such academic areas as agriculture, biology, chemistry, medicine, psychology, physics, and many others, German Studies are relatively invisible in and isolated from social consciousness and social processes in the United States. Even as part of the humanities, we are easily and understandably overshadowed by our English-teaching colleagues and by the big two foreign languages, Spanish and French. Everybody is concerned if Johnny cannot read English, but who cares if he cannot read German?

There are some who do. We are not entirely without friends. But unfortunately the 1960's with their cornucopias from unexpected quarters did not force us to cultivate them or to take care of our public image. Now is the time to realize once again that our relations with the society at large are very important for our own welfare and to understand that all our theoretical arguments and all our "proofs" of the value of foreign language study will not help us unless we find effective vehicles to carry our plaints to those in a position to affect our professional lives directly: the local school boards, the university and college regents and administrators. We cannot really do it ourselves; we need a public voice and public support.

The direct way to achieve this end would be to become involved in social and political activities—a route easier to prescribe than to take. A simpler way would be to let others help us as help is needed. But before we do this, we have to make sure we are ready for the public—there will be no hiding once we let the public in—and to decide who should be addressed as our best potential allies and intermediaries.

As to being ready, we need three ingredients: (1) Indispensably—the development of high quality programs and our ability to articulate their *raison d'être* to the society at large. (2) Our ability and willingness to act as mediators of cultures and not simply as transmitters of a foreign culture (a job of German cultural attachés and the Goethe Institute). (3) Our willingness to spend more time and effort in developing programs and activities that have a public bearing (such as open houses, public lectures, newsletters, etc.). Our best potential allies and intermediaries are, in my opinion: (1) our students and the parents of our students; (2) our former students; (3) Americans of German extraction or with other ties to Germany and German culture.

I cannot conceive of any advertising or media campaign that would be as effective as the direct testimonial of our students and their parents, especially at the high school level. I do not mean that we have to indoctrinate our students in public relations, or that we have to overwhelm their parents with publicity blitzes. We simply have to do a good job as educators—being not only aware of what we want to or have to give but also of what our students (and their parents) expect from us. If we develop a simple dialogue with our students and their parents and try to articulate our mutual needs and expectations *vis-à-vis* the study of German, we will have combined effective education with effective public relations.

This leads me directly to the second group—our former students. How conscious have we been of their public relations potential? What public image are they projecting of us? How well have we kept in touch with them? Except for those who continue with us—and they are a distinct minority—what do we know about the vast majority who stay with us for a year or two, maybe three? Or even about those ex-majors who went into other vocations? This would be a useful set of questions to explore, though the answers are not guaranteed to be flattering; we may be faced with quite a few unpleasant surprises. But all this would be worth knowing—we might be able to improve our programs and our public image in the process. A business executive, a public official, an educational administrator, or simply a parent who has good memories of his German studies and with whom we have kept in touch can mean all the difference that is needed when it comes to a foundation grant, public funding for language and humanities programs, the retention of a German teacher, or a prospective student's choice between German and some other subject. Conversely—a disgruntled former student can mean all the difference when it comes to a negative decision. We can do with an occasional disgruntled student, but we cannot afford a host of them at a time when we have to fight for every student and every program we have.

Just as our former students may—or again may not—refer their children to us, there is another group in society that exerts some influence over such decisions. Many of us are aware that oftentimes a choice of language does not depend as much on a logical or practical consideration but simply on a student's ethnic background. At a time when ethnic consciousness in our country and elsewhere is rising, we should give adequate recognition to it in our efforts to enlist public support. For the most part those of us at colleges and universities, as representatives of *haute culture*, have been aloof from the local German ethnic groups. There have been reasons other than the cultural level: the rather narrow nationalistic and political outlook of many of these ethnic groups have made them less than ideal vehicles for furthering our aims and voicing our concerns as educators. The new ethnic consciousness, however, comes with new, more mature, and more liberal attitudes toward ethnic characteristics and their interaction in a multi-ethnic setting. We can not only hope that these attitudes will eventually affect the nature of German ethnic groups in this country, but we can also further the process through our own efforts as cultural interpreters and mediators. For it should be only natural that Americans of German extraction and German ethnic groups in America should be among our allies in our efforts to gain wider public recognition. But it can only happen if our goals are not at odds.

This takes me to the last point under this heading and returns me to one of the three ingredients mentioned earlier: our role as mediators and interpreters of culture. In the larger societal context—not just the ethnic one—our future viability will depend to a great extent on our becoming better integrated into the cultural life of the United States. While it is true and necessary that we should not only be aware of but also involved in what is happening in *Germanistik* and German culture today, we must also not forget our primary responsibilities as *American* educators. As long as we are considered and consider ourselves as a *Germanistik* in diaspora, we can never really hope to gain the support and the understanding from the American public that we need. And we can never really hope to perform our functions as American educators as long as we march to the drumbeat of a different drummer.

Students and Programs

It should be axiomatic, but after the surfeit of the 1960's it needs repeating, that students form the basis of our existence as a profession. Additional jobs, tenure decisions, and, in some cases, retention of even tenured positions will depend to a great extent upon enrollments. We may hate calculations of faculty/student ratios and student hours taught, but we will not wish them away. Those parts of our programs will be most vulnerable which have the lowest enrollments. In universities that means: the graduate programs. If they are to survive, our undergraduate programs will have to be healthy enough to pick up the slack. Low enrollments will have to be compensated somewhere.

As our overall enrollments dwindle (between 1972 and 1974 the decrease of German enrollments was about 14% nationwide[5]), it is imperative that we look into the problem and ask why and under what circumstances this has happened.

[5] *ADFL Bulletin*, 7:2 (November 1975), 40. During the same period, French showed a comparable decrease of 13.6% but Spanish lost only 0.7%.

The enrollment decline is by no means uniform for all languages, nor does it affect all German programs similarly. Studies to discover some of the reasons would be most instructive and might give us cause to reassess what we all or some of us are doing wrong. These studies could very well tie in with those suggested earlier to determine the attitudes of our former students toward our programs. Yet even without such studies some areas can be pointed out as problematic, or at least needing additional attention.

We have talked much about motivating students to take foreign languages, in our case—German. But what happens usually to the students once they are motivated to choose German instead of some other subject, or, in the case of a foreign language requirement, instead of another language? Experience and statistics show that attrition rate of students once motivated—at some effort!—is tremendous. We simply are not holding on to our students. And this is not only a phenomenon between high school and college as a result of bad articulation.[6] It is also a phenomenon within our college programs. Very rough statistics from my own department show that we enroll half as many undergraduate students in our second year language courses as in our first year courses and half again as few in our third year courses with language, literature, and culture options.[7]

Keeping in mind the fact that the future pool of students which will supply our input will decrease, even keeping up with present levels of first-year enroll-ments will become increasingly difficult—assuming we do no more than we have been doing up to now. Better public relations efforts will scarcely make up the deficit. This deficit will have to be made up and can only be made up by holding on to our students longer, something we obviously are not doing well enough.

To be sure, this drop-off of students does have several perfectly reasonable explanations, primarily the patterns established by the language requirement,[8] but even with the best explanations the problem is only rationalized. The simple fact remains: many of our students do not stay with us for more than a few semesters. Many do not stay with us even sufficiently long to acquire that "intermediate proficiency" justifiably criticized by Peter Heller (pp. 88–90). To argue—rather feebly—that at least we have given them some "exposure" is to be euphemistic. At best they will retain a few fond memories of some quaint German customs that seem to form the cultural component of our elementary

[6] Concerning the articulation problem see Frank Grittner's essay in this volume.

[7] The actual first-semester enrollments in German courses at the University of Wiscon-sin-Madison:

	First-year courses	Second-year courses	Third-year courses
1973:	452	274	156
1974:	500	258	152
1975:	570	263	125

[8] The College of Letters and Science of the University of Wisconsin-Madison requires for B.A. candidates either 4 sequential units (college semesters or high school years) of one language or 3 units of one language and 2 of another. B.S. candidates need 3 sequential units in one language.

instruction and ten years later shake our hands, exclaiming, "Why gates?" Yes, indeed, why, if they do not lead anywhere?

For it is primarily a question of gates—both gates of access and gates of progress. The normal access gate to our upper level courses has been through up to four semesters of college or four years of high school language. And once that gate was passed through, we provided one or two gates for further progress—usually quite disproportionate to the entrance gates, so that most of our students in language courses headed for the nearest exit as soon as feasible.[9]

That may have been a good enough model for the 1960's when we had problems finding enough qualified staff to take care of our bulging programs and when the sheer number of students was enough to crowd those few gates we provided for further progress. Now many of our programs have to fear exactly the opposite: more than enough teachers—with many more waiting in the wings—for less than a sufficient number of students.

To hold on to those students we will have to expend a great amount of ingenuity and—above all—hard work. Our programs must become attractive, valuable, and challenging for our students. They will have to be much more flexible, much more capable of multiple application—to different clienteles with different interests and needs—than in the past. A great amount of effort will have to go into devising the necessary curricula and teaching materials. A prudent distribution of effort will be called for to achieve the best possible results in the shortest possible time. Small and marginal German programs—those in the greatest danger of extinction and with the greatest need to be flexible and innovative—will especially need help in this regard.

My assumption that greater flexibility and greater stress on service functions will be needed is based on two simple considerations: (1) that most of our language students—most of whom are *not* potential German majors—would like to learn and would benefit from learning a foreign language to do something with it and not simply as a vaguely "broadening" experience; (2) that there are students, especially at upperclass college and graduate levels, who for some reason did not learn German, could not learn it, or learned it only in a rudimentary fashion and still are attracted to the *content* of what we are teaching. These considerations also suggest two possible areas which should be explored:

1. diversification and broadening the subject matter and providing a greater variety of or greater flexibility in our upper level courses for those of our students who primarily want to learn the German language for use in other disciplines;

2. exploring the possibilities of courses in English (such as German literature in

---

[9] Eva and Jere Fleck, p. 102 of this volume, use a similar simile to describe the same phenomenon. Whatever the simile, the problem needs solutions, and Flecks offer some practical suggestions to that end.

translation) or bilingual courses which can enroll both our majors and others with less than full command of German.

As language teachers we are in the rather unique position that we can teach practically anything that can be expressed in language. All in all we should adopt the—admittedly less than missionary—attitude that, as long as we do a conscientious job and maintain high standards, there is very little that is improper in language teaching, not only on the elementary but on intermediate and advanced levels as well, including non-traditional reading materials, courses, or German-language lectures as part of our curriculum, be they in botany, biology, geology, history, or anything else that our resources and ingenuity allow.[10] We cannot provide our students with Germany in America,[11] and only a limited number of our students can spend a year or semester, or even a summer, in a German-speaking country while still in school; but, by addressing our students' immediate academic or vocational interests, we can provide them with the incentive to stay with us a while longer.

In a narrower sense—as members of the humanistic (and to some extent the social) discipline—we can and should develop curricula that are interdisciplinary in nature and allow us both to participate in and attract students from related areas of academic endeavor. In other words—we must develop alternatives to literary and language studies in the broad area of German culture, particularly for our high school and college teaching majors but also for students in German or European history, political science, art history and other fields.[12]

Lest someone misunderstand me, let me emphasize: I am not talking about phasing out our literature programs; nor am I talking about taking students away from the traditional curriculum. Such reallocation would be merely an expenditure of effort in a quest for futility. What I am talking about is—the development of alternate programs for students who would not have gone into our traditional programs anyway. The success of diversification will have to be measured in

[10] The University of Wisconsin-Madison gave a course in botany in German in 1970/71; a German lecture series in the biological sciences in 1975/6 drew steady audiences of around 80; a geology course in German is planned for 1976/7. Professor Ursula Thomas pioneered in this area. A history course in German was developed and taught under a U.S. Office of Education contract by Helmut Keitel, Hamilton High School, Sussex, Wisconsin in 1969. See also Charlotte Brancaforte's essay in this volume, especially pp. 72–73. For career-oriented education in German read Barbara Elling's contribution.

[11] The Southern California German Semester (Rudolf Hirschmann, *Report on the First German Semester,* Los Angeles: University of Southern California, 1974), the Middlebury method, the Deutsche Sommerschule am Pazifik and other attempts at total immersion notwithstanding . . . Our best efforts to this end, even with sufficient funding, will have to be an ersatz for the total, immediate cultural environment that a stay in Germany can provide.

[12] There is ample discussion of the philosophic, administrative, and pedagogic aspects in the essays by Louis Helbig, Sidney Johnson, and Eberhard Reichmann in this volume. Walter Lohnes and Charlotte Brancaforte describe practical experiences at Stanford and Madison.

terms of (1) numbers of students added, or retained, and (2) the satisfaction these students express. Both are probably interrelated, and both are determinable.

As the interdepartmental nature of our programs becomes better defined and as interdepartmental cooperation grows, we will be faced with students who are attracted to what we do in our upper level courses but are at various stages of unpreparedness in German. Our pragmatic sense should tell us that turning them away would be wrong. But would it be right to allow the use of English to erode what is, after all, our professional basis—the German language and the transmission of German culture through the language? Clearly—no. The use of English as the language of communication or even the primary reading language should not become the rule, but it also should not be a rare exception. We have to develop a healthy sense of bilingualism in which "doing it in English" and "doing it in German" depend on the students, the situation, the level, and the goals to be attained. We need literature and culture courses in translation to set goals for those who do not (yet!) know enough German (oftentimes through no fault of their own) and for those who are just learning German. We are dealing, not only in college but in high school as well, with young people whose intellectual curiosity and ability far outstrips their German language ability. This curiosity should not be killed but fostered while the language is being learned. And we should also think of the language laymen in related fields who would benefit from our advanced courses if they were not exclusively geared to German speakers.

A practical problem will arise, of course, where enrollments will not allow parallel instruction in German and English. But it should be possible—ingenuity again needed!—to devise courses in such a way that students with varying levels of German proficiency can all derive maximum benefits both as far as subject matter and German practice is concerned.

I have not mentioned one temptation that we should avoid at all costs: the temptation to try attracting students by giving easy courses and easy grades. Such a policy might yield short-term results, but in the long run it can only erode our programs, public support, and the respect of our colleagues in other disciplines. If anything, our courses must become more challenging and our grading policies stricter. The only feasible long-range policy is to strive for excellence in our students and solidity in our programs.

Professional Interdependence

What I have said about our programs implies a great deal of professional cooperation and mutual assistance both among various levels of instruction in German and between German and various other disciplines. It also implies competition for a limited number of students: most additional students in any given program will come from internal shifts—from less attractive programs to more attractive ones. There is nothing wrong with healthy competition as long as it does not obscure the even more basic need to cooperate. Our cooperative efforts should occur in four areas: (1) intraprofessionally, (2) interprofessionally, (3) intradepartmentally, and (4) interdepartmentally.

Intraprofessional cooperation means primarily cooperation among German teachers at various institutions, particularly those representing various levels and kinds of instruction: university and college, college and junior college, liberal arts and vocational colleges and schools. These efforts should be primarily directed toward the development of

1.   a sense of professional communality;
2.   strategies, structures, and materials for the advancement of the profession and its work;
3.   effective resource pooling and communication as a means to increase professional efficiency and quality.

Far-sighted leadership, creative initiative, and smooth administrative functioning of the AATG and its chapters are indispensable to achieve these aims fully. But ad hoc activities outside the AATG which further the overall goals of the profession should also be encouraged, as every Faust needs his Mephistopheles. There are many resources that can be drawn on, and many chances that offer themselves, not strictly within the purview of the AATG, that should nevertheless be utilized. Too much organizational control can result in a membership waiting for Godot; the professional organization should not primarily direct but encourage and coordinate the diverse activities and energies of the profession.

As we develop strong intraprofessional ties, we should also participate actively in various organizations that further interdisciplinary goals and voice interdisciplinary concerns, be this the matronly MLA, or the youthful ADFL, or the ACTFL and its affiliates, to mention just a few. Our activity in these organizations will strengthen their ability to further common interests and at the same time strengthen our own place in the professional community.

Intradepartmental cooperation is primarily cooperation among members of a German department or German section of a foreign language department at a college or university. Ordinarily this should be the simplest of cooperative efforts, but in the 1970's and 1980's we will be facing great and unusual stresses that could jeopardize the functioning of some departments, quite aside of personal conflicts and departmental politics.

The greatest adjustment will be needed from those members of our departments who have primarily or exclusively taught on the graduate level. If they are American-educated colleagues, they at least have a knowledge of all our programs since they themselves have been through them, but there are some colleagues who came to us with German doctorates and were given assignments that did not allow them, or made it unnecessary for them, to get acquainted intimately with the whole range of our offerings, their special methodological requirements and problems. They will have to do it now. And if they have not yet done so, they will also have to become more involved in the academic life of our universities and the American situation in general. It is natural that they participate actively in the intellectual and professional life of the German-speaking countries, but it is not natural that they don't do it in our own country.

We—and our graduate specialists—will also have to realize that with enrollment trends as they now are, certain inequities will result in our teaching loads. As graduate enrollments dwindle, graduate courses and seminars will become less populous, therefore more rewarding to them and to the students. Unless the university administration decides to close down a graduate program when its numbers no longer justify it, a certain minimum of courses and seminars will have to be maintained to enable students to complete a program.

But this is surely a prodigal approach to education. No matter how much *we* may be convinced of the value of our teaching, and no matter how averse *we* are to even trying to calculate this value in monetary terms, even the most idealistic of us will have to realize that at some point an accounting has to be made, will be made. In a university such an accounting will be made, and deficiencies will be made up, when a department's overall enrollments are calculated. If, let us assume, a department's output of services demands, on the average, a class size of 20 to earn its own way, then a graduate course with five students will have to be made up on a lower level with a class of 35, or two classes of 28, or three of 25. This in turn means that the job of those teaching lower levels will become more demanding and less rewarding. Any feelings of animosity toward the stars of a department can thus easily become exacerbated—and with some justification, especially if those teaching the bulk of the students are untenured or short-term employees.

One solution to this problem is an equitable distribution of teaching duties along the entire spectrum of courses. Much better than any theoretical arguments, teaching an undergraduate language course or an introductory literature course would give the graduate teacher a practical sense of what is going on and whence his gifted students emerge. Above all—it would give the undergraduate student the rare (and usually deeply appreciated) chance to be taught by an expert in his field. Qualified junior colleagues, too, would benefit by such an arrangement: the chance to practice what has been learned in four or five years of seminars and thus to grow professionally. The entire department would benefit and function better together.

And that is not the only benefit. With little faculty mobility and numerical growth in prospect and with graduate and major courses cut down to a minimum, stagnation can easily occur unless there is some internal mobility within a department.

Such mobility can be expanded to include other disciplines and areas within a university or college. Guest lecturing in other departments, participation in interdepartmental programs, accepting split and administrative appointments all can help to diversify our staffs and add some younger members during the lean years. If a department succeeds in obtaining split appointments for two of its members, the department may possibly add—or promote—a younger member. Quite aside of such fringe benefits for the department as greater visibility and maybe even greater influence in university affairs.

In general—those of us in colleges and particularly universities would benefit by greater involvement in academic and administrative affairs. Cooperation in formal interdisciplinary programs is only one way of doing it. We should also encourage interdisciplinary symposia and workshops, team teaching of interdisciplinary courses, and other less formal interdisciplinary endeavors as a means to overcome the dangers of parochialism that are to some extent endemic in universities with their large number of students and colleagues and their stress on specialization. Even in the largest universities knowing our colleagues is important when it comes to getting something done. As a first step, why not visit other departments and find out (1) what they and their students think of our courses as far as their needs are concerned; (2) what in their and their students' opinion we could do to improve our offerings; (3) what assistance and what resources they have to offer to help us to do a better job? We started such visits at the University of Wisconsin-Madison and were almost overwhelmed by the goodwill and help we encountered.

The 1960's with their abundance were good for us. The 1970's and the 1980's may even be better if we approach them realistically and with confidence. And with the knowledge that we are neither weak nor—alone.

GERMAN STUDIES AS CULTURE STUDIES:
THE BLOOMINGTON MODEL

LOUIS F. HELBIG
Indiana University

In the beginning there was a German model: *Germanistik.* Today, in the 50th year of the American Association of Teachers of German, an American term is about to become the disciplinary label for all our professional activities: German Studies. This development is hardly accidental. First, it is not only an expression of the current emphasis in the humanities and the social sciences on social and cultural history as seen from a decidedly contemporary, interdisciplinary view; it is also, after all, an expression of the self-defined purpose of the AATG, namely: "to promote and improve the teaching of the language, literature, and culture of German-speaking countries."[1] Secondly, this development is a counterreaction to the misleading claim that language and literature studies alone would in fact be culture studies. This traditionalist claim is misleading because German culture comprises more than the processes of language communication and aesthetic mediation. What is at stake, then, in German Studies as culture studies is an enlarged concept of culture (*erweiterter Kulturbegriff*): "die ganze Spannweite zwischen den geistigen Grundlagen und Traditionen der Kultur und der daraus erwachsenden Zivilisation."[2] This is the basis of the Bloomington Model.

German Studies as developed at Indiana University since 1969 focuses on the social, cultural, political, and economic developments in the German-speaking countries over the last thirty years. In this paper I wish to argue that our profession needs this approach, if it is to remain viable in these times of foreign language retrenchment, shrinking funds, and increasing difficulties for the liberal arts ideal.[3]

No doubt, we are in trouble. One reason for our difficulties, to me at least, is that we have been unable or unwilling so far to take a hard look at ourselves and our profession, our safe shell. We are like those chicks in Günter Grass's poem *Im Ei*: "senile Küken, Embryos mit Sprachkenntnissen/reden den ganzen

---

[1] "AATG Constitution and By-Laws," *The German Quarterly,* 48 (1975), 3.

[2] *Bericht der Enquete-Kommission Auswärtige Kulturpolitik* (Bonn: Deutscher Bundestag, Drucksache 7/4121, 7. Okt. 1975), p. 8.

[3] Portions of this paper were presented at the 1974 Annual Meeting of the AATG in Bonn-Bad Godesberg.

Tag und besprechen noch ihre Träume"—who, as apathetic victims of circumstance, are about to succumb to the inevitable—

> Wenn wir auch nur noch vom Brüten reden,
> bleibt doch zu befürchten, daß jemand,
> außerhalb unserer Schale, Hunger verspürt,
> uns in die Pfanne haut und mit Salz bestreut.
> Was machen wir dann, ihr Brüder im Ei?[4]

Indeed, what shall we do then, o brothers and sisters in the egg? More precisely:
How can we prevent our American *Germanistik* from getting fried, sunny-side
down, before it is too late?

Although I do not believe that German Studies as culture studies, in and by
itself, should be considered a panacea, it seems that this approach may prove
helpful—if for no other reason, then because the Bloomington Model is an
American model. Our professional situation is quite different from the one in
West Germany. Nothing comparable to the reform movement for a *Neue
Germanistik,* propagated at the *Germanistentage* since 1966, has happened in
our country.[5] To this day, German Studies as culture studies, though practiced
at some American colleges and universities, has remained a largely uncoordinated
effort of a few academic teachers. In short, there is as yet no *Neue Germanistik*
in our country which could be compared, for example, with similar efforts in
West Germany, or with the *civilisation allemande* revolution in France, or with
German Studies in England and Sweden.

However, it is precisely against the background of this broad, international
reform movement in the field of *Germanistik* that the Bloomington Model of
German Studies should be seen. We, too, like Pierre Bertaux in France, believe
that the task of such a *Neue Germanistik* is "die Studenten mit der heutigen
Kultur der deutschsprachigen Länder vertraut zu machen—Kultur im aller-
weitesten Sinne, also Kunst und Wissenschaft, Wirtschaft und Technik, Gesellschaft und Politik. Und zwar die Kultur von heute." Bertaux continues: "Die
Kenntnis der Vergangenheit ist der Erkenntnis der Gegenwart untergeordnet, hat
ihr zu dienen und sich nach ihr zu richten."[6] We, too, like Robert Picht in West
Germany, believe that the purpose of German Studies is to provide a synoptic
view of German culture: "Die deutschlandkundliche Fragestellung zielt . . . auf
die Zusammenhänge, in denen die jeweiligen wirtschaftlichen, gesellschaftlichen,
politischen oder künstlerischen Phänomene stehen."[7] And, like Eberhard Lämmert, also in West Germany and again with an eye on Pierre Bertaux, we would

---

[4] *Günter Grass* (Neuwied and Berlin, 1968), p. 87f.
[5] Cf. *Germanistik—eine deutsche Wissenschaft;* Beiträge von Eberhard Lämmert,
Walther Killy, Karl Otto Conrady und Peter v. Polenz (Frankfurt/Main, 1967).
[6] *Die Zeit* (Sept. 8, 1967).
[7] "Thesen zur Deutschlandkunde," *Die Kultur der deutschsprachigen Länder im Unterricht,* ed. Wilhelm Siegler (München, 1972), p. 124.

also like to see a *Neue Germanistik* which is "...dem Rahmen und der Zielsetzung nach eine Kulturwissenschaft, zu der Philologie, Geschichte, Landeskunde, Soziologie und andere Disziplinen im Hinblick auf einen bestimmten Kulturbereich verbunden sind."[8]

In all those international attempts, as in our own case, has it been necessary to initiate a national reform movement directed toward, but not against, our traditional language and literature oriented *Germanistik*—not in order to stage a movement of heretics within its traditional boundaries or to practice separatism as a new discipline, but so that German Studies can begin to encourage no less than "eine Reform an Haupt und Gliedern."

Inasmuch as the Bloomington Model of German Studies finds itself in principal agreement with those international reform endeavors, and inasmuch as the result of our efforts can be only a specifically and typically American solution, my thesis is this:

> If our *Germanistik* is to continue as a viable liberal arts discipline, then it must give up its language and literature fixation in favor of a triple focus which is to include culture; our *New American Germanistik* must become an interdisciplinary science of German culture based on the American concept of culture; American *Germanistik* must become *kulturwissenschaftlich.*

As a reform initiated from within, the Bloomington Model has already had a considerable impact throughout the country. On the national scale, however, this impact has been somewhat less evident than in France (with its centralized education system) or in West Germany (where *Germanistik*, contrary to its marginal existence in the American academic spectrum, plays a central role as befits that largest German-speaking country). For this reason many of the professional analogies between Germany and the U.S. do not hold, especially on the practical side. But our basic premises are quite similar: as in Germany, our *Germanistik*, having started in the 19th century as a universal, interdisciplinary study of German culture, must become all-encompassing again.

In our effort to implement this design two important points must be considered: culture content and language competence. As far as content is concerned, German Studies in America should feel obligated to deal, as dispassionately and as impartially as possible, with all four German culture areas—the Federal Republic to Germany, the German Democratic Republic, Austria, and Switzerland.[9] With regard to language competence it must be remembered that the German major at the American college—usually after initial exposure in high

---

[8] "Das Ende der Germanistik und ihre Zukunft," *Ansichten einer künftigen Germanistik,* ed. Jürgen Kolbe 2nd ed. (München, 1969), p. 91.

[9] This point has already been presented: Louis F. Helbig, "The Concept of a German Studies Program," *Teaching Postwar Germany in America;* Papers and Discussions, German Studies Conference, Indiana University, March 24–25, 1972 eds. L.F. Helbig and E.

school—will be primarily a language student for two more years. In his third year he will take a masterpieces course in German literature, but only if given the chance will he take a civilization course as well. The most critical problem, however, is this: More likely than not, the student's German department will not have an expert in German culture—be it at the junior rank, including associate instructors who taught him, or among the senior professors who probably did not. I mean those who extricated themselves from the "menial" job of language teaching or the "amateurish" task of teaching German culture, usually without complaining any less about the further decline in German majors. Who is to teach German culture? This, too, is a key question.

It seems more than obvious that under present circumstances the student's exposure to German culture will be limited to an occasional remark about the literary context and other aesthetic expressions of the German spirit—not counting touristic experiences which everyone loves to relate. If any thought at all is given to the matter of teaching German culture, then one of the most astounding beliefs, if not to say fallacies, of our profession comes to light: the claim that the interpretation of German society through literary authors would be the only viable view of that society. The rest, so one is led to believe, is to be transferred by intellectual osmosis or could easily be absorbed by looking into the German newspapers, or by a trip to Germany.[10] To avoid any misunderstanding it should be made clear that, as in the case of the high school student, the German major in the American college will of course improve his ability to speak and write German as well as his knowledge of some literary works. But he will not know much, if anything of significance, about German culture in the last one hundred or the last two hundred years, let alone earlier periods, or, and this is even more critical, about contemporary society in the German-speaking countries.

One reason for this is that the German department at the American university has not changed much (with some notable exceptions) since the fifties and sixties. Its concept of graduate studies, for example, is still a reflection of the academic growth period in the wake of the Sputnik-shock. To this day, graduate studies are dispensed under the assumption that there are jobs for all Ph.D.s in our institutions of higher learning and that all persons with a master's degree will, with nothing but their language and literature background, produce enough potential German majors through their teaching effort in the high

Reichmann (Bloomington, 1972), pp. 1–11; (same), "German Studies: Zehn Punkte zu einem neuen kulturwissenschaftlichen Modell," *Deutsche Studien,* 11 (1973), 341–49, reprinted in: *Die Unterrichtspraxis,* (1974), 118–25.

[10] Maria P. Alter, *A Modern Case for German* (Philadelphia, 1970), p. 23: "A trip to Germany on a Christmas charterflight, or even a thorough study of a German newspaper will do more than the most brilliant lectures on the German national character or civilization." It seems symptomatic that here this otherwise useful survey appears to play down the need for excellence in teaching. Without being facetious, I think good lectures are worth a try.

school. The typical graduate student in our field is still forced to take a more or less specific series of courses and seminars. This tends to make it almost impossible for him to enroll in courses dealing with Germany that are offered by other departments. If he studies for the Ph.D., he will still spend a considerable amount of time on Gothic, Old High and Middle High German, without which he cannot get his doctorate; but without ever having taken a course on German social or political developments—he can. A strange situation indeed! Nothing makes the need for curricular readjustments more obvious than this state of affairs.

It is a fact that our American *Germanistik* still follows in the footsteps of a traditional German *Germanistik*. The problem is, however, that we do not seem to understand that our ignorance of certain changes in our field in Germany may well be just one result of our inability (or unwillingness) to familiarize ourselves with the whole range of social, cultural, political, and economic developments during the last thirty years. We simply do not know enough about our rapidly changing subject matter—and neither do our students. Therefore, what may be unnecessary for a student of *Germanistik* in Germany, namely taking a course in past or contemporary civilization because he grew up in the midst of it (although this is not the most convincing argument either), becomes an absolute necessity for the American student of *Germanistik*—and for his teachers. By the same token, the argument that many students, especially the better ones, usually study in Germany for some time does not really hold. German professors should not teach our future Ph.D.s; we should be doing that ourselves. Only an American approach will be successful in our classrooms.

It is particularly regrettable that the traditional German department is not showing greater flexibility in its curriculum and in its teacher training and retraining programs, but that there is, on the contrary, a marked development toward greater rigidity. Although attempts to save the department may be justified, we should realize that we may thus increase, not decrease the problems we have as a profession. If a department is to survive, then I don't believe it can be saved by way of administrative measures.

Instead, we should, as a profession, throw our doors wide open to let the winds of change carry new ideas, new impulses, and a new sense of direction into our work. Reduced financial and popular support calls for expansive new ideas. *Germanistik* in America *can* be saved with new ideas. Let us not retire to Günter Grass's chicken existence:

> Wir leben im Ei.
> Die Innenseite der Schale
> haben wir mit unanständigen Zeichnungen
> und den Vornamen unserer Feinde bekritzelt . . .[11]

---

[11] *Günter Grass*, p. 86.

Instead, we should leave that prison shell and venture forth onto new territory! Unfortunately, this is more easily said than done. In our profession we have to contend with certain fallacies: individual, departmental, and professional ones. Among the *individual* fallacies the verdict that teaching culture courses would lead to amateurism and dilettantism is most frequently heard. This is quite clearly a prejudice; for without the necessary intellectual, academic, and methodological preparation any classroom presentation is bound to become dull and amateurish. Nevertheless, the apparent lack of theory of culture studies in our field tends to put language and literature studies into a stronger position. Without such a theory the danger of dilettantism looms large indeed. It is therefore an understandable reaction if some colleagues flatly deny any competence in teaching culture: "Language, or literature, is all I know about; that's what I have been trained in; culture studies are not for me." Whereas a disclaimer of this sort may be honorable, the problem remains a real one. Obviously, the implementation of the necessary course work at the graduate level would remedy the situation in due course. More difficult to disprove is another individual fallacy, namely: the claim that a viable overview of one culture, let alone two cultures, would be impossible. But if we realize that any academic pursuit must remain piece-work, then we should at least try for such a synopsis.

Among the *departmental* fallacies the most serious one is the statement that, "since it is difficult to change the curriculum, culture courses can only be offered as options." Here we have hit upon a very important administrative hurdle which German Studies must overcome if it is to succeed. Unless culture courses become a truly integral part of the whole slate of courses offered by a typical German department, by putting them, as it were, on the same footing in terms of credit and creditability with language and literature courses, our students will be unable to afford such courses outside their narrowly defined major. At least a "Certificate in German Culture Studies" may therefore be a good idea. Another departmental fallacy is the fear that teaching interdisciplinary courses will cause conflicts with other disciplines. To this we must say that culture courses are not intended to replace those in other disciplines as, for example, in history or political science. But since those departments also offer courses dealing with German affairs, there is absolutely no need, to my mind, to back down from what is rightfully ours and to be less aggressive than some competing departments.

All those fallacies are serious indeed. But the most self-damaging ones are those which I call *professional* fallacies. They have become deeply engrained in the very philosophy of our profession. It therefore seems symptomatic that two of those fallacies are included among a list of "36 Traditional Reasons for Retaining FL Requirements" in the booklet *A Modern Case for German:*

> —FIs provide the only genuine access to the culture of foreign nations, for language and culture interact one with another, and both reflect the spirit of a people.

—They are needed as tools for other disciplines.[12]

If language and culture interact with one another, as indeed nobody would deny, then there is no reason why the English language should not be qualified to interact with German culture. Why should it not be possible to gain access— genuine or not so genuine (what does this mean, anyway?)—to the whole intellectual, socio-economic and political essence of German culture by reading, studying, and researching this field thoroughly and substantively, using *also* the English language as a tool, rather than frustrating the intelligent student with insufficient language preparation? This, to me, would be like inviting someone to a sumptuous dinner and insisting that neither knives, nor forks, nor spoons be used, only perhaps toothpicks. This neither makes the meal any better, nor does it forever encourage people to acquire the more refined tools necessary for consumption. In addition, even the most palatable cultural pie has a tendency to become less attractive with age. Therefore we should give our students at all levels a better chance for a larger piece of that pie while it is still tasty. Once the student has discovered that it is (but we've got to give him a chance to find out first!), it could indeed become a steady diet. Therefore we should not dismiss this suggestion as nonsense: to use English *initially* for a more substantive, more challenging, and more rewarding treatment of German culture in our classrooms.

The second professional fallacy, that German is indeed a tool for other disciplines, is by no means totally erroneous. Let us use it unfallaciously wherever applicable. But we should realize—this has seldom been mentioned and almost never heeded—that, after all, German is not so much a tool for *other* disciplines as it is, first and foremost, the single most important tool for *our own* discipline. This confirms the continued importance of language teaching, under- scoring at the same time an observation made by Victor Lange at the historical German Studies meeting sponsored by the Goethe-Institut in Munich in 1970, namely that there would be "zahlreiche und gewichtige Stimmen, die die Kulturkunde zum eigentlichen Ziel des Fremdsprachenunterrichts erklären wol- len."[13] The Bloomington Model is moving in this direction.

Whether *Kulturkunde* or *Landeskunde, Deutschlandstudien* or *deutsche Studien, civilisation allemande* or the Bloomington Model of German Studies—all those movements will, in varying degrees, contribute to the making of a new type of *Germanistik*. German Studies will most certainly be based on sound language instruction. But even the pure language teachers among us should see themselves as teachers of German culture in this new sense because it is they who teach the basic skill in our discipline. The expert on literature has always

---

[12] Alter, p. 13. It should be stressed that those arguments are from a list of widely held beliefs; they are quoted here to illustrate typical professional attitudes, not those of the authoress, which are not specifically stated.

[13] "Die Kultur der deutschsprachigen Länder in der amerikanischen Germanistik und im amerikanischen Deutschunterricht," Siegler, p. 25.

been closer to German culture, although his interest in aesthetic and intellectual culture tends to dominate over socio-economic issues and the activities of everyday culture. Therefore, the main feature of what might some day become a *New American Germanistik* will be the complementary inclusion of culture studies, so that the traditional double focus on language and literature can be expanded to encompass culture. On those three pillars—language, literature, and culture—the new approach must be built. German Studies must be based on the concept of culture which is derived from American cultural anthropology and which comprises all material and non-material aspects of a culture.[14]

Greater awareness of the culture component in German Studies will bring about a number of changes. I would hope that, before the end of this decade, we will be "American Teachers of German Culture." Perhaps we should start calling ourselves "German Studies teachers"—analogous to the teachers of Social Studies or American Studies. Wherever we are organized in departments, we might gradually move away from the tape-worm name of the "Department of Germanic Languages and Literatures." "Department of German Studies" sounds better and may soon be more accurate anyway. The term "Department of German" I consider a misnomer. Who has ever heard of the Music Department being called the "Department of Scores"? Or the Mathematics Department the "Department of Numbers"? It is likely that the somewhat stuffy image of our departments would improve if we were to give up advertising the tool instead of the substance, the medium (language) instead of the message (culture)—which are not the same in our case, no matter what Marshall McLuhan would say.

Language and literature are not the exclusively "genuine" alleys leading to an understanding of our cultural target area. It is my firm belief that a culture-oriented *New American Germanistik,* with language as the basic skill and literature as an example of written culture, will regain some of the lost ground within a modern liberal arts education. It would seem parochial to me, if a contemporary educational model were not to include prominently, though not of course exclusively, a *contemporary, interdisciplinary,* and *cross-cultural* focus. Those are the signs of the times. We should read them right.

With the help of this new "cultural approach"[15] the danger of dilettantism is bound to disappear. If conceived as cultural studies, a German Studies course would be able to discuss a great variety of cultural and social phenomena (in this case relating to West Germany): *Mitbestimmung* and *Industrieverbände, Mehrwertsteuer* and *dynamische Rente, Lastenausgleich* and *Sozialversicherung.* All those features, if explained well, would contribute more to the students' under-

---

[14] Cf. S. Winston, *Culture and Human Behavior* (New York, 1933), cit. A.L. Kroeber and Clyde Kluckhohn, *Culture: A Critical Review of Concepts and Definitions* (Cambridge, Mass., 1952), p. 43.

[15] Helbig, "The Concept of a German Studies Program," p. 11.

standing of German culture than could ever be transmitted by the most advanced language course. In addition, there is the possibility of a cross-cultural comparison: Why is it, one might ask, that in our current American debate over social security and a universal system of health care our elected representatives are drawing their arguments from the British or Swedish systems—not the German one, on which both are based?

There will also have to be administrative and curricular change, if a *New American Germanistik* is to establish itself. At the college level, culture tracks should be introduced to provide an alternate route to the bachelor's degree. If a "B.A. in German Culture" should not be practical, then at least a "Certificate in German Culture Studies" could be instituted. At the graduate level, immediate steps should be taken to make culture an integral part in the training of all future M.A. candidates in teaching. Ph.D. candidates might be offered a "Concentration in German Culture Studies" with somewhat reduced requirements in philology in exchange for greater options in interdisciplinary studies. The Bloomington Model already allows for such an option.

Change, especially curricular change, will not become feasible unless departments across the country designate at least one colleague for the purpose of preparing for the task of teaching comprehensive culture courses and seminars. In my estimation, this task of retraining ourselves to meet the new professional demands may well be the most arduous and, quite likely, the single most essential effort that lies ahead for our profession. In this effort we shall continue to depend on outside assistance, especially from various agencies in the realm of foreign culture policy in the Federal Republic. During the time of adjustments a generous number of stipends and fellowships to assist American Germanists in their reorientation efforts would be most helpful. A new *Deutsch-Amerikanisches Institut* in the Federal Republic—which could be modeled after the already existing *Deutsch-Französisches Institut* and which could serve all English-speaking countries—would be an ideal place for summer seminars as well as pedagogical and research projects.

This much seems certain: no amount of help from outside will allow us to sit back; no matter how generous it may be (and in that case doubly appreciated), the work must be done by us. The Bloomington Model of German Studies will continue to assist in this effort.

GERMAN STUDIES PROGRAMS AND GERMAN DEPARTMENTS

SIDNEY M. JOHNSON
Indiana University

While some German departments may wish to transform themselves into Departments of German Studies (see pp. 78–87), others may prefer to remain more or less traditional Departments of Germanic Languages and Literatures, yet recognize the developing area of German Studies in other ways. The solution will vary with the nature, size, and resources of a given institution. German Studies may be an alternative to the language and literature major *within* the German Department, or it may take the form of an interdisciplinary program under the administration of a committee. It could also be a sub-area under a general program of West European Studies, or it may become an independent Institute of German Studies. Whatever arrangement is established, there will be a significant impact on the administration of the German department. The purpose of this paper is to discuss that impact.

Since there is no clearly defined German Studies Program per se, I shall make several general assumptions that will probably be valid in the majority of cases: (1) A German Studies Program will involve teaching by members of the German department; (2) there will be financial requirements that will have to be met wholly or in part by the German department; (3) courses offered under the German Studies Program will impinge on those offered by the German department and may indeed compete with department courses for students. These assumptions form a common denominator affecting the relationship between a German department and the German Studies organization, which I shall hereafter call simply "GS Program."

Many of the administrative problems involved between a department and a GS Program are obvious, but they will be most easily resolved if there is first and foremost a clear-cut decision by *both* the department and the administration of the institution that a GS Program is a good idea educationally and that it will be supported financially. I should like to stress the necessity of the commitment on the part of the German department, because without it the door is wide open for jealousies, rivalries, and misunderstandings. The decision of the administration is just as important. A GS Program will be an extra expense. It can not be run successfully out of the hip pocket of the German department or by begging teaching support from History, Political Science, or Economics. There must be guaranteed support from the administration, and that will come only if the administration can be made to see the necessity or desirability of a GS Program. Of course there is always the possibility of financing or starting to finance a GS Program with an outside grant or "soft" money, but such funds will be terminated at some point, and a lot of hard work could be in vain unless there is a commitment to assume the costs when the soft money is no longer available. I have no magic formula for convincing administrations or departments of anything, let alone of GS Programs, but it must be done if there is to be any chance at all of success.

Let us assume that adequate financing has been secured and that the German department is committed to a GS Program. Now comes the problem of staffing the GS Program. Not every faculty member holding the Ph.D. degree in German is automatically qualified to teach interdisciplinary courses in a GS Program, and without an adequately trained staff the program will run grave risks. Of crucial importance is the selection of a director of the GS Program. He or she would not necessarily have to come from the German department but should be someone with a broad background whom the department would respect and who would have an appreciation of the work of the department. The same would have to be true vis-à-vis other departments if the director of the GS Program came from German. An imaginative director who is dedicated to German Studies and who can persuade, cajole and, if necessary, help train his colleagues is most important for a successful program. Needless to say, he or she must enjoy the full confidence of the chairman and the administration.

There will undoubtedly be comparatively few people fully qualified in German Studies until GS Programs (both undergraduate and graduate) will have had time to train them. For the present, therefore, we shall have to make do with team-teaching in the unifying interdisciplinary courses and make provisions for re-training the faculty we have now. The latter is certainly not impossible. Support for such faculty development should become increasingly available nationally or locally. In fact, it should be budgeted as a GS Program expense. Team-teaching, provided a compatible team can be assembled, *can* be an exceptional experience for both students and teachers, but it is not necessarily efficient in the quantitative terms of student/hour ratios conventionally used by statistically minded administrations. In smaller departments staffing may be especially difficult because the variety of interests and talents necessary for a GS Program simply may not be available. This is no reflection on smaller departments, merely a function of the number of faculty members to choose from. On the other hand, smaller institutions frequently have faculty members who *are* trained to teach in more than one field and *do* so on a regular basis. In any event, conflicts will surely arise when the faculty members committed to the GS Program are urgently needed to teach specific courses in a given semester in the department. Nevertheless, schedule-juggling *has* been done before.

There can be problems too between GS Program faculty, if it becomes a discrete group, and regular department faculty members. Traditional Germanists may become jealous or suspicious of GS Program faculty. The field of German Studies is only slowly emerging, and many faculty members will not look kindly on it, in fact may not consider it a respectable academic discipline at all. Charges of dilettantism may be hurled at GS Program faculty, and such negative attitudes can have a devastating effect when a department's recommendations are sought in promotion and tenure decisions. Conversely, GS Program faculty members may come to be regarded as some sort of super-scholars merely because they are involved in an interdisciplinary program. It is easy to imagine how problems of departmental morale can multiply for a chairman!

And what about the students? Aside from the fact that GS Program courses constitute additional dishes on the smorgasbord of course offerings and presumably are welcomed by the students, what will happen to enrollment statistics in the German department? Will students be siphoned off from the traditional senior survey of German literature? Or will the GS Program actually have the effect of attracting more students to the department and of encouraging them to take more courses in language and literature? I do not think we should waste time in such idle speculation or fear to initiate a GS Program because of possible adverse effects on the German department's enrollment figures. Programs of excellent quality (like excellent departments!) have always attracted students. At the very least a GS Program will encourage or require students to take German beyond the minimum foreign language requirement. Furthermore, we may well provide teaching opportunities in GS programs for some colleagues, thereby increasing employment openings in the department.

My comments on GS programs and their impact on German departments have all been made from the point of view of the departmental chairman. If problem areas have been identified, they are the problems common to all interdisciplinary programs in their relationship to traditional academic departments. And like all innovative programs some GS programs will succeed and others will fail under almost identical circumstances. Despite my apparent concentration here on some of the problems of GS programs, it has not been my intention to argue *against* German Studies. On balance, I see many advantages in such programs and am particularly interested in fostering interdisciplinary programs. We should not be afraid of such programs. We have had considerable experience with Comparative Literature, Humanities programs, and, at some institutions, with area programs. They can be exciting experiences for students and faculty when the quality is high, but they do not succeed without considerable administrative effort. Wherever faculty members, students, programs, departments and administrations must interact there will invariably be problems, but if we keep the possible pitfalls in mind, we can assess our individual situations more accurately and thus make more rational decisions about GS programs for our own institutions.

GERMAN CULTURE STUDIES: PEDAGOGICAL CONSIDERATIONS

EBERHARD REICHMANN
Indiana University

While in the 1960's the principal pedagogical concern in foreign languages was the development and implementation of a modern methodology for the purpose of training students in communicative *skills*, the 1970's have shown a decided shift toward cultural *substance*. But whereas the skill-oriented audio-lingual movement—based on a somewhat simplistic acceptance of mechanistic learning concepts—seemed to provide a working methodology within a short period of time, the present culture emphasis movement is making slower progress in this respect. This is, however, not due to a lack of responsiveness but rather to the fact that the grammar of the message (culture) is more complex for our profession than the grammar of the medium (language). We can agree, therefore, with a voice that recently warned against the bandwagon type of rush to culture program development that "might lead, as before (with audio-lingualism) to chaotically conceived, ill-defined goals, and could thus contribute even more than before to our instability within the context of the total college or university curriculum."[1] Indeed, there is a host of conceptual, curricular, methodological, and personnel ramifications that defy patent solutions for our pluralistic educational system in both its vertical and its horizontal dimensions. In this paper, I shall limit myself to principal pedagogical issues posed by the increasing interest in German Culture Studies (GCS) on the college level.

Conceptually, we have witnessed changes in professional thinking about the nature and scope of culture within foreign language programs. Traditionally, the approach to culture had been determined by a historical-aesthetic-literary triad, provided that culture was taught at all in an organized fashion.[2] The dominating historical element of this triad was presented and studied more as a matter of chronology than of dialectic processes. Content (*Stoff*) was more important than

---

[1] David P. Benseler: "Culture, Civilization and the College Curriculum of the Future," *Essays on the Teaching of Culture*, eds. Howard P. Altman and Victor E. Hanzeli (Detroit: Advancement Press of America, 1974), p. 174.

[2] See the report on the state of culture teaching in the 1960's: "The German Culture and Civilization Course at American Colleges and Universities: A TAP Survey for the Year 1967–1968," *UP*, 2:1 (1969), 91–99.

analysis and understanding of historical and cultural development. And—analogous to the dominance of the classical-romantic canon in literature and the dominance of the medieval period in the History of the German Language course—the modern, contemporary era received little attention.

Under the influence of anthropological, sociological, behaviorist, and socio-linguistic ideas, this practice and its underlying historistic-elitist *Kulturbegriff* of the *cultura major* came under attack, first in 1953 when the MLA's Interdisciplinary Seminar on Language and Culture recommended a strong emphasis on everyday, behavioral, and contemporary culture.[3] But the pendulum did not swing toward *cultura minor*, the contemporary small "c" culture, until the 1960's when iconoclasts blasted big "K" culture. The polarization of the concept of culture had its validity and it served a purpose, no doubt. For serious college teaching, however, this *big "K"–small "c"* antagonism needs to be overcome. We would, so it seems to me, benefit more from a structuring of the *Kulturbegriff* in three spheres that complement and permeate each other both synchronically (in their respective contemporaneity) and diachronically (in their respective historicity):

C_1 = the private sphere of the individual with its group affinities;
C_2 = the public sphere of the society and nation;
C_3 = the intellectual-aesthetic sphere.

Pierre Bertaux (Sorbonne), the most influential reformer of French *Germanistik*, demands that the culture concept must "so weit wie möglich gefaßt werden und neben Literatur und Kunst auch Wirtschaft, Wissenschaft und Technik, Gesellschaft und Politik in sich begreifen."[4] Louis F. Helbig, in addressing himself to the subject of post-1945 GCS in this country, wants to see them based "on the American concept of culture which comprises all material and non-material traits of a given culture."[5]

The demands for the totality of the culture concept with its implied interdisciplinary character, the subdivision of the German culture area in four nations, the lack of scientifically and didactically sound strategies for GCS, and the shortage of qualified teachers—all this tends to compound the difficulties for the GCS movement, not only in the United States but worldwide.[6] Cautious program development is thus indeed imperative.

---

[3] *PMLA*, 68 (1953), 1196–1218. A shorter version is reprinted in: *The Teaching of German: Problems and Methods*, ed. E. Reichmann. (Phildelphia: NCSA, 1970), pp. 68–71.

[4] "Die Kultur der deutschsprachigen Länder in der französischen Germanistik" (Korreferent Gilbert Krebs). In: *Die Kultur der deutschsprachigen Länder im Unterricht*, Bericht über ein Internationales Seminar des Goethe-Instituts München, 16–20. März 1970, ed. by Wilhelm Siegler (München: Max Hueber, 1972), p. 58.

[5] "The Concept of a German Studies Program," *Teaching Postwar Germany in America*, Papers and Discussions of the German Studies Conference 1972, eds. Louis F. Helbig and Eberhard Reichmann (Bloomington: Institute of German Studies, Indiana University, 1972), p. 10. See also pp. 47–55 of this volume.

[6] See "Schlußprotokoll" of the Internationales Seminar des Goethe-Instituts, readily accessible in the reprint by *UP* 4:1 (1971), 32.

While we may readily agree, in abstracto, with the wide culture concepts offered in the preceding, we will find no unison over the question of the role of culture in the curriculum. For this question is inextricably tied to the view we may hold in regard to our discipline as a whole, other practical factors notwithstanding.

Theoretically, we may discern four basic *Germanistik* concepts with correspondingly differentiated functions assigned to culture:

Concept of Germanistik	*Function of Culture*
I. A linguistic and literary science	subsidiary
II. A linguistic, literary, and social science (viz., with the sociology of literature)	subject immanent
III. A linguistic, literary, and cultural science	integrated
IV. A cultural science with languages and literature (among other components) as expressions of culture	dominant

We recognize in Model I the pattern still predominant in North America; Model II reflects the specifically West German features of the last ten years; Model III is spreading in the United States but still in the experimental stages; Model IV will strike many as remotely utopian. I submit that these models of *Germanistik* and Culture need to be examined in regard to their academic promises and dangers, and to their chances for curricular and didactic realization—or rejection. A sober assessment would, I venture to say, benefit not only the culture component.

If we, as we must, take into account the significant differences between a vernacular discipline (e.g., *Germanistik* in Germany) and a non-vernacular discipline (e.g., *Germanistik* in America), the need for the culture component in the latter is obvious. Most advocates of the culture cause are therefore favoring the model that puts culture on an equal basis with language and literature. This provides not only a more substantive background for students of literature but it is also capable of attracting students whose interest in "things German" is not necessarily linguistic or literary.

We may define our goal for a triple-track system first in terms of the undergraduate major program. GCS would then constitute the third track in a curriculum offering advanced undergraduate work in language, literature, and culture. There are three possible avenues: (1) The course offerings are exclusively provided by the German Department (internal track); (2) The GCS program avails itself of suitable courses offered by neighboring disciplines (external track); (3) The German Department collaborates with other departments (interdisciplinary track). Clearly, there are pros and cons for all three options. The internal track is almost prohibitive for a department with small third and fourth year enrollments, both in terms of maintaining defensible faculty-student ratios endangered by an additional program component, and in terms of faculty time and expertise. The *external* track will remind some readers of the not too successful Area Studies Programs of the 1950's. (They failed, however, not because of the Area Study concept per se, but for lack of clearly identifiable programming for student *groups*, and for lack of a home base within the German Department.) The exclusively external track would, furthermore, constitute an abdication of our responsibility toward the culture segment of our discipline, an attitude that is indefensible in the 1970's. The *interdisciplinary* track with its combination of resources from within and outside the department offers the greatest degree of flexibility in program design and utilization of faculty expertise. It also can provide a richer educational experience for the student. The minimum contribution of the German Department would be one core course (with or without outside guest lecturers), and systematic scheduling of courses taken outside, done by the GCS specialist whose coordinating skills and follow-up activities through regular colloquia are essential for program cohesion. Two practices are subject to particular caution: (1) A guest lecture series, as intriguing as it sounds, is not a basis on which to build a solid program. As the very name implies, it lacks permanence. (2) Enrollments in courses outside the department need to be controlled so as not to have an adverse effect on upperclass enrollments in German proper. Early counseling in the major's career will permit judicious utilization of credit hours from the general humanities requirements. The Stanford experience with interdisciplinary GCS (see the report by Walter Lohnes pp. 78–87.) is proof, on the other hand, that there need not be a "student drain effect" as long as the program in German Studies enjoys popularity and prestige throughout the university.

Provided we have the faculty resources, an undergraduate GCS program can be developed without great risks by expanding the offerings normally provided by the German Civilization course, a standard course in many institutions today. The first step may be the two-course sequence, e.g., "German Culture to 1918 (1945)" and "Contemporary German Culture." This offering may then be expanded again at a later date by one or two special topics seminars, and/or augmented by suitable courses in other disciplines (preferably not by giving German credit).

With the framework for GCS defined as the totality of German culture past and present, selectivity (*Mut zur Lücke*) becomes of crucial importance. But this is true in any course endeavor of any subject. Unquestionably, however, a knowledge of the historical forces is indispensable for the understanding of the continuity as well as the changes in a given culture. Only the extent to which history is to be incorporated is a matter of individual decision.

The emphasis in various GCS programs is not, and need not be, identical. Depending on staff qualifications and preferences, the primary stress in a course may be in the C_1 area, thus being principally concerned with patterns of behavior, values, traditions, and clichés; or it may be in the C_2 area with its corresponding sociological, political, economic, and historical issues; or in the C_3 area with its artistic, philosophical, religious, and literary manifestations. Whatever the dominant features of a course or seminar may be, the total GCS program will have to strive for an overview, with particular attention to contemporary German culture. For here lies the true contemporary significance of GCS as compared to the 19th century concept of *Kulturgeschichte* with its equal emphasis on all past epochs.

As regards methods, the statement made by Pierre Bertaux in 1970 is still valid: "Was nun die Methode des kulturkundlichen Unterrichts betrifft, so bekenne ich freimütig, daß wir uns hier noch weitgehend im Stadium des Experimentierens befinden."[7] This comes as no surprise. After all, GCS are expanding the traditional confines of *Germanistik* proper—for which we were, and still are, primarily trained—and we are confronted with a truly interdisciplinary complex, culture. This requires not only a considerable expansion of our knowledge, but even more so a certain familiarity with a number of subject-specific methodologies of which the sum total will not equal the methodology needed for GCS. In the absence of a systematic GCS methodology to date, only our collective experience will, in time, lead toward a viable scientific and pedagogical theory.

The one promising principle in methods that deserves to be singled out is that of contrastive analysis with its subcategory of cross-cultural comparison. The contrasting of phenomena within one culture, within the German culture areas, or between any or all of the latter with our own American culture is legitimate and also valuable for the student's keener awareness of the nature and tendencies of his own society. Topics for contrastive presentation and inquiry in GCS are innumerable, from the dualisms of early history and to the most current issues. Here are some examples: *Herzogtum und Königtum; Kaisertum und Papsttum; Rittertum und Bürgertum; Der deutsche Drang nach Osten und der amerikanische Drang nach Westen*—all good illustrations for phenomena such as *Föderalismus und Zentralismus, Staat und Kirche, Sozialer Wandel, Formen der Kolonisation; Blockbildung und Neutralität: die deutschsprachigen Länder zwischen Ost und West; Modelle der Landwirtschaft: Bauer, LPG Bauer, Farmer; Von der Feindschaft zur Partnerschaft: das deutsch-amerikanische Verhältnis; Minoritäts- und Rassenfragen: Neger, Jude, Gastarbeiter; Das Deutschlandbild in Amerika und das Amerikabild in Deutschland* (Sources: *Geschichtsbücher, Lesebücher, Zeitschriften, Filme, Fernsehsendungen, Enzyklopädien*); *Verhaltensmuster hüben und drüben* (Source:"American meets German—Cultural Shock in the Classroom," *UP* 2/72, and the commentaries in subsequent issues of *UP); Bundeswehr und NVA; Konvergenztheorie, friedliche Koexistenz und ideologische Abgrenzung; Soziale Marktwirtschaft und Sozialistische Planwirtschaft; Ideologie und Sprache: ein Vergleich der Duden-Wörterbücher in Ost und West.*

An individual topics series, at present being developed by the AATG in collaboration with the Goethe-Institute New York and the Institute of German

---

[7] *Die Kultur der deutschsprachigen Länder im Unterricht*, p. 59.

Studies at Indiana University, will provide a wealth of textual materials for in-depth study of key issues of contemporary German culture, and frequently with segments suited for cross-cultural comparison. Naturally, with any contrastive cultural analysis, caution is called for. The communication science formula—who says what, to whom, over which channel, and with which intent?—reminds us that the narrower the basis for comparisons, the more limited the validity of the results.

As regards teaching and learning modes, we should seek a reasonable balance between lecture and discussion, survey and topical concentration, use of secondary materials (viz., didactically organized presentations in textbooks) and original (documentary) materials. Exemplary learning with fewer topics that permits transfer of methods of investigation to other topics—thereby offering lifetime training—is to be highly recommended. For training the student in research, he must be introduced to the GCS collection in the college or seminar library. Above all, he must learn to work with primary sources, lest he fall prey to uncritical acceptance of views and biases expressed by textbook authors and teachers.

Since we conceive of GCS as an interdisciplinary cultural science, the question arises whether the strictures posed by the widely held principle of exclusive use of German in third and fourth college years should be maintained, relaxed, or abandoned. If they are upheld, GCS are destined to remain inaccessible to most students from other fields, and our educational mission and appeal within the humanities will be drastically limited. If, on the other hand, we keep the door open for *Hörer aller Fakultäten* through using the vernacular (as is common in the majority of European universities), our own GCS majors may feel deprived of the much needed exposure to German. At present, few institutions can afford to offer both a GCS program in German for inside majors and one in English for non-German speaking students. With English as the language of instruction, compromises are possible: the inside majors may do a goodly portion of their reading, writing, and individual (or group) consultation in German. And with expanded offerings and growth in enrollments, there may be room for a seminar done exclusively in German. However important these language considerations, the respectability of a GCS program—analogous to a literature or linguistics program—is not measured by the degree of language exposure and language practice it affords but clearly by the degree of academic standards it achieves.

Having recognized the need for a GCS track, many a department is still frustrated in its planning efforts beyond the merely quantitative puzzle of dividing a relatively small number of students into a three-track program. We hear the cries for "culture specialists," and we hear of the fears of being stigmatized as "dilettantes" dabbling in subjects we presumably know little about, and, finally, of academic justification in terms of both quality of instruction and of "transgression" into other fields of knowledge, that is, into other departments. Teacher qualification is indeed a serious issue, and it is also true (but we need not apologize) that we are *not* historians, social and political scientists, economists, art and music historians, and philosophers. We are, at best, generalists, good amateurs, in some neighboring disciplines bearing upon German culture in its contemporary and historical dimensions. But this generalist status does not disqualify us from teaching culture courses. For the interdisciplinary nature of GCS must not be equated with subject-specific courses in other disciplines. We are *not* offering course sequels matching or paralleling those of other departments; we are, however, called upon to treat responsibly *aspects* of German history, politics, philosophy, art, etc., as they relate to and are essential for the understanding of the German-speaking culture area. Besides, our general humanities background as professors of German or of comparative literature extends well beyond the confines of language and literature—and so do our interests. As teachers of literature we are compelled to explore the intellectual, aesthetic, social and political climates of many epochs. And as comparatists we are used to transcending national literatures and cultures. Potentially, we have indeed the core qualifications to teach culture. Not everybody, of course, is destined to become a culture specialist. Individual inclination, continued autodidacticism, and participation in culture workshops and seminars will provide GCS-minded departments with the staff needed to embark on an attractive program for undergraduates.

In the long run, however, individual departmental responses to the challenge of undergraduate GCS must be augmented by program design and teacher training on the graduate level. Speaking on this very problem in France, Gilbert Krebs, secretary of the French Association of Germanists, makes a point that is pertinent to us as well:

> Der Umstand, daß die kulturkundlichen Themen im 3. und 4. Studienjahr [equivalent to American graduate programs] in den meisten Instituten verschwinden, hat noch einen anderen Nachteil. Dadurch werden die meisten Studenten davon abgehalten, kulturkundliche Themen als Stoffe für ihre Diplomarbeit und später für ihre Promotion zu wählen. Und eben der Umstand, daß es zur Zeit unter den Germanisten wenige Spezialisten für Kulturkunde gibt, wird immer wieder angeführt, um zu erklären, warum man nur mit Anfängern Kulturkunde treiben kann, denn mit älteren Semestern müßte man höhere Ansprüche an Wissenschaftlichkeit haben. Keine Kulturkunde für höhere Semester, weil es keine Spezialisten gibt; wenige Spezialisten, weil Kulturkunde nur in den ersten Semestern getrieben wird: es scheint ein circulus vitiosus zu sein.[8]

Krebs then suggests a short-range solution: the use of video-tape culture programs prepared by specialists for the generalist's teaching situation.

For our long-range planning in GCS in America—let us avoid a repetition of

[8] Ibid., p. 63.

the overly optimistic mushrooming of foreign language graduate programs in the 1960's. For the training and retraining of teachers of culture we will be better served by channeling our manpower and financial resources into a few graduate centers for GCS.

We have considered the upper undergraduate level; we have touched upon the as yet untackled graduate level; but specialization in GCS within German Studies eventually can and must begin on the lower undergraduate level. Three and even four-year programs in GCS are feasible. There are many high school graduates throughout the country who enter college with an excellent preparation in German. Unfortunately, however, we are often unable to have them continue within our conventional two-track option of language and literature. Strong undergraduate GCS programs would surely attract a number of these students. Why not modify the Marine Corps recruiting call to the high schools? "German Culture Studies need a few good men and women." For our ideal GCS product is the student well versed in German culture, *and* with a fluent command of German.

BEYOND THE LANGUAGE REQUIREMENT:
GERMAN FOR ALL SEASONS OR
The Wheel of Fortune in Its Upward Movement

CHARLOTTE LANG BRANCAFORTE
University of Wisconsin-Madison

The analysts of the melancholy state of the profession are not doing badly—their metaphors of malaise are definitely reaching beyond the literary: from business they borrow the "falling stocks," the "fight against recession," and the hope in "conglomerates"; philosophy supplies the "Angst," and "sickness" and the remedy of courageous "leaps"; humble household experience warns us not to "cook with unknown equipment," promises indigestion in case of too diversified a "menu," and tells amateur cooks to "stay out of the kitchen" unless they are willing to retrain and join other cooks.

May I propose to add the well-known "Wheel of Fortune" to the apparatus descriptive of our present status as teachers of German language and literature? If we can agree that at the moment we are close to the nadir in enrollments, finances, maybe also in morale and ideas, then we might also expect that there is only one way to go—upwards. We have lost popes, emperors, burghers and beggars in the course of our downward turn, but new forces are waiting to scramble onto the spokes. A good deal of inertia is at work but also some healthy pushes will do the trick. We have to hold on, to help push—if possible, with a modicum of optimism.

"Cautious optimism" is the underlying mood in the attitude of the Department of German of the University of Wisconsin-Madison in its dealings with Fortune and change. As one of the three largest foreign language departments (with Spanish-Portuguese and French-Italian) on campus, but moderate in size compared to the other disciplines in the College of Letters and Sciences, it is one of the Ph.D. granting departments in the University of Wisconsin System. The faculty of around fifteen is supplemented by teaching assistants who must teach for at least one year as part of their Ph.D. requirements. Since the College still maintains a foreign language requirement, a good deal of departmental effort is devoted to the service aspect of basic language instruction.

Change in the undergraduate policies and teaching practices of the German

Department during the last ten years has been remarkable. Departmental decisions have been promoted by legislation in the College of Letters and Science, by
financial restrictions, limitations on hiring of new faculty, a contract with the
Teaching Assistants Association, to name the most important developments.
Graduation requirements also have been redefined.[1]

Although in general there has been a reduction in German enrollments, the
Department has expanded its course offerings on the undergraduate level in
response to perceived needs and has gone from the traditional language and
literature studies within a fairly rigid framework of ascending courses to more
flexible approaches that allow for interdepartmental cooperation and introduction of courses dealing with the culture and civilization of German-speaking
countries.

In contrast to the Bloomington and Stanford models of German Studies,[2]
which involved a complete restructuring of programs and, to some extent, a
reorientation in the priorities of their faculties, the Madison model of expansion
is characterized by its caution. Although the Department is committed to the
concept of and, eventually, an undergraduate degree in German Studies, courses
are added and dropped in a slow process: an experimental section is carried,
evaluated, taught again, modified, and only if deemed successful in subsequent
semesters, finally added to the general course offerings. No university funds are
committed initially, and the potential crossover from a traditional to a new
course and back into the traditional course sequence is left open to any student.
The evaluation of a new course by the Department is aided by extensive student
questionnaires, and the final commitment to a new course depends on the
careful justification of its necessity and desirability before the Divisional Committee of the Humanities.

The main purpose of this paper is to present—by example of the "model"

---

[1] The college reduced its language requirement in 1971 from four semesters plus an
additional 10 credits of either language at the third-year level or calculus to a four-semester
requirement for the B.A. and a three-semester requirement for the B.S. High school work
can be applied toward the requirement. At the same time liberalized rules governing credit
by examination were introduced, which resulted in students' being able to earn graduation
credit for previous work in a foreign language. The College has an Honors Program, and the
University participates in a number of Junior Year Abroad programs, including the Junior
Year in Freiburg (cosponsored jointly by Michigan State, Michigan, Wayne State, and
Wisconsin-Madison) and a smaller program in Bonn. The College requires 120 credits for
graduation, of which 80 must be outside the major (students with first-year foreign language
credits are allowed an extra eight credits in their foreign language major). These rules allow a
student to earn two majors (see discussion later in the paper). The breadth requirements
include 12 credits each in the humanities (including 6 credits in English or foreign language
literature), social studies, and the natural sciences.

[2] See the articles by Lois F. Helbig, Sidney Johnson, and Walter F. W. Lohnes in this
volume.

course offerings of one department—another approach towards change and diversification. A frank discussion of the positive and negative aspects of this change—as seen from one faculty member's point of view—may aid other departments in their deliberations. The discussion of course offerings is limited to the undergraduate level and excludes literature and culture/civilization courses in the English language.

Underlying our whole German program is the realization that the "care and feeding of undergraduates" is not only (or: no longer) a necessary adjunct to the graduate program. "Success" and "excellence" of a department must include a certain quantitative measurement today: Hundreds of students begin their basic German studies every year in high schools and at the university. College requirements, previous experience, or initial interest bring them to our departments. It is up to our program and to our faculty to keep this initially captive audience beyond the time of servitude. Success should be measured in part by their motivation to remain in contact with our departments, not necessarily as majors, but as participants in the study of aspects of language, culture, and literature. We enrich the students' performance in their own discipline, and we strengthen our departmental position within the university community in the process. The training of German majors and future teachers will always be the most important aspect of our undergraduate program. The Madison model sets out consciously to involve as many students from other disciplines and from outside the University as possible in the ongoing process of defining Western culture and civilization via the language and culture of the German-speaking countries.

Basic Language Instruction

We define "Basic Language Instruction" as the preparation students acquire during four years of high school German or four semesters of college German. We assume that this includes a thorough training in grammar; that the students read and write basic sentences correctly; that their active vocabulary enables them to carry on a simple conversation. They can read and analyze brief stories, and translate a German non-literary text with the help of a good dictionary. After their fourth year of high school or fourth semester of college they will have read an anthology of short stories, some poetry, and several plays by modern German authors; or they will have translated selected scientific texts.

At Madison this basic type of foreign language preparation is considered sufficient to fulfill one of the options of the foreign language requirement for a B.A. degree.

Needless to say, there are wide variations in the academic background of the students. The fourth semester grade report, or the advanced placement test, or their own decision to start a fifth semester classifies them as more or less belonging to a group with the same competence. Quite a few students have traveled in a German-speaking country or have participated in the American Field Service exchange program, and there are, especially in Wisconsin, always a handful of students whose parents trained them to speak German since child-hood, but who had minimal formal training in the language.

At this level of competence very few students are motivated to continue their German training because of the beauty of the language and literature alone. A certain "lassitude" characterizes their responses, one might say similar to that of the forced laborer who has finally reached the end of his bondage, i.e. who has fulfilled the requirement. Further probing, however, reveals that the students are aware that a certain plateau has been reached, and that now they ought to work on "everything." They are intent on speaking and understanding, they want to sharpen their translation skills, and in a general way they are interested in reading more about the culture of the country whose language they are so laboriously conquering. Rare is the student who knows after four semesters of college or four years of high school German that he wants to major in German or, for that matter, who knows what specific advantage a further study of German might bring him.

Thus it is clearly to the advantage of the student as well as the department to have detailed advising at this point. Yearly forays of university departmental advisers to selected high schools, and yearly meetings with beginning under-graduates on campus to discuss further possibilities of study are a necessity. In addition, at this juncture of basic and intermediate study, individual advising by the departmental adviser is imperative. Even if it takes more time than we think we can devote to an ever-recurring round of questions, even though we will not end up with signatures on "major forms," these interviews give the students a chance to find out about differences in course offerings, to air their apprehen-sions and complaints, to indicate their preferences. The adviser will be able to assign the student on the basis of an interview to a language, literature, or culture course with much more success than can be achieved with raw scores and grades alone.[3] Especially in a big university such a personal interview is much welcomed by the students.

A strong "motivating" factor in getting students to consider further German courses is the recent College policy of granting "Credit-by-Course-Examination." It is the foreign language departments' variation of the liberalized College rules concerning credit by examination. In brief, an entering student may earn college degree credit for foreign language proficiency acquired elsewhere (high school,

---

[3] The student has to make the final decision as to placement. He usually informs the adviser within fourteen days after the beginning of classes if the course does not "feel right" and a reassignment is necessary. Informal visiting of classes is encouraged to give the student a better idea of what is going on in the various courses and to enable him to arrive at an informed decision.

foreign sojourn or travel, etc.) by getting a B (or C, depending on the department) or better in a University of Wisconsin-Madison foreign language course above the level for which the credit is earned. Thus, for example, a student with four years of high school German who passes the intensive honors course at the fifth semester level can accumulate 21 degree credits in his fifth semester: 16 credits (at four credits for each year) for the preceding four years "by examination," and five credits for the course which he took to prove his previous knowledge. Such cases are by no means rare.

The new policy has encountered resistance on the part of colleagues who feel that college credit should not be give for skill courses taken in high school. The positive aspects of the "Credit-by-Course-Examination" rule are, however, considerable. It rewards independent study; it gives the student the psychological and financial motivation to save time and tuition money on the college level by using his high school years to pursue a foreign language; articulation with the high school curriculum is strengthened by student reactions to the high school language training they received.[4] The German Department gains highly motivated and eager beginning students at the intermediate level of German and thus gains a chance to interest and keep these freshmen beyond the semester that decides, by the quality of the final semester grade, whether credit for previous work in German should be granted.

For this group of freshmen, and for the top students in college classes, the "Honors Course" system is a further incentive. The College Honors Program offers the intellectually stimulating option of taking certain courses within the major programs and during their undergraduate career, and to graduate with University honors. Very few German majors choose to stay in this program through the entire undergraduate program. But the program is flexible enough to permit outstanding students not in the Honors Program to enroll in these accelerated, small courses, where equally interested peers, daily contact with the language and literature, and—on the upper division level—seminars guarantee dedication and achievement. Many German majors begin university work with German in an honors course, since it is possible to telescope the normal four-semester basic language instruction into three semesters of honors courses.[5]

---

[4] What this means for articulation between high school and college is described by Frank Grittner in this volume, p. 204.

[5] Students are allowed to enter the honors sequence at intermediate points with a grade of A in the prerequisite course; they have to drop out of the honors sequence if they earn less than a B. The first semester of the regular and honors sequences coincide. The acceleration starts in the second-semester honors course and continues in the third-semester course. The crossover points are from third-semester regular to third-semester honors and from fourth-semester regular to fourth-semester honors (which is a literature course covering the same ground as the regular fifth- and sixth-semester literature courses); to get back to the regular sequence, a student would go from second honors to third regular and from third honors to fifth regular.

Beyond Basic Language Instruction

The student's choice of fifth and sixth semester intermediate level courses will fall into one or more of three areas: literature, culture and civilization, language training.

a. German literature:

The fifth- and sixth-semester courses offer readings in the 20th and 19th centuries in all genres and give the students basic tools for literary analysis. The literary works are set in their historical and political context; understanding the literature is the main purpose of the course.

The corresponding honors course covers similar material in one semester by intensive study. Classes are smaller, and five contact hours per week as well as individual and group projects, papers, etc. facilitate an in-depth study of literary works and trends.

b. Culture and civilization of German-speaking countries:

These courses are considered alternatives to literature courses. Literary as well as "non-literary" texts deal with the development of German-speaking countries since 1945. The political and historical backgrounds of the two Germanies, Switzerland, and Austria are stressed in order to understand better the development of their different political and social philosophies. Artistic life as well as common problems of these industrialized societies are examined. In the assigned readings, literature in the sense of *belles lettres* is seen as only one among many possible forms of human expression.

The division between literature and culture/civilization courses on the fifth and sixth semester level is not so marked that a crossover from one track to the other is impossible. In either track the student receives humanities and literature credit to fulfill College requirements.

An interesting distinction between the two tracks developed by accident: Culture/civilization courses attract different types of students, typically juniors and seniors, but also mature students who are returning to the University to get their degree later in life, as well as foreigners who are studying in the United States. In some classes the age difference between the youngest and the oldest student has been twenty years. The students' ability in the language ranges from the minimum fifth semester competence to that of native German speakers. A majority of students major in the humanities and arts but also in fields preparatory to public careers, such as pre-law, political science, international relations, history, economics, or the individual major of Peace Studies. Thus we are addressing students who choose culture and civilization courses specifically because they provide a broader background to and a better understanding of their own major field of study.

The teaching methods in these courses must consider the multi-level preparation and interests of the students. Independent preparation of reports, small papers on topics of interest in their own fields, group research projects are integral methods in these courses, as are audio-visual aids. A departmental library geared to the interests and capabilities of these students is gradually being perfected.

c. Courses that stress language as a means of communication:

Conversation and composition courses are the traditional means of any fifth and sixth semester language instruction program. Our three-credit courses fulfill that purpose. The instructional material comprises selections from German newspapers, short-wave German language radio programs, videotapes and slide-tape shows prepared by the faculty in cooperation with the Laboratories for Recorded Instruction. The absence of an international agreement that would permit the use of cultural programs prepared for television in the German-speaking countries for instructional purposes is deeply felt.

It is not only the beginning undergraduates who need to improve their fluency in German. Graduate students in other disciplines of the humanities and in the sciences still need to pass German language examinations; faculty members and students need to do research in German; native speakers of German in the University and Madison communities are interested in keeping up or sharpening their language skills. For their benefit, and with a gratifying number of participants, the German and Zoology Departments in the fall semester of 1975/76 sponsored a fourteen-week, one credit/no credit lecture series in the Biological Sciences. Native and non-native speakers of German lectured in German on topics related to their scientific research specialty. Glossaries, summaries, questionnaires, and discussions in English and German helped the audience over difficulties both in German scientific vocabulary and listening comprehension. This lecture series, cross-listed with Zoology, and classified in the "Independent Study" category, provided for all participants a non-pressure alternative to the traditional grade-oriented study of German. The students were exposed to different German dialects; psychologically, there was an incentive to pursue language competence, since English and American scientists proved that their university language training enabled them to lecture in German. The mixed audience of old and young, undergraduates, professors and non-faculty participants provided the "outreach" and "interaction" climate so necessary for the growth of communication. The Department will continue this unique program of German studies in the future.

An intensive, multi-level, multi-media language course during the interim between the second semester and the beginning of Summer Session, which also makes use of shortwave radio programs, tapes, and videotapes is regarded by the students to be a most effective course in speaking and comprehension. It also serves as preparation for the high school student who will enter the University in the fall semester. "German for Travelers" is taught by the University Extension German Department as a night course.

At this level in the students' language learning, when both active and passive vocabulary are increasing, the social aspect of language learning ought not to be downgraded. Unfortunately, there is no longer a "German House" on campus that might provide a focus for extracurricular German activities. In the late 'sixties and early 'seventies, because of changing student interests and a decreasing number of faculty members, the German Club was taken out of the realm of faculty duties, and student volunteers now carry the responsibility for long-range planning of its cultural and social events and their administration. The ad-hoc quality of student commitment (and here one must regret the discontinuity of efforts when students go abroad for the Junior Year) makes for very uneven scheduling. There are attempts at German dinner tables; there are German language discussion groups on the upper division and graduate level; but for the beginners and intermediate students a more structured framework would be necessary. In downgrading the pedagogical together with the social aspects of "Club" life, faculty and students deprive themselves of a valuable teaching and learning tool.

The offerings of the fifth and sixth semester level of German study—literature and culture/civilization with concurrent formal training in the language—are repeated every semester in traditional or multi-level courses. Decisions about the students' further language study are made during that time. A small number of the students who attend courses in the German Department for credit-by-course-examination, or to fulfill their humanities or literature requirement, or to gain or keep fluency in spoken and written German decide to declare a major under the auspices of the German Department.

The German Major

The student who decides to make German his major field of undergraduate study has three options, two of which require the same background in courses:

a.   the traditional B.A. in German language and literature
b.   the "double major" in German and another discipline
c.   the Secondary Education major, which leads to certification to teach German on the secondary school level.

a.   The B.A. in German Language and Literature

The accelerated literature honors course described above fulfills a dual function: beside serving as an honors course, it also facilitates entry into the advanced literature courses for German majors. If they obtain their basic language preparation entirely in college, they need to take advantage of the honors sequence to complete their major in four years. If they enter college with most of the basic preparation completed in high school, they can take the more leisurely pace of the regular sequence.[6]

---

[6] The major in German requires a minimum of 18 credits above the third-year level. Though it is theoretically possible to compress these credits within the last year, course

All majors are urged to plan to spend their junior year in Germany with the Junior Year in Freiburg (or Bonn) program. Although the Department deprives itself yearly of a group of good students, the students gain immensely by such immersion into German language and culture: fluency of expression, breadth of interest, and general motivation.

During the year abroad the student usually has time to take the minimum of three "cultural enrichment" courses required for all majors who do not choose to exercise the other requirement option, intermediate proficiency in another foreign language. In consultation with the adviser they must take at least three upper level courses in European (German, Austrian) History, or the Arts, or Philosophy.

b. The Double Major

The College does not recognize an undergraduate minor. However, by design, and sometimes by accident, students may graduate having fulfilled the major requirements for two departments. Since the College began granting credits-by-course-examination, the number of degrees with "double majors" has increased. Some of the students are quite versatile, fulfilling requirements for the German major as well as for another department in the humanities, the biological, physical, or social science, even pre-medicine. The degree is considered by the students to be more prestigious, since it improves their chances upon graduation both on the job market and in applications for graduate study. Some of the numerous award competitions for senior students on campus also seem to favor this versatility.

Double majors lead into the temptation, however, to spread one's basic education too thin. Students tend more to skip the Junior Year program (in order to fulfill laboratory or sequence course requirements for their science majors), they reduce the number of German courses taken to the bare minimum, and thus they sometimes defeat the very purpose of the "double major": fluency in the spoken language and acquaintance with the culture. The pure literature courses quite often do not meet their specific long-range needs.

c. Secondary Education Majors

For the benefit of the "language-oriented" majors and the secondary education majors for whom training for high school and middle school teaching careers necessitates acquaintance with language and culture of the German-speaking countries, courses in philology and linguistics have been introduced. Advanced conversation and composition courses may be repeated for credit to improve the students' fluency in the language. Two advanced-level culture courses which combine historical and literary documentation for the cultural history of German-speaking countries from the year 800 to the present are offered as alternatives to literature courses and as background to advanced level

---

sequences, prerequisites, and the intensity of taking three advanced courses per semester prove to be a practical obstacle for most students.

literature courses. Graduate students from other departments for whom the knowledge of German is indispensable frequently enroll in these courses.[7]

The secondary education major who also has to take required courses in the School of Education and fulfill obligations connected with two or more months of student teaching in the senior year, tends more and more toward the language/civilization/philology options of course offerings. For him, study abroad is imperative; returning students quite frequently exercise the option to change from secondary education to German literature or vice versa.

The sheer mechanics of administration of a varied program of instruction in a relatively small department at a large university are sometimes at cross purposes with university policies. One illustration will suffice: although the option of an "Individual Major" for students was officially instituted (students make up their own undergraduate program which is interdepartmental and supervised by a special committee), the concept of independent study on the undergraduate level is harder and harder to realize. During the academic year, when a faculty member is already teaching three courses per semester and burdened with administrative duties, there is little incentive for him to add independent study students to an already crammed schedule. Independent study supervision and teaching does not count towards the official teaching load. Thus, the "tutorial" aspect of independent study is virtually disappearing.

However, students are encouraged from the intermediate courses on to work independently or in group projects within a given course throughout their career in the German Department. Third semester basic language instruction is highly individualized. Multi-level courses on the intermediate level lead naturally to that pedagogical method. Seminar courses have great appeal on the junior and senior level, and are ideal for directed individual study. The last option of truly "independent" character, the Senior Honors Thesis to be written with an officially appointed thesis adviser, is not very popular with the students.

The future of undergraduate study of German at Madison—beyond the requirement—is not as dark as it appeared at first when the requirements were reduced. The policy of credit-by-examination does necessitate communication with high school administrations concerning foreign language training. Departments are also prodded to take the idea of "service to the University community" seriously. Interdepartmental communication and cooperation in course offerings and guest lectures is the natural result of tightening financial resources. The admission that literature is just one of several means of expressing the culture of a country is not really asked of a department of languages and

---

[7] The Department is planning to offer a major with a concentration in German Studies as soon as the entire culture course sequence has proved itself in practice.

literatures; only the admission that non-literary communication also is a facet of living. Our students are telling us that they want to learn to use a language for their future professional training. Graduate studies in business are being coupled with demands for fluency in one or more modern languages. The scientific community is reemphasizing the value of communication in another language. And if we are as convinced as we profess that the most important educational aspect of foreign language learning is the appreciation of one's own culture by comparison and contrast with another culture, then the future of German Studies as an expanded concept is assured.

GERMAN STUDIES: THE STANFORD MODEL
THE EVOLUTION OF A PROGRAM

WALTER F. W. LOHNES
Stanford University

The following account[1] is presented here as one possible model for realizing the potential of German Studies in a major American university in the late 20th century. The description proceeds from the recent development of the department, beginning about 1960, to the dynamics of the current situation and to potential further evolution. Two factors must be borne in mind: (1) Stanford University, with over 11,000 students, is a relatively large institution, and (2) Stanford has an unusually large number of experts in the area of Central European Studies in a wide range of academic disciplines. Without these two factors, many of the courses and programs described would not be possible.

The traditional structure of German departments in American universities is that of a pyramid, with large numbers of students in the beginning language courses at the base—taught by a multitude of teaching assistants, lecturers, "native informants," and an occasional professor, usually of the untenured variety—and with a very small number of advanced graduate students at the top—doctoral candidates taught by tenured faculty who very often have not encountered a freshman since they were promoted to associate professor. The doctoral students are trained as research scholars for the pursuit of lofty goals, only to find themselves, upon achieving the ultimate aim of their student careers—the Ph.D. degree—back down at the base teaching German 101 or Masterpieces of 19th-Century German Literature. Then they commence the second arduous ascent toward the pinnacle, which only very few ever reach.

This situation has existed for many decades, but now, in the late seventies, we suddenly find that the carefully orchestrated routine has been disrupted. The profession has been rudely awakened to the fact that the base of the pyramid has been badly eroded and no longer has room for all those low people on the totem pole. The entire structure has become top heavy and is perhaps in danger of crumbling altogether.

---

[1] This article evolved from a paper presented at the 1973 Annual Meeting of ADFL, December 26, 1973, in Chicago, and published in revised form in the *ADFL Bulletin*, 5:3 (March 1974).

Only very recently has the profession begun to ask whether its pyramidal structure, oriented essentially toward the single goal of producing Ph.D.s, can be maintained, and, indeed, whether this structure was ever really justified. We have doubtless done justice to the few who reached the top, but we have paid very little attention to all those that fall by the wayside. But, if some of our large university departments start with up to a thousand students per year in first-year courses, and if no more than ten of these end up with a Ph.D. in German literature eight or ten years later, are we then not obliged to provide for the remaining 99% as well, and not just in a perfunctory fashion but with the same zeal and dedication we devote to our Ph.D.s? Are those who only take our basic courses not important to us? And what about the majors (and non-majors) in our upper-division undergraduate courses?

One major reason for our preoccupation with the doctoral program has, of course, always been the false equation of American German departments with the *Deutsche Seminare* at universities in Germany. We have rarely thought of German Studies in America as a discipline *sui generis* rather than as an extension of German *Germanistik*. We tend to forget that for almost all of our students German is a second language and not their native tongue, and that our American students do not have the language background of the German *Abiturient* (or at least the background he used to have); we forget that even many of our Ph.D.s did not start to learn German until they were freshmen in college; and we disregard the fact that American higher education, that curious blend of the German and the British systems, encompasses a far broader population than the German university ever did.

We also too often fail to consider that the overwhelming majority of the students in our introductory language classes have no interest whatsoever in German literature; instead, we have regarded them only as potential recruits for our—narrowly conceived—graduate programs. But our students' reasons for taking German are manifold: some just want to clear the hurdle of a requirement, be it college-wide or departmental; some take German because they have a grandfather who was born in the Black Forest; some want to learn German in order to better appreciate places like Schwabing or St. Pauli; some want to study history or physics or political science at a German university; others see themselves as members of the diplomatic corps or as junior executives in a multinational corporation; and still others want to teach German in high school, where they will be regarded as the ultimate authority on German politics and the German cuisine (if there is such a thing), on the Bavarian dialect, on the *Völkerwanderung,* the life and times of Goethe, and "Please, what does *VEB* stand for?"

These preliminary remarks could, of course, be amplified, but such elaboration is done elsewhere in this volume. Let them here stand as the background against which the attempts of one department should be seen—attempts to restructure itself in such a fashion that not only the Ph.D.s are well-cared for, but that the several other large groups of our clientele leave the department with the feeling that they have not been mere adjuncts to one major enterprise.

The far-reaching implications of this notion led, quite consciously, to the change of the department's name from "German" to "German Studies" in 1970–71.

The original pyramid has now been replaced by a stack of cubes that can easily be rearranged or added on to. The right angles of this new system have produced a number of plateaus which can be clearly defined as to objectives and achievements. The introductory and intermediate courses, the undergraduate major program, the M.A. and the Ph.D. programs, all have become much more recognizable units within themselves, while also providing continuity for those who want to proceed all the way to the top.

At the same time, we have diversified our offerings, both within the department and in the form of interdisciplinary programs. This outward-bound movement was a logical consequence of our restructuring and has greatly helped to eliminate what provincialism there may still have been in the department ten or fifteen years ago.

We have thus, if the mercantile comparison be permitted, moved away from the exclusive manufacture of one very fragile product, a process which produces an undue amount of waste and is subject to constantly changing market conditions, and we have established a conglomerate that enables us to shift our productive energies as needed.

I do not mean to imply that we have abandoned literature and literary scholarship. On the contrary: the eminence—though perhaps no longer pre-eminence—of literary studies is as strong as it has ever been, and no student beyond the basic language courses leaves the department without having been exposed to at least some aspects of German literature. By adding to the original core, we have infused new strength into literary studies, while at the same time providing many more opportunities for those students whose aim in life is not a college teaching career.

Such diversification, one might argue, is simply a ruse and a maneuver to increase the size of our classes at a time when students have become scarce—and I would be speaking less than the full truth if I claimed that this thought never crosses our minds. What is more significant than such a mercenary and utilitarian motive, however, is that we started moving toward German *Studies* during the most affluent of times, and long before the current recession began. I myself have argued for a broader concept of German Studies for almost 25 years, and when I came to Stanford fifteen years ago, I found an openness toward innovation and experimentation that was largely due to the far-sighted efforts of F.W. Strothmann, who then presided over a mammoth Department of Modern European Languages, the largest department in the School of Humanities and Sciences.

By 1960, Strothmann had initiated the Stanford Humanities Program for undergraduates and graduates, which is still a going concern. Several members of the German faculty are deeply involved in the program, teaching large undergraduate classes and graduate seminars, and supervising undergraduate honors theses in Humanities. In addition, we offer a joint Ph.D. in German Studies and Humanities, a degree earned by some of our most outstanding students, which requires the most rigorous preparation in a wide field.

By 1960, Strothmann had also invented the Stanford Overseas Campuses programs. The establishment of a campus in Germany in 1958 was quickly followed by campuses in France, Italy, Britain, and Austria, until more than fifty percent of each Stanford graduating class had spent at least two quarters in Europe, not as foreign language majors, but as general students who would become engineers or mathematicians as well as historians or Germanists. Starting in 1968 or 1969, a slow decline in interest in overseas study set in—doubtless part of the trend that also brought with it the vanishing language requirement and the sharp drop in foreign language enrollments. As of 1975, however, numbers were increasing again, accompanied by a sudden upswing in beginning German enrollment, but, ironically, this renewed interest clashed head-on with severe restrictions on the overseas budget, due to fiscal problems at home and inflation and dollar devaluation abroad.

In 1961, the Department initiated a special program for 10–15 advanced undergraduate and first-year graduate students at the University of Hamburg as part of a Ford Foundation-sponsored Three-Year Masters Program. The program in Hamburg was continued even after the grant ended and was moved to the University of Bonn in 1973. It is open to students in German Studies as well as in such programs as German History and Art History, but students in other fields, for example in mathematics and physics, have also successfully participated. Directed by a member of our faculty, the students take courses in their own field at the University of Bonn. In 1975, we added a direct exchange of graduate students with Bonn: we send one or two Germanists, and Bonn sends us Americanists who pursue their own studies at Stanford and simultaneously serve as teaching fellows in the Department. A regular faculty exchange with Bonn is now in the planning stage and should commence in 1977. For the summer semester 1976, one of our colleagues was invited by the Land Nordrhein-Westfalen to hold a research professorship in Bonn on the occasion of the American Bicenntennial.

In 1960, the Department conducted the first second-level NDEA Institute abroad for 80 American high school teachers of German, and in 1963 we conducted a third-level institute in addition, the only one in any language ever held. By the time of the last institute in 1969, we had established close contact with over 800 teachers, about seven or eight percent of those then engaged in the teaching of German in American schools.

It should also be mentioned here that for many years, and since long before the audio-lingual crusade, language teaching (and, by implication, the care and feeding of freshmen and sophomores in our beginning German classes) has been one of our foremost concerns. We have always believed that the strength of our lower division governs the strength of the entire departmental structure: *finis origine pendet*. We do not grant a Ph.D. to anyone who has not taught beginning language classes. Teaching assistants, contrary to a common misconception, are not cheap labor, and we could do better—and achieve more continuity—if we replaced most of our T.A.s by lecturers. But we continue to insist that our students teach.

All Ph.D. candidates take a course in contrastive syntax and a course in methods of teaching German, which also serves as a general introduction to the profession. This course was first given in 1962, but the tradition is much older: the first methods course ever mentioned in our course descriptions appears in the 1906 catalogue. All staff members teaching beginning language courses— professors, lecturers, and teaching fellows—meet once a week to discuss teaching problems and strategy and to plan common examinations. Within this structured framework, however, teaching fellows are completely on their own and not in a lock-step operation. All Ph.D. candidates are required to teach six quarters, but never in their first graduate year. For one or two of these quarters, they may also serve as research assistants to members of the staff. Graduate students may also assist in the preparation and teaching of upper-division literature courses, not for remuneration but for course credits.

Most graduate students are enthusiastic teachers; they usually prefer teaching assistantships to fellowships, and about half a dozen of them have gone on to write dissertations in the field of contemporary German language. In 1972, one of them, a native American, was appointed to a tenured professorship at the Central Foreign Language Institute of a German university.

I have mentioned these early innovations in order to make it evident that our trend toward German Studies is not a fleeting bow to relevance or to student demand, but a genuine realization that a department of foreign language can be many things to many people without losing strength and cohesion.

The 1960's saw expansion primarily on the graduate level, due at least in part to the sudden demand for Ph.D.s in the post-Sputnik era. Whereas prior to 1960 we had granted one or two Ph.D.s per year, and sometimes none at all, that figure increased from four in 1965 to thirteen in 1973 and is only now leveling off. As the number of graduate students rose—the highest number of registered students at any one time was 55—teaching and research activities branched out considerably. Today, even with a much smaller number of Ph.D. candidates, this broad range of interests persists very strongly: the Department's connection with the Humanities Program has already been mentioned; there is considerable involvement with the program in Comparative Literature, and one member of our staff has a double appointment in German Studies and Comparative Literature; some of our courses form part of the program in Modern Thought and Literature, a program that combines the study of literature with other disciplines in the Humanities and Social Sciences; the degree of involvement with the

Department of Linguistics is indicated by the fact that one colleague is an affiliated member of the Linguistics faculty. Many of our courses are cross-listed with these other programs. Around 1970, an effort was made to officially establish an interdisciplinary program in Central European Studies, and while this proposal has been temporarily shelved, the cohesion established among the Central European group continues to exist.

During the mid-sixties, the Stanford Library appointed a special curator for the German collections in its Resources Development Program who, together with the West European curator in the Hoover Institution, oversees the acquisition of books, journals, etc., in the Central European field. Also in the sixties, the Department began publishing *Stanford Studies in Germanics and Slavics* (Mouton) which has now been superseded by *Stanford German Studies* (Lang),

Within the Department, the traditional graduate courses in periods and genres were de-emphasized in the sixties, and a new trend developed toward literary theory and methodology. This new emphasis made sense at the time, because many of our Ph.D.s obtained positions in large research-oriented university departments. Today, such courses are still given on the advanced graduate level and are usually interdepartmental in nature. But we have re-introduced a core program in German Literature and Culture, a three-year sequence of nine courses which exposes all graduate students, whether they take all courses for credit or audit some of them, to the entire continuum of the cultural history of the German people. These courses treat the major periods of German literature from the early Middle Ages to the present. They are intended to convey to the student a sense of the developing traditions that have shaped German literature. By focusing on a specific period, the literary and non-literary (cultural, social, political, philosophical) contexts can be established within which individual authors, works, and movements are situated. Since these courses, like a number of others, are also open to advanced undergraduates, duplication of courses is avoided—a vital consideration at this time of low graduate enrollments.

Recognizing the strong interrelationship and interdependence between literature and thought in the history of German letters, we introduced (in 1969) a new track, *Geistesgeschichte*, into both the undergraduate major program and into graduate studies. A basic series of three courses acquaints students with the history of German thought since 1750, covering such authors as Herder, Hegel, Marx, Nietzsche, Freud, Wittgenstein, and Adorno. *Geistesgeschichte* by now is well established as an area of graduate specialization, as is Germanic linguistics. In the linguistic area, courses are offered in the older dialects, from Old Norse to Early New High German, as well as in contemporary synchronic linguistics. Students may concentrate in either diachronic or synchronic linguistics, or in language study and pedagogy.[2] Regardless of their area of specialization, however, all students are required to take a number of courses and seminars in *all*

---

[2] Early in 1976, the Institute for Basic German, under the direction of J. Alan Pfeffer, formerly at the University of Pittsburgh, was relocated in the Department. Its vast corpus provides a mass or raw data for future research in contemporary German.

fields so as to avoid narrowness of training which might easily lead to narrow-mindedness.

Two other components of the Department's program also date back to the 1960's. We became aware quite early of the need to recognize the significance of the cultural developments in the German Democratic Republic and started offering courses contrasting the diverging cultures of East and West Germany and others dealing with the literature and cultural politics of the GDR. Over the years, these courses have undergone repeated changes, but are now settling into a definite pattern.—For about fifteen years, we have taught at least one course per quarter outside the confines of the Department, conducted in English and with all readings in English, on major authors like Nietzsche or Kafka, or Joyce, Proust and Mann, and on such topics as "Nazism and Literature," "The Fantastic, the Grotesque, and the Uncanny," and "Manners, Morals and Mores in the Middle Ages." We have never felt that these courses took students away from our regular courses; some of them have attracted a great number of students, and they have always been truly university-wide courses.

In 1970 we changed the name of the Department to "German Studies" to reflect the widening of our curriculum. The name change coincided with a revamping of the undergraduate major program that brought with it several far-reaching changes.

At the time, there were already three options for the undergraduate major: language/linguistics, literature, and thought. These, of course, are not three completely separate programs, but each has a core around which the student arranges his courses. Nor do these course options prepare specialists or professionals in these three areas. We still conceive of our B.A. as a general education degree that serves primarily to give young people an extended outlook on themselves and on their culture. That this notion is not entirely false is attested by the fact that the majority of our majors, like those in most other fields, do not go on to graduate work in German, but rather into law, medicine, business, and so on. It makes little sense, therefore, to consider the B.A. in German as *primarily* a first step toward a German Ph.D.

It was considerations such as these that led us to the introduction of yet another undergraduate option—which by now we have extended to the M.A. level.

For a number of years, students returning from the Overseas Campuses had been anxious to learn more about the Germany or Austria in which they had just spent six months. Obviously, they turned to the German department for more courses, but it was always "Goethe and Schiller, yes" but "Willy Brandt and Ulbricht, no." Most of them couldn't care less about Goethe and Schiller, but they were vitally interested in "German Studies," that is, in studying Germany rather than just German language or literature.

For the three "traditional" tracks, we require 50 quarter-units beyond the basic courses. For the new German Studies major, students need to take only 30 units within the Department, and an additional 25 units outside the Department, but in courses that deal with the geographical area of Central Europe. Actually, since we require that all students in this track attend one of our overseas programs, most students accumulate far more than the required total of 55 units.

The program is now in its sixth year, and about 50% of our majors are choosing the "German Studies" option. It is interesting to note that most of these German Studies majors would not have chosen a German major at all had it not been for this new track that allows a student, up to a point, to write his own program.

There are two dangers inherent in this scheme: first, unless carefully supervised, students might put together a program that would resemble the kind of area studies sometimes practiced fifteen or twenty years ago—an exercise in superficiality that might join together medieval German history, baroque music, and contemporary religious thought. We try to avoid this kind of pseudo-general education by asking the student to outline a well thought-out plan of study in accordance with his interests and with a possible future career in mind. Thus, a student thinking of going into international law or international business will select outside courses in modern German history, German government, East and West German law, etc. A student who is considering high school teaching—the one who will have to be a Jack-of-All-Trades—will choose a broad spectrum of related courses. If we did not have a large number of Central European specialists in all the relevant departments, we could, of course, not possibly teach all these courses within the Department without becoming superficial and overextended indeed.

The second danger posed by the German Studies option was that, in effect, we reduced the number of units taken within the Department. Fortunately, this was offset by the considerable number of new majors we gained through the new program. In fact, a number of students who started out in German Studies have since switched to literature or thought, thus adding strength to the old central program rather than taking it away.

To strengthen the "German Studies" track within the Department, we introduced several courses, for example a very popular course on current German newspapers and a course on Centers of German Culture, taught enthusiastically for several years by the late Dora Schulz. In 1975, we initiated a new core course: a three-quarter sequence on contemporary German culture and civilization. These courses survey geography, people, and institutions of the German-speaking areas of Central Europe: the contemporary situation and its origins in history. Topics include: governmental structure in the BRD, the DDR, Austria, and Switzerland; population; stability and migration; the *Gastarbeiter* problem; social structure of East and West Germany; the education system; communications systems; urbanization and its consequences since World War II; government and the arts. Extensive use is made of films, slides, etc. These courses are conducted entirely in German, but will be given in English in alternate years and will thus be available to all students.

At the same time at which we introduced the German Studies major, we started yet another innovative project, a program in translating and interpreting.[3] This program was conceived quite independently of the German Studies major, but the two have become very compatible indeed. It is directed by a *Diplomdolmetscherin* trained at the University of Mainz; during the academic year 1975–76, we "borrowed" an interpreter from the European Community in Brussels as an additional staff member in the program.

We do not offer a bachelor's degree in translation, nor do we consider doing so. Instead, we offer certificates in general translation on the B.A. level, and in either advanced translation or interpretation on the M.A. level, so that the students may participate in the program regardless of their major field.

At the beginning, we thought of this program as leading to translating careers much more than we do now. In our current thinking, the T and I program creates an ancillary skill that can, of course, lead to professional translation, but in most cases will be used by students going into some form of international relations—be it law, diplomacy, or business. To our great surprise, three of our first four certificate holders actually decided to continue graduate work in German—all the way to the Ph.D.

Several students who started the T and I program as juniors rather than as sophomores received their B.A. a year before the translator's certificate and continued to work towards master's degrees in German Studies. They are among the growing number of graduate students who are working for their M.A. only, a major departure from our traditional policy of accepting graduate students only if they planned to go all the way to the Ph.D. Also, during the last few years, there has been an ever-increasing number of co-terminal B.A.-M.A. students in the Department; thus, paradoxically and contrary to the general trend, our graduate enrollment has somewhat increased.

The growing number of M.A. students has raised a troubling question: what should we be training them *for*? It is true, of course, that some of them will go on to teach in high schools and junior colleges, but the majority, especially the co-terminals, do not anticipate teaching careers. We are therefore currently discussing the possibility of reorienting the "German Studies" option of the M.A. program toward non-academic careers. This might well take the form of joint programs with, for example, the Graduate School of Business, the School of Law, or the Department of Communication.

The latest restructuring took place in 1975–76 on the beginning language level. Until then, we had offered a standard six-quarter sequence, covering two academic years and using a global approach to all four skills. Shifts in student interest as well as the necessity to provide more flexibility in the number of credit units students were able to take prompted us to loosen up this somewhat

[3] For a detailed description, see *ADFL Bulletin*, 4:4 (May 1973).

rigid structure. We now offer, in addition to the standard course, a three-unit sequence in conversational German and another three-unit sequence for those students who are primarily interested in developing a reading knowledge of German. It did not come as a surprise that the latter option has been elected by quite a few students, positive proof perhaps that the audio-lingual approach was not as universally appreciated as we have at times been led to believe. Parallel to these courses, we have for several years run an individually programmed first-year course, which has been highly successful and is most popular with those students who, for whatever reason, need to work at their own pace. Also on the introductory level, we have introduced Dutch and will be adding, in cooperation with the Linguistics Department, beginning Swedish and Norwegian in the autumn of 1976.

Perhaps the most intriguing innovation on the introductory level was the establishment of a year-long series of lectures designed to acquaint students with the culture and civilization of Central Europe. We had long felt that, from the very beginning of their contact with German, students should become aware of the cultural matrix in which the language functions. Therefore, an initial decision was made to devote one hour of class time per week to *Kultur- und Landeskunde*. It soon became apparent, however, that it would not be feasible, without a considerable administrative apparatus, to present the same material in as many as 15–20 sections; furthermore, not all instructors would be equally qualified and would have to be specially trained for the purpose. The solution was to combine all sections once a week. Then it became possible to engage as lecturers Central European specialists from various departments. The additional bonus derived from this is that the students not only learn about the German-speaking countries but are also exposed to senior members of the faculty, some of whom they would not normally encounter in their entire undergraduate career. The topics of these lectures have ranged from an anthropologist's view of "Cultural Change and Urbanization in a German Village" and a Germanists's look at "The Films of Leni Riefenstahl: German Art or Nazi Propaganda?" to a linguist's discussion of "Language Change, Dialects, and the German Family Tree," an historian's description of "Regional Culture and the Berlin Style," and a political scientist's analysis of "Austrian Politics since 1945."

Over a period of about fifteen years, we have transformed—sometimes repeatedly—every level of our departmental structure. Perhaps we now have a program that will last unchanged for a decade or more, but we are willing to continue to invent and to experiment, to improve what we can, and to further both scholarship for its own sake and its application to what we teach. We believe that we have defined each component of our total program in its own terms; we are quite sure that at each level students can leave the Department with the feeling that we have provided them with an experience commensurate with their own educational goals and, above all, we feel that we have become an *American* Department of German Studies.

BEYOND INTERMEDIATE PROFICIENCY:
A LOOK AT OUR BASIC PROBLEMS

PETER HELLER
State University of New York at Buffalo

It is dangerous for a sick man to be ignorant of his condition; for only by recognizing his troubles can he hope to find a cure. The troubles confronting our profession are threefold: the inadequacy of training in basic language skills; the inadequacy of an undergraduate major restricted to literary studies; and the inadequacy of a graduate program deprived of relevance by its isolation from larger—Anglo-American, Western or interdisciplinary—contexts required for a meaningful pursuit of studies in the humanities and social sciences at this juncture. The remedies entail consequently: (1) a shift from an untenable defense of tokenism in basic language instruction, epitomized by the notion of "intermediate proficiency," to an aggressive advocacy of a substantive and solid training leading to a usable language skill or true proficiency; (2) a shift from the single track in literary studies available to the German major to a pluralistic approach to "German Studies" which would include—along with the literary track—several other tracks serving interests, concerns and demands in such areas as politics, history, economics, business management, et al; (3) an analogous shift to a pluralistic approach to programs on the graduate level where the study of German literature ought to be pursued—again on various tracks—in a broad Western context determined by perspectives of Comparative and English literature, and in combination with other disciplines such as history, philosophy, psychology, political science, etc.

The deficiency in basic language training is a problem peculiar to the United States rather than to the English speaking countries generally; for this deficiency does not plague higher education in Britain or even in Canada. A corruption and neglect of standards—at times defended as if it were a necessary concomitant of "democracy"—is pervasive throughout American education from high school onward. Though the world is increasingly in need of understanding other nations and cultures, our secondary schools have grossly neglected to train pupils effectively in basic foreign language skills. Hence the burden of basic instruction had to be shifted to colleges and universities where the foreign language departments have felt it incumbent upon them to assume the impossible task of inculcating a basic linguistic "proficiency" in two years of non-intensive training in a foreign language such as German (or French or even Russian), typically with no more than 5 weekly class hours in the first year and with three weekly meetings in the second year. However, in spite of the perennial fuss over—alleged or real—improvements in teaching techniques and the excessive claims made for gadgetry on which university administrators used to like to spend a good deal of money, the impossible has remained impossible. The so-called "intermediate proficiency" attainable after two years of non-intensive training provides as a rule no more than a preparation for the acquisition of usable basic skills in a foreign language; and as long as this is not recognized and the basic deficiency is not remedied, the foreign language departments in the United States will rest insecurely on the morass on which they have been built.

It is true that the intermediate preparation—at which most of our takers of language courses stop—entails a mental exercise which is no less beneficial per se or in terms of incidental benefits derived from foreign language study for the command of the student's native language, than the rudimentary training in some other disciplines. However, the radical inadequacy of Americans with regard to the command of foreign languages is only slightly affected by these four semesters (or less) of basic language instruction. For as far as the command of a foreign language such as German is concerned, "intermediate proficiency" leaves the majority of our customers in a limbo where they know too much to have learned nothing but too little to get any appreciable use out of their skill. Provided with "intermediate proficiency" they can neither write nor speak nor understand nor even read German with a degree of facility that will be of substantive use to them. Nor are the rudiments of a language likely to impress many students as a thing of beauty in and by themselves. There are other employments of the mind—e.g. a more thorough training in the grammar and use of English or a course in logic—which will seem to many quite as useful and less frustrating in that they will not leave them with an unusable semi-skill.

It is as if a course in driver education stopped short at an "intermediate level" where a man would have learned enough to get his car out of a garage but not enough to drive it to his place of work and to park it there ... But what should we do about this unsatisfactory state of affairs? "Intermediate proficiency" has at least provided a basis for our programs for undergraduate and graduate majors, much as instruction on the elementary and intermediate levels has provided the financial basis for our TAs. What good will it do to criticize the inadequacy of the levels attained in basic language instruction, as long as they furnish the sine qua non for our more ambitious endeavors? Shouldn't we, in fact, fight to get back the old language requirements?—Or should we rather try to get it through the thick heads of educators and students that insufficient command of a language does no one much good, while a true command is truly a useful attainment? And then, perhaps, there would be some honesty restored to our enterprise by a sizeable student body who could be expected to get to a point where their language skill would be of some substantive use to them?

The kind of "pragmatic" mentality that defined "intermediate proficiency," continues to operate even in further and upper ranges. It is in tune with the standard American prejudice concerning language skills. For it is as becoming to an American to admit he never did do well in languages as it would be unbecoming for him to admit an inability to operate a motor vehicle. And that block and the pride in that block about languages continue to affect the upper reaches of our programs, along with the real inability of those who got their "intermediate proficiency." And consequently our scene is fairly crowded with people who never mastered the foreign language in which they majored; or acquired such tenuous mastery that they lost it after a few years—which is when they meet you at a party proudly with "Vee gayts, vee shtayts!" or some such solitary idiomatic remnant retained from their precious college experience.

This much I found to be true: just as the virtuosos of "intermediate proficiency" lack basic command of the language—though they are likely to be tested even in their first year on such relative rarities as double infinitives and the finer distinctions in the uses of subjunctives, so likewise do the German undergraduate majors lack—not a basic command but the fluency and ease which they would need if they were really meant to engage in a serious study of German literature and civilization. And even our crowning achievement, the graduate student, still tends to suffer from that same deficiency.

But what if the study of languages were finally to be put on a sound basis? What if a notion of true proficiency gained as widespread acceptance in this field of ours as, say, in training programs for pilots or parachutists? American students entering the field without previous training would then accept as a matter of course what students elsewhere have long taken for granted: namely that the elementary and intermediate training must be intensive or prolonged, that it must involve a far greater number of contact and study hours than are normally required at present. And our prospective undergraduate majors would then be treated in the way foreign language students in European countries are treated; they would be expected to undergo and would receive the best and simplest of all linguistic preparations by total immersion in a German speaking environment, preferably for two semesters, minimally for one, either in an artificially created setting (such as Middlebury summer school) or, preferably, in a German speaking country. For so far this has done more for students than years of exposure to the most laboriously devised and most cunningly advertised methods, textbooks, labs, and gadgets.

The profession has always condoned tokenism and has become inured to trained incapacity. The present period of retrenchment might serve to wake us up and to make us realize that our basic problem and insufficiency lies in the field of language training, which makes whatever is built on this shaky basis a shaky affair. Nor is the subject of insufficient language training exhausted by the above remarks. For there is the tie-in with departments of education which insist on their right to certify language teachers without requiring substantial command of the target language (and indeed: they tend to discourage such command by their very insistence on the priority of "teaching methods" divorced from substantive skills). And there is the tie-in, within a larger context, with an entire concept of education divorced from any notion of substantive skill or social and intellectual utility, and dedicated to the conviction that education, and especially the college, is, and is meant to be, a beautifully wasteful baby-sitting operation designed to keep the young off the labor market for a spell. "Let them enjoy a good time; let them let off steam, and—since we must have the luxury of the "humanities"—let them acquire some useless "adornments" (the more useless the better). We (being wealthy) can afford this." Especially the languages were frequently seen in the light of some such implicit concept of honorific conspicuous waste—which, to be sure, was also a cover-up and thus a symptom of fear and distrust of incisive skill and insight in all but the purely technical fields. Yet at present the old conception of the usefulness of useless educational adornments does not seem to work anymore. The notion that a liberal education should be characterized by a genteel futility including a non-functional or non-"operational" smattering of a foreign language, deserves to be discarded. What needs to be recognized and stressed is the increasing need for people who have an operational command of a major foreign language and a substantive knowledge of the area and civilization to which this foreign language pertains. And with this recognition we have arrived at an enlarged conception of the German major as it has been put into practice at the Stanford German Department, which appears to provide a model for the profession (see pp. 78–87).

An inadequate correlation between supply and demand has been characteristic of our profession as of most of the humanities. Typically, members of a German department have been aware of demand only in the educational field itself, that is: of the demand for German teachers at various levels, and even in this domain attention has focused typically on the needs of full-fledged colleges and universities, with the requirements even of junior colleges and, especially, of high schools entering, if at all, only marginally into the orbit of our awareness. However, given the far flung enterprises of Americans abroad and the high degree of interaction characteristic, say, of ventures in business and politics, or in journalism and the media, it is obvious that there has been a very substantial demand for personnel with a knowledge of both English and German capable of working in German speaking areas or of making judgments pertaining to German affairs. And it is equally obvious that, by and large, this demand has not been filled by our profession. For unlike, say, chemical concerns which are wont to recruit chemists on campus, the American business firms maintaining a branch or connection with Germany, or a Federal agency, such as the State Department, maintaining personnel in German speaking countries, have not been in touch with us—nor we with them. Instead, it appears that the considerable demands relating to the German speaking areas were filled—unless they were neglected and disregarded altogether—by native German personnel capable of communicating in English. Indeed, an American employer in Germany would, one suspects, rather hire a German with a real command of English than an American with a German major who is in fact incapable of carrying on a business correspondence or a technical discussion in German. Yet above and beyond this consideration which pertains to the insufficient linguistic training discussed above, the lack of connection between American enterprises in German areas and the academic German departments would appear to be due to a condition of mutual indifference. For in concentrating on German literature (and somewhat marginally on the pedagogy of language teaching), the German departments trained primarily teachers of German language and literature, and did not look toward business or government agencies; much as the members of the business establishment or the political bureaucracy did not look to academic German departments to fill their needs.

A great deal remains to be done in these and other fields. As mentioned above, there are in the area of German Studies demands which could be met by us but are, in fact, met by others, as in the case of the German natives with a command of English assuming functions which could be performed by Americans with a command of German. And there are also desiderata which are not met properly at all; and it would be easy to cite instances for this. E.g.: try to find an American lawyer or tax expert who could interpret implications of German law or tax regulations for citizens of this country; or a group of American journalists who could participate in a forum discussion in German with their German peers and a German audience (instead of depending on the ability of the Germans to communicate in English). Quite generally, a blatant disregard and ignorance of foreign cultures and language communities have played a very substantial part in the series of international failures of the United States which have marked the decades since the close of World War II. To be sure: these have been and continue to be long range failures, and precisely because they are long range they never attract sufficient attention at the time when the damage is done. To give a—minor—illustration: In the fifties the U.S. maintained a large and expensive network of Amerika-houses in Germany and Austria—much larger and much more expensive than anything the French or the British did. But unlike the French or the British, the Americans staffed these institutes with incompetents—men and women ignorant of the language and culture of the natives, and consequently entirely dependent on their native employees. And while the skimpy French and British establishments enjoyed by and large a good deal of respect among the more intelligent natives, the chiefs of the Amerika-houses and the cultural "niveau" or lack of niveau of these establishments provoked a good deal of contempt. Yet *we* were never in touch with the State Department or Federal agencies of *Kulturpropaganda;* we never had an opening to connect us with these extended enterprises except by way of occasional guest lectures.

If we may assume that the U.S. is not simply an imperialist power bent on establishing colonial dependencies, but rather a powerful nation willing to enter into a genuine dialogue with other nations inhabiting the globe, there is indeed a place for Americans with a true command of German and a true knowledge of German civilization not only in *Kulturpropaganda* but in cultural exchange as well as in foreign affairs, business, journalism, the media. Yet we have hardly begun to consider the demands and needs in these areas. So far, our lack of connections has prevented us even from knowing the precise nature of these needs, let alone from filling the demands, from supplying necessary skills. Moreover, even within the university community we have been less than eager to initiate programs oriented toward perspectives other than those suggested by a major concentration on German literature. Undoubtedly, the masterpieces of German literature should and will always remain *one* on our primary concerns, both because of their intrinsic merit and interest, and because the study of German literature provides a *via regia* to an appreciation of some of the most significant aspects of German culture. Yet we should also create alternatives in close cooperation with such departments as history, economics, political science, sociology, business management, the natural sciences, etc. Various options for undergraduate programs in German Studies are dealt with elsewhere in this volume and need not be specified here. Suffice it to say that they must be predicated on a true linguistic proficiency and that they should be developed by way of intradepartmental diversification as well as by way of interdepartmental cooperation.

Analogous considerations concerning the need to open up the somewhat musty quarters of the traditional German department and to let in fresh air apply also to the higher and highest reaches of graduate training in our field. Here again we need to embrace a pluralistic approach ranging from a much needed training program (and degree) for competent language teachers, who would, hopefully, also enter into and reform the language programs of our high schools, to the Ph.D. programs in genuinely comparative and interdisciplinary fields. With notable exceptions the German departments in this country have been deficient in originality, frequently combining spinelessness with rigidity within an encompassing framework of mediocrity. More often than not, we have been spineless vis-à-vis German *Germanistik,* a dubious academic discipline which, at last, has become subject in Germany itself to the critical and polemical scrutiny it so richly deserved for many a decade. By and large, we have sought to do what the Germans, with a higher degree of intimacy with their own language and literature, were inevitably able to do better than most Americans. And so we deprived ourselves of the substantial advantage of the informed outsider who can observe the phenomena of another culture from a vantage point of his own. Unlike a Tocqueville looking at America, unlike a Veblen reviewing Imperial Germany, unlike the German Romanists, unlike even the British Germanists who have ever been ready to take their insular idiosyncracies to be the measure of all things, we rarely developed points of view of our own. Why didn't we? Was it because many of the American Germanists, though not native to the German traditions, were disassociated also from Anglo-American literary contexts and from participation in major currents of American intellectual life?

Defensively rigid in their associations with other fields, including other foreign language departments and, above all, the English departments which, in an English speaking country, inevitably exceed us in weight of numbers as well as in vitality and distinction, the German departments have been typically among the—respectably—parochial enclaves within the American academy. Yet in terms of intellectual impact German authors—e.g. Kant, Hegel, Marx, Burckhardt, Nietzsche, Freud, Weber, Husserl, Heidegger, Wittgenstein, et al.—have loomed very large indeed. Why, then, did we fail to derive more substantial profit from this massive impact? With spineless rigidity we adhered, by and large, to an idiosyncratically "Romantic" and sentimental conception of antiquated German Germanists who sought to exclude discursive writing from the heartlands of *Dichtung* and thus set up a barrier against the very genres in which the greatest literary achievements of prose have ever been recorded, from the Bible to Plato and Plutarch, from the scholastics to Luther, from Montaigne to Voltaire. As if the prose of Schopenhauer and Nietzsche had not been greater literary events than all of the German novels from Arnim down to Fontane put together! But was Nietzsche really and properly "literature"? As for Marx and Freud, most Germanists were certain they were not—until recently. And so, again with notable exceptions, the American Germanists cut themselves off from the very authors who were of greatest interest to the literate American (even and especially when he received them from the hands of French intermediaries) and who could have helped to liberate American *Germanistik* though, indeed, such liberation would not have been agreeable to some of the most influential men in the profession who felt quite honestly more secure and more in harmony with a defensive, ready-made *Germanistenweltanschauung,* or, generally, with an intellectual provincialism protecting them from the troubled climate of contemporary literary and intellectual currents.

What is to be done? We can act on what we surely know: namely that the era in which it might have been meaningful to study literature under a predominantly national perspective is past; that we should therefore learn to collaborate with other foreign language programs to establish a predominantly transnational or supranational—proximately: Western, ultimately: global—perspective. In practice this will mean an increased emphasis on comparative literature and a more selective approach to German literature (e.g. a readiness to allow a student of the 18th century to do without Gellert's *Schwedische Gräfin* but not without some firsthand acquaintance with Voltaire) and, perhaps, a development away from the autonomy of individual language departments and toward interaction within a foreign language division. For—though there are also other alternatives—cooperation and interaction might be facilitated by the creation of such transnational units. If these worked poorly in the past and led to jealousies among the representatives of the various national literatures as well as to favoritism toward the one which had the support of the divisional chairman, this proves only that the faculty of foreign language departments failed to realize that their intellectual and material advantage—including that of political weight as administrative entity in the larger context of an American university—could be promoted substantially by cooperative interaction. Instead of resisting the trend toward reinstatement of the foreign language division, natural in the present context of retrenchment, we should perhaps assume an active role in shaping such transnational units. Instead of guarding against Comparative Literature, we should join and strengthen the kind of program which, at present, still leads a precarious existence on the margins of several departments of literature but is clearly destined to take on a leading part in an age in which the conception of foreign literatures in terms of national traditions is bound to become subordinated to a larger Western perspective.

The other need that has become obvious at this time is that of systematic broadening of the area of our professional concerns so as to include the range of German Studies relating to history, politics, society, media, fine arts, music, et al. (as distinct from a restriction to language and *belles lettres*). And again these interdisciplinary emphases will entail selectivity and flexibility in our reading lists. Moreover, in close association with this broadening, an effort should be made toward a systematic development of interdisciplinary programs, e.g. in literature and political science, sociology, psychology, anthropology, philosophy, theology; literature and history; literature and linguistics. For much as in the area of literary studies the times have passed when the *predominance* of national perspectives was acceptable, the times are gone when one could advocate the study of the humanities in isolation from one another or, particularly, in isolation from the social sciences. The very distinction has become problematic; the need for interaction is plain. The humanities stand to gain greatly from this association (for when kept in isolation, the humanities lose their relevance to the vital concerns of men); the social sciences should benefit in turn by being enriched and somewhat humanized.

So far, the development responding to the need for interdisciplinary perspectives has frequently resulted in the humanists, e.g. the interpreters of texts, providing themselves with their own versions of psychology, philosophy, sociology, anthropology, and the like. An instance of this would be an English department or a German department developing their own programs in literature and psychology or literature and sociology by drawing exclusively on some of their inside members who had cultivated a secondary interest, say, in Marxist sociology or in Freudian psychoanalysis. Such programs, however useful as steps beyond the usual departmental barriers, fail to provide interaction with faculty who are bona fide sociologists or psychologists. They maximize the ever present dangers of dilettantism; and the professionals in the other fields will—rightly or wrongly—look down their professional noses at humanists dabbling in a psychology for literarians or in a *belles lettres* version of sociology, etc. At any rate, the genuine interaction between representatives of separate academic fields will not take place in this fashion. And yet, that genuine interaction and the reintegration of men's intellectual endeavors is needed most urgently. For we have been rebuilding the tower of Babel and are faced now with the threat posed by excessive specialization and the resulting state of intellectual alienation which is itself a symptom and an agent of dehumanization. Consequently, the modest task of implementing truly interdisciplinary programs and ventures in different fields could be a very worthy undertaking, however unaccustomed and painful the representatives of widely divergent fields of enquiry might find it to be forced to listen to one another. If the teachers and scholars in our field could take an active part in this endeavor to reintegrate the various branches of literary studies with the body of the humanities and social sciences, we would have finally overcome that intellectual isolation and pervasive provincialism which has threatened again and again over the decades to restrict our entire profession to a mental level as inadequate within the larger range of the humanities as an "intermediate proficiency" has been inadquate on the level of basic language skills.

To be sure, the radical changes and reforms advocated here cannot be accomplished overnight. Nor can they be accomplished merely by our own efforts. Their full implementation requires and presupposes radical changes and reforms throughout our entire system of higher education which is plainly in a crisis at this point from which it will only emerge if and when it becomes more truly cooperative with respect to the interaction between increasingly separated fields and departments of knowledge within the universities and more truly responsive to the needs of the society which it is meant to serve. However, these larger considerations should not keep us from taking whatever initiative we are capable of in our own limited sphere of activity.

GERMAN STUDIES IN AMERICA:
THE EXPANSION POTENTIAL

EVA MARIA FLECK
JERE FLECK
University of Maryland–College Park

When conversation turns to the state of the profession, over the past five years we have been hearing very little other than "academic horrors": collapsed departments, truncated programs, mass firings of junior staff and, first and foremost, enrollment loss or, at best, stabilization. This grim list would suggest that it is hardly the time to be talking expansion. With the administration's eyes on our present condition, many feel that we should not rock the boat, that we should tighten our belts, bite the bullet, grin and bear it, and other trite phrases which amount to: "Consolidate to defend the embattled *status quo!*" In this paper we would like to reinforce a realization that is gaining momentum: that the *status quo* has been an untenable position for decades. It is the result of our discipline's lack of foresight in the fifties, when interest focused suddenly on foreign language study and expansion was encouraged with ready funds and employment lag. At that point, instead of diversifying our product to meet a new and basically different demand, we put all the old wine into old skins, built up graduate departments and expanded undergraduate programs without changing the real product at all. Or, to put it another way, instead of responding to a genuine demand for something new and practical, we embezzled from our own future to build a monument to our professional past. The "Post-Sputnik Mentality" demanded a new program of pragmatic education in a world "getting smaller all the time." Our answer to the next decade of language students was to jam an enlarged wad of the same old education down their throats—not what they wanted, but what we wanted to give them. There are really little grounds for surprise that the boom went bust; the fact that it went bust in other academic disciplines as well suggests that we were not the only part of the university system to provoke an intellectual brown-out. And despite this incompetent management, things seem to be levelling out at present—we are not to be wiped out after all—we are simply being reduced to the state of things before we took the wrong turn at the crossroads of the fifties. Divested of our largely self-engineered disaster, we should now be ready to try again. Certainly it is true that this time we will not have the thrust of a broad-based intellectual awakening on our side (fed by wide-eyed articles in *Time* magazine to tell Americans that speaking a foreign language is not really a social disease, etc.)—we will not have virtually inexhaustible funds forced upon us by a government embarrassed by its own monolingual State Department. But it is time for us to do some serious positive thinking about a disciplinary expansion potential of a healthy and viable sort.

The principle of growth for growth's sake—that the only healthy enterprise is an expanding one—has been questioned seriously in the past decade. We are well into a period of general skepticism characterized by massive social realignment, revamped life-styles and shuffled priorities, highlighted by a new attitude toward population growth. This general trend rejects a goal of "more of everything" and tends toward a more rational ideal of "more efficient utilization of what we already have." In such a time, in order to be genuinely productive, expansion cannot be directed simply according to some abstract disciplinary master-plan; it must seek to satisfy demands which have had to take a back seat during the past and misdirected boom. Our return to a less pressured pace forced by present recession raises the premium on responsive tailoring of the product to the market demand.

Our profession in not unaware of this change. The first mood of deep hurt resulting from the trauma of foreign language requirement reduction or abolition was almost as short-lived as it was utterly unrealistic. Five years ago our colleagues were avidly discussing ways and means to preserve the foreign language requirement or reinstate it where it had fallen. The image was that of the prosperous blacksmith awakening sluggishly to the shock that horseshoes— yesterday a necessity of life—had become obsolete overnight. There was much "this can't happen to me" thinking, characterized by dicta to the effect that foreign languages were an absolute necessity in any form of education and that rejection of this tenet was barbarism. Others picked up their cross with an attitude of saintly innocence and accepted martyrdom in the name of their persecuted but undiminishedly holy vocation. The wisest smiled and prophesied that the pendulum was simply on a minor swing away from us and that soon the vogue would switch to another equally unjustified target. Let us hope that by now the more realistic members of our discipline agree that all of these attitudes are unresponsive as well as irresponsible. To begin with the fundamental flaw, the foreign language program common in the United States and Canada is generally not the source of an educational component which is indispensable to a meaningful degree. In fact, the accusations of irrelevancy levelled at us so frequently were and are based on a valid evaluation of the facts. We cannot state with any degree of honesty that college language training suffices for even modest dependence on the skill it professes to supply, nor that our graduate programs are supplying the world of academia with those professionals trained to cope with the demands of the future. There is surely no glory in this world for academic martyrs who went to professional death with unbroken faith—who did not retreat one step in the name of accommodation or compromise. And the hope that soon the students' vacillating rage will tire in our direction and move on to new and greener pastures is meaningless. Even if we were to observe a sudden deep-seated student need to turn against, for example, mathematics as irrelevant next year, this would not mean that they would swarm back into our unimproved language programs.

The evidence that change is underway can be read from the attitude toward use of realistic language in describing our woes. Five years ago terms such as *market, demand, packaging, product merchandising* or *diversification* drew scathing abuse to the effect that: "The university is not a marketplace!" But the exigencies of budget responsiveness to enrollment variation have proven far more convincing than constructive criticism from within the individual department could ever be. One gets the impression that far more ears among those still left on academic payrolls are open to thoughts formulated in the terminology of the world of commerce than there were in the past.

We should also expect that, once the problem has been identified, steps toward its solution should be in evidence. Here too there is a marked change. Departments, which might have scoffed haughtily at any proposal to tailor academic offerings to student needs, are now experimenting with *Commercial Language X* and *Reading Skill in Otherwise Unoffered Language Y*, etc. In some cases entire curricula have been reorganized, not without success. But certain basic attitudes still hamper potential expansion. And it is these attitudes which must first be questioned before constructive suggestions can be made.

Above all else, our foreign language programs are crippled by a complex stumbling block to expansion which can be labeled "major-centrism." During the period of forced enrollment under the language requirement, the sheer factor of numbers assured us that a certain number of students (not necessarily the best overall students, but at least those who did better in our courses than elsewhere) would continue beyond basic training. These students were then our *majors* and our program was geared to serve them. As advanced courses required advanced standing within the department, our justification for offering such advanced courses depended on our drawing majors to take them. And since we were much more interested in offering advanced courses to our majors than offering lower-level courses to others, concern with majors became obsessive. Major growth was equated with departmental growth. Of course it was admitted that a wide base was needed to support such growth. But for the most part teaching of general access courses—that is to say, courses which can be taken without departmental prerequisites, such as first semester language training or culture courses in English—was held in disdain by the true scholars of the department. Such work, often called "plumbing," was relegated to graduate students and junior faculty. Their time was as cheap as their talents were low—and it was a privilege for them to be permitted to teach at all. Majors, on the other hand, could be entrusted only to the cream of the department; they inhabited those academic realms where the course number grows in inverse proportion to the number of students enrolled. Of course, non-majors were permitted to enroll in such courses "if they could hack it," but the number of courses developed specifically to attract the non-major to continue language work was always miniscule in comparison with the cultivation put into the major.

And the concentration in the major program was literature. In fact that concentration was (and still generally is) so obsessive that many students who confess that they "aren't interested in the literature" are forced to major elsewhere. This stress is defended as the only valid preparation for graduate programs in which literature plays the same overwhelming role. And such programs, in turn, produce teachers who have learned to venerate literature. Who can be surprised that the products of this approach feel slighted by being obligated to teach "language and stuff" until they have the departmental stature required to teach literature. The resulting frustration is passed on to the next generation in the form of badly taught non-literary courses—conversation or composition classes which the repressed literary pedagogue has remodeled as courses in conversation about that very literature he (or she) does not get to teach.

As is frequently the case in self-serving structures, our foreign language major programs have led to intellectual inbreeding, goal-disorientation and overall input and output degeneration. Just how long this process might have continued—the structure itself surviving artificially, stuffed with warm bodies by means of the foreign language requirement—is a moot point. It might have toppled over under the weight of its own dead wood at any time, or, pot-bound by its self-limitation to literature, it might have choked itself off. And, of course, it might have lasted until it was felled by the results of a population drop not yet seriously felt but looming up on the horizon. That is to say, students might at some point, completely independently from any general change in university requirements, have become unwilling in larger numbers to submit to the crippling effects of being given only one direction in which to grow; that would have left us with only those who feared failure in other fields more dynamic than language. Or the simple decrease in the numbers of university age youth could have reduced overall enrollments to the point at which the faculty count might exceed half or one-third of the major count, making the continuation of such an academic luxury indefensible.

But the fact is that the impetus *has already* come—and in the form of decreased enrollments due to abolition or reduction of language requirements and further from pressure from the top, namely: the market glut of potential language teachers. Unfortunately, some of the reactions to these pressures have been self-defeating. Lowering standards or internal requirements for the major draws the very poorest type of student, both in native ability and motivation. On the other hand, attempts to vitalize the program by "better courses" and "wider offerings" at the top are equally counterproductive. Students used to the "old grind" cannot be promoted magically to a higher level by raising the quality of senior level courses. Since an increased number of offerings does assure a decrease in class size—an improvement academically, but a disaster when considering student-teacher ratios—if the number of potential customers (that is, majors) remains the same, no true growth can be realized.

The obvious response to the diagnosis above is the diversification of both undergraduate major and the graduate program. Here a Department of German is in an excellent position, especially if it is nominally or *de facto* a Department of Germanic Languages and Literatures. Always assuming that it is unwise to attempt expansion in competition with other departments, the lack of programs in Comparative Literature, Linguistics, Indo-European Studies, Scandinavian, European Area Studies, etc., delineates expansion potential. Three major areas of expansion present themselves immediately.

1. *Inclusion of Languages other than German.* Here, obviously, the Germanic languages (naturally, English excepted) are target areas. The modern Scandinavian languages are very similar in structure to English and have a potential market on any campus. Dutch can be floated at least once every few years. And German departments should never forget the appeal of Yiddish. But this is by no means the end of the list. In the absence of a Linguistics Program (or in the event of its exclusive concern with Chomskian Linguistics), traditional Indo-European Studies can be considered. In this context it is interesting to note that in the Washington, D.C., area four universities presently offer Sanskrit; at three of these it is taught by Germanists. Finally, there is the possibility of an interdepartmental Language Studies Program in which language skill in several languages rather than language and literature in one constitutes a major. In such an arrangement German is likely to come out a winner.

2. *Inclusion of Area Studies.* The idea that students may be more interested in life-style, past and present, in the German-speaking countries rather than in their *belles-lettres* is often abhorrent to the literarocentrics as is the idea that interest may be focused on the language itself rather than on the aesthetic content it has communicated. But such interest does exist. Where a "German Civilization" course succeeds in establishing itself as such—rather than as a slightly "other arts too" oriented "Survey of German Literature" course—enrollment among non-majors can be expanded. In fact, there is no reason why an enterprising department should not be able to sell as many "Periods in German Area Studies" courses as it does "Periods in German Literature." There is once again no reason why offerings should be limited to the German area alone. Any department which does (or could) offer language training can also house the area studies component, such as "Scandinavian Civilization." At the University of Maryland—College

Park—we now have a "Periods in Germanic Area Studies" number; to date only "The Viking Era" is actually taught,[1] but we may hope that other periods (including recent ones) will follow.

3. *Inclusion of Comparative Literature.* If no Comparative Literature program exists on campus, there is no reason why a German department should not take the initiative and offer introductory courses in the comparative method, literature courses in translation covering any language the department does (or could) offer, and, eventually, seminar-level courses. Of course such growth can hardly be purely a "German concern"—here interdepartmental effort is almost mandatory, including departments of English, Theater/Drama/Film and perhaps Music as well as the foreign languages. Although the literary colleague may at first shudder less at the thought of a Comparative Literature track within the German major, we must remember that the comparatist position cannot give a preeminent position to German literature—that German can only be the "first among equals" for a student majoring in Comparative Literature in our department.

The great advantage of such diversification of the major—at least as far as gross numbers are concerned—is that it represents not only an improvement for the major. Just as the singular obsession with German literature must be overcome in order to permit healthy expansion, so must the obsession with the major student be abandoned. Even if an expanded major program—one with Language and Linguistics, Area Studies, Comparative Literature and German Literature tracks—were to be strikingly successful (to pick a random but plausible figure, let us say that it had doubled the previous number of majors), it would still not bring back the broad-based support lost with the foreign language requirement.

In order to increase our base we must think in terms of *Upper-Level Access for the Non-Major* and give up the "reward at the end of the funnel" principle. In order to reach that lush blossoming of courses (at least of literature courses) open to the junior and senior, the student must creep in sequence through at least four semesters of four-skill language training. Consequently we cannot count on even the most attractive selection of senior-level courses as an enticement to departmental enrollment. We tend to forget that, unless the student comes to the university with German skills, he must take first semester German in his first semester if he is ever to be qualified to take a fourth year course at all. In other words, we assume that students will look at our exciting array of upper-level courses (their titles often in German) in the catalog and *predict* their devotion to German Literature before they have learned a word of the language—and that they will consequently register for "Introductory German"

[1] J. Fleck, "The Period Option in Germanic Areas Studies: A Sample Course in the Earliest Period," *PSGP Yearbook 1975*, pp. 30–52.

without delay! Of course, seen from that perspective, this position is patently ridiculous—or, at best, painfully elitist. It makes it easier for us to understand why we often have upper-level literature courses in which native Germans (who have been through the same texts in high school) outnumber the non-natives most in need of the course. We cannot afford to take an "all or nothing" approach—that is, eight semesters. The principle of access entails our making it possible for a larger number of students to take our upper-level offerings than our normal (major-oriented) language training program produces.

There are various ways of accomplishing this. Few departments will be able to mount both major and non-major offerings of the same course (the latter in English), although some departments do this with the "German Civilization" course. More efficient is the offering of a general interest item such as "German Literature between the World Wars" in English, but demanding that majors read the texts and write papers or exams in German. On the other hand, we can make German language texts more accessible by offering a two-semester "Reading Skills Only" track as an alternate to the four-semester four-skill option—in which case, lectures, papers and exams would still have to be in English to accommodate the non-major.

Another important step in the process is the *Acceptance of German Studies as an Ancillary Discipline.* Our "major-centrism" is most destructive in its purest form, namely: "Only a student devoted entirely to our discipline deserves the blessing of our teaching!" The concept that for the great majority of students at any given university, German Studies can never be anything more than "pleasant electives" or "ancillary skills" is generally ignored. And the suggestion that we should make active efforts to cater to both the seeker of an attractive change of pace and a vocational skill is another "social blunder." But to use numbers again to bring the issue into focus, let us assume that at a certain university there are about fifty German majors. All in all, including everything from first semester to doctoral research, that department racks up some seven hundred registration units per semester. Students on the lowest level rarely contribute more than one unit per semester (unless they have access to departmental offerings in English)— and a graduating major can contribute four or even five units to the count. The potential of increasing enrollments within that frame of reference is rather limited—even doubling the majors would produce at best another 150 units. But when one considers that the university in question may have in excess of 40,000 students on campus (and with an average of four courses per student, that is a pool of 160,000 enrollment units), the question becomes obvious: "How do we tap that enourmous resource of students who *never* take *any* courses from us? Certainly *not* by offering them even an enlarged German major. The answer lies in the concept of German Studies as an ancillary discipline; realizing any part of this largest expansion potential entails discovering the presence of an interest factor, tailoring a course to fit it, reaching the customers with convincing but honest advertising, and sending them away satisfied with a good product.

Such a suggestion will at first draw vehement cries of "prostitution" or "materialism" from our more conservative colleagues—there is a reason for that to be mentioned later. But it is "professionalism" and "realism" rather than "prostitution" and "materialism" to be proud of the fact that the educator is offering a valuable service on the commodity market and that the product can be tailored to the demand without any compromising of quality. We, for example, at the University of Maryland have developed a reading skills course for Swedish, Danish, and Norwegian in one semester which regularly draws over 75% students who otherwise have never taken a course in our department.[2] About a third come from Library Science with a second group coming from the behavioral sciences and history, plus an assortment of language buffs, students of Scandinavian ancestry and German students. The librarians are quite pragmatic in their expectations: they must be able to understand the languages in order to catalog books in them correctly. The Historians and those from Political Science and Economics need to be able to read expository prose. An occasional student from Interior Design wants to be able to handle Scandinavian catalogs of textiles and furnishings. Most of the German students are interested in reading the literature in the original or join the language buffs in their interest. If the students are satisfied (and they are, judging by their course evaluations and examinations), a genuine contribution to their education has been made and that is an *honorable professional success.* There can be little question as to the almost self-policed academic stature of such a course: if it doesn't work, word gets around very quickly! In fact its only blemish from the perspective of the traditionalist is that it is intentionally and blatantly ancillary.

The negative response to a course tailored to serve as a pleasant elective for students from another discipline must be based on the assumption that "it can't be medicine if it tastes good." Academicians are always very suspicious of popular courses, assuming that if a course offered by a certain teacher has a tendency to draw consistently high enrollments, something must be wrong. This is clearly not the case with our "Viking Era" (hardly ever likely to close out with two sections of fifty students during preregistration!) which draws its regular complement of hard workers, of whom, once again, only 25% are from our own department. We find it hard to understand why a tenth century areas studies course taken for pleasure should be inferior academically to a nineteenth century literature course taken to fulfill the major sequence if both entail similar student effort and represent a full semester's material.

Let us assume that a direct effect on departmental enrollment, including major and ancillary, can be exerted by curriculum diversification as suggested above. If that were all there was to it, we would be dealing with nothing more than utterly unfounded resistance by old-line conservatives and convincing (or

[2] J. Fleck, "Scandinavian Studies and German Department Enrollments," *Die Unterrichtspraxis,* 6:1 (Spring 1973), 63–70.

overriding) them would solve our budgetary problems. But few fundamental dilemmas can be resolved entirely by a change in thinking. The problem remains: Who will teach these new courses, should enrollment demand their being taught? That brings us to the bitter pill—the underlying realization which makes such hardened resistance to curriculum change understandable. Obviously *we* must teach these courses. Certainly not for long, because if demand proves that we are right, we will soon be turning out a new generation of fresh *doctores philosophiae* who have taken such courses from us and will be just as anxious to teach them as they were to take them. We are the bottleneck.

Let us assume that for the sake of argument the assumptions of this paper are justified—that a Department of Germanic Languages and Literatures can come close to doubling its overall enrollment in direct response to curriculum diversification. Allowing four undergraduate and three graduate years for that new generation to emerge, we are faced with our own "seven lean years" to suffer through. What would this entail beyond a "change in thinking"?

As administrations are now generally geared to reducing our numbers rather than expanding them, the lean years would entail substantially increased teaching loads, although we might look for trained personnel among the ranks of our colleagues who are "elsewhere" due to present conditions. After these few years we would be over the hump, able to relinquish course after course to younger colleagues. But in order to make time free for more teaching over the lean years, shelving of individual research would become necessary. This would represent a considerable sacrifice to many of our colleagues—in particular to those who see in research their true *raison d'être* and consider classroom teaching an unwelcome minor commitment of the profession. As harsh as it may sound to some, in times such as these publication of another weighty tome on another obscure poet amounts to fiddling while Rome burns. It is a form of arrogant narcissism in the face of the job to be done. German Studies in the United States and Canada might well survive seven years without American research—the question is: What will conditions be if German Studies is to survive another seven years without a substantial rededication to improved classroom teaching?

But what is in some way an even greater sacrifice is entailed in the process of academic self-reeducation that curriculum diversification would require. Academic dons who have done their Goethe in the fall and Schiller in the spring since the dawn of time would be faced with the moral obligation to shoulder their part of the load—to expand their own teaching programs, *not* according to their personal research interests or the supposed needs of a literature (and only literature) major, but according to the demands of the expanding program. And that means even more work outside the classroom than in it. Not only must the new courses be prepared—they must also be publicized. In most departments curriculum components will be envisioned for which there is no "staff specialist." Rather than sending the chairman out to interview, talent must be found within the department to bridge the gap. If we are really educators—if education is our product and teaching our trade, we should be able to develop our new courses quickly if we devote our full energies to the task. And this may be the far-sighted fear of those who scoff and scorn at diversification suggestions—the realization that they are justified; and if justified, must be implemented; and if implemented . . . that will send us all back to school.

This reschooling is not limited to the *Klassik*-aesthete, who may have to prepare an attractive and academically rewarding area studies course on the German-speaking world around 1800. It includes the philologist, who must expand his program to include an "Introduction to Indo-European Studies" or "Historical Linguistics" among his offerings. The methodologist will be kept busy making variant access tracks work and cooperating with native informants in offering on demand languages not normally part of the program. And so forth down the whole line. But perhaps above all else, colleagues must accept as axiomatic that no part of the departmental program is more *noble* or more *valuable* than another, or that servicing any one student is more important than servicing any other—that every course offered must be taught as well as reeducation and devotion permit, and always with the educational goals of the students taking them in mind rather than personal preference or the departmental major program. Students who emerge as majors or with graduate degrees from departments where such thinking is general will be far better equipped to serve in turn the professional demands they will meet in the future.

When it comes to sweetening this bitter pill, we can offer only one suggestion. We are all together in the same boat—and when we reach shore (if we do), we will probably discover that, all in all, we are not an untalented group. Once willingness to pioneer in good faith is assumed, perhaps the next step is more a question of logistics than anything else. As long as we do not feel that university is competing with university in developing diversified curricula, there is no reason why we should not treat the matter as a group effort. Then those of us more skilled at organization, publicity, material collection, etc., could be of genuine help to our colleagues. In less abstract terms, we suggest a clearing-house for new courses—either one we run ourselves or one structured through a present organization, such as ERIC. Every attempt should be made over the next years to channel summer grants not into personal research, but into summer workshops offering extremely pragmatic pedagogical preparation for offering one or, at the most, two such new courses. Participants would receive a packet containing a practical syllabus, teacher and student reading lists, sample exams, visual and audio material, publicity layouts from which to mimeograph publicity flyers, etc. The workshop would be devoted to giving the teacher an opportunity to become familiar with these materials and observe alternate methods of using them in a classroom situation. If successful, then such a workshop should return the teacher to his own campus not only with a large part of the most unpleasant spade-work already done but with a more positive attitude toward teaching the course in preparation.

The suggestions offered by this paper may at first glance seem either too drastic or too idealistic—but they are neither, as comparisons with conditions outside our own profession illustrate. We are used to thinking of the higher educational system as "the heritage of Greece and Rome, given academic form by the Christian Middle Ages, and flowering incredibly in our own century with the information explosion." What we often consciously ignore is that education is a consumer service, and that it is the obligation of every producer of a service to understand and satisfy the needs of his customers. The constant upheaval of the world of commerce often forces the overhaul of an entire operation—or even of an entire industry—an eventuality one hardly looks forward to; but once unavoidable, it often proves ultimately rewarding. Demand changes, and the need to satisfy that demand—to run a few steps out in front of it and possibly even to lead it—has trained the world of commerce to strive for extreme flexibility. If we had such aspirations, perhaps we would not be jamming our fingers into crumbling dikes and hoping for the imminent return of the hand-crafted horse-carriage. Instead of wasting further time with fortifications to protect our ruins, we would accept the challenge which changing times have offered us and sally forth to turn the advantage to our favor. Certainly the future of German Studies in America lies in moving with the times rather than in denying them "their truth." Educators are not professionals who have completed their educations and may then shut down the input before taking on the task of educating others; learning should be one of the greatest rewards of teaching. Perhaps if our discipline can make that principle its motto, we will develop new skills to be proud of—and greet the next academic upheaval (regardless of when or whence it comes) with less of the ostrich and more of the hawk.

THE REWARD SYSTEM FOR THE
AMERICAN UNIVERSITY TEACHER OF GERMAN

HENRY H. H. REMAK
Indiana University

Nowadays few teachers want to wait for their rewards until they go to their reward. Gone are the days when teaching was viewed both by its practitioners and society-at-large as a secular equivalent of preaching, a calling whose joys had to be purchased at the expense of materialistic penance. Not long ago a teachers' strike was considered with the same horror as the spectre of a striking clergyman: both striking against God's children. The remark of an Oxford don made to me years ago that he was not in favor of paying his own kind a better salary because a good income would attract the wrong sort of people to college teaching would elicit today, if not indignation, certainly amused smiles at so quaint an anachronism. Nevertheless, many of us, even though we hesitate to say so aloud in negotiating with administrators, trustees, state officials, and legislators, *are* aware that good-sized portions of our work are intellectually, spiritually, and personally satisfying to a degree not vouchsafed to many other fellow-citizens, that they do correspond to an inner urge in addition to a materialistic requirement. In comparison with many other university teachers, we enjoy the advantage of better contacts with individual students on account of the smaller size of our classes. But these intangible though very real rewards are not the ones to be evoked here. What you want to read about are the recognition of our competence in terms of salary, fringe benefits such as insurance, retirement pay, etc., working conditions including teaching loads, office space, clerical help, library and visual aid resources, appointment terms, reappointment, tenure, promotion, sabbatical leaves and the like.

Since there is so much rhetoric about the subject and the record is full of pious resolutions, dramatic protestations, and transparent special pleading, I would be wasting your time and mine if I piled more clichés on the huge, odorous but essentially sterile heap of attractive commonplaces that make us feel good the last day of conventions but don't leave us a whit better off a day, a month, or a year afterwards. So I will be very candid with you at the risk of not catering to some of the most cherished biases of our profession.

I owe it to you to allude to my own biases. I cannot possibly enumerate them all, for they form an impressive list, but I can at least give you occupational and service data that may provide some clues for them. I have been a teacher of German in America on the university level since 1938, but, except for guest roles elsewhere, at one university only. I continued to teach every semester, though on a reduced scale, while in administration. Since 1948 I have also been a teacher of comparative literature (which at Indiana comprises not only connections among various national literatures but also the relations of literature with the arts, sociology, political science, etc.), and since 1966 of West European Studies, an interdisciplinary field addressing itself to the total configuration of West European civilization. As to administrative bias or experience, I have, at various times in the 1950's and 1960's, served as acting chairman of the Comparative Literature Program and, on one occasion, of the German Department, for four years (1967 to 1971) as director of the Middlebury Summer School of German, for four years as chairman of West European Studies, and for five recent years (1969 to 1974) as Dean of the Faculties (something like Academic Provost) of the Bloomington campus of my university. For three or four years, right after the war, I was a member of the American Federation of Teachers. For about twenty-five years, I was active on the campus, state, and national levels in the American Association of University Professors. Whatever I may have learned or not learned or learned but forgotten, my interests have not been parochial, but I can divulge to you that in my heart of hearts my most personal commitment has been to German.

My first message to you is that the teacher of German is not as different from a teacher of other Humanities subjects, or from any other teacher in the university, for that matter, as he likes to think, or fears, he is (and please note that in order to avoid the cumbersome repetition of he/she or she/he, I mean to include "she" in this essay when I say "he"). The reward system is essentially the same for him as for any other university teacher. The same university rules and policies apply to him as to anyone else of his status. Hence there is no need to go into every facet of the reward system but only into those where endemic differences seem to exist.

Although this equality may, in fact, exist, the psychological perception of the university teacher of German is apt to tell him differently. Like many Humanities teachers he feels like a stepchild in American society. He perceives ours as a basically pragmatic nation in which useful, visible, tangible, measureable, vocational subjects like the sciences, professional curricula, and, to some extent, the social sciences get preference. Though the German teacher may desperately stress (and, I believe, exaggerate) the usefulness of our subject, he knows that our fundamental raison d'être is the expansion of linguistic, literary, and cultural horizons of the student, the fulfillment of his personal potential, a co-determinant element in shaping the significance of his life. That there will be some collective benefits is likely, but these are unpredictable, depend on chance combinations and opportunities, and occur *after* the university experience. Whatever personal benefit an individual derives from a foreign language, literature, and culture occurs *during,* though does not end with, the university stay and cannot be taken away from him whatever his future occupation because it has become part of his total personality.

Sciences, social sciences, and professional training are, of course, also able to affect the *Gestalt* of the student while student, but in addition their post-university benefits to society are more obvious. This means that for the university teacher of German the impact he makes on his students in classroom teaching and personal contacts is more crucial for the prosperity of our cause than similar effects achieved by a teacher of science, social science, or professional subjects. Suppose a teacher in one of *these* areas is not overwhelming. Every student of his will, nevertheless, be aware of the market-place opportunities in these subjects which lend their own motivation. A look at the daily newspaper convinces him that science, social science, and professional accomplishments are indeed very relevant to the country and to his personal job prospects. Much less reinforcement of this kind comes to the Humanities teacher and student, and still less to the teacher of a foreign language such as German. The proof of *our* pudding is in the eating. In our American civilization foreign language instructors must be better teachers than those of most other subjects. It may be personally therapeutic to lambast this situation, but otherwise deploring it is a wasteful exercise. Our quandary may even be a blessing in an admittedly thick disguise.

It is futile and therefore silly for us to demand that our society turn around and consider the Humanities, let alone foreign languages, on a par with the sciences, medicine, economics, the law, business, etc. The basic complexion of our society is what it is, namely based on the British modified by the American experience, and we have got to make the most of our opportunities within the system rather than daydream about creating a utopian one of which we might be the center. Besides, it is not such a bad system. If I had to choose between a fundamentally sound political, social, and economic structure tested for two hundred years, in which the Humanities have to struggle and constantly prove themselves but are vigorous, and a political, social, and/or economic system that is questionable but in which the Humanities are or seem better off, I would choose the former without any hesitation. Moreover, when one looks at the development, quantitatively and qualitatively, of the Humanities in American university departments and programs since the 1930's, the evolution is truly spectacular despite our quantitative, economic setbacks (relatively speaking) in the last few years. I was asked in France, some years ago, why the American Humanities were among the liveliest, the most enterprising in the world of the university even though the place of the Humanities on the American social totem-pole was inferior to that in France and Germany. My answer was that we were healthy and ingenious because our position in society was more precarious than in other western countries, that therefore we had to clean house and search our souls and try new approaches and teach like positive hell and, in general, behave like that other endangered species: missionaries—which we are.

What has that got to do with the reward system? Plenty, insofar as it requires special recognition, all the way from the department to the top dogs on campus, of the teaching function in our endeavor, particularly of elementary courses. There must be increased appreciation of the fact that our instruction, even in comparison with the other Humanities subjects, is complicated by our having to teach the medium before our clients can get the message. We must do this laborious chore extra well for we are hitting near-adult young men and women with the ABC of the foreign language which is more attuned to six-year olds, and must somehow make this primitive exercise palatable and interesting to students thousands of miles and a lot of dollars away from the place where that language springs to life as part of a culture.

On top of it, German is known as a tough language. Nor does it benefit from the cultural prestige of French or the geographical proximity of Spanish. So our task is, in some respects, more difficult, though we must in fairness acknowledge that, in others, it is easier, because German, with its "tough" reputation and the presence of a lot of science students in our classes, tends to attract better students than Spanish, and because the German "way of life" is much more congenial to many Americans, young and old, than French or Spanish or Russian civilization.

However—and it is a big "however"—we cannot hope, nor do we deserve, to profit from this special recognition of our mission if German departments do not become serious and professional about delivering the evidence for outstanding teaching. The failure of university departments (not just German, of course) in assembling a truly analytical, critical, differentiated, comprehensive evaluation of the teaching of their faculty to the powers-that-be constitutes one of the biggest hypocrisies currently in operation on university campuses.

Why "hypocrisy"? Criteria for promotion and tenure at my university (as probably in most other public universities with graduate schools and research facilities) require "outstanding" performance in one and "satisfactory" performance in the two other categories: teaching, research, service. It is, however, a commonplace, heard in numberless departmental meetings and corridor conversations, that no matter how much lip service the "administration" pays to teaching, when the chips are down what counts is "publish or perish." I remember an open meeting of the AAUP chapter at my university about fifteen years ago at which the then Dean of the Faculties answered the same allegations. He was in a difficult position because he did not want to discuss publicly the reasons why some faculty members had not been promoted or even the foibles and strengths of those promoted. Nevertheless, he managed to demonstrate that the majority of those faculty members promoted to the highest rank during the past academic year were known as outstanding teachers rather than as outstanding publishing scholars.

Six years later, when I was chairman of the Committee on Teaching charged with making a complete survey of the teaching situation at my university, I got permission to scrutinize all faculty dossiers used in promotion cases the past two years (over eighty) in order to determine whether teaching had not indeed played second fiddle to research. When such was the case, I found that the fault lay almost always with departmental lack of documentation on teaching. The use of facile epithets: "great teacher," "one of the most popular," "universally appreciated," etc. abounded. I even discovered that a department with a short memory described two different faculty members coming up for promotion in successive years as "the best teacher in the department." Teaching evidence in the dossiers was mostly hearsay and grapevine, plus some dithyrambic student letters or occasional collective student evaluations (solicited for the occasion?). In an enterprise dedicated to scholarship, this can hardly be considered serious documentation.

While dean of the faculties, I chaired the all-campus faculty committee on promotions for five years. In that period we dealt with over six hundred dossiers. Looking at the outcome superficially one might indeed conclude that research counted more than teaching or service since more faculty members were denied promotion or tenure for lack of research than for inadequate teaching or service. This overlooks several factors. First, the promotion and tenure criteria in my university (and I suspect in most universities in our category) were formulated by *faculty* decisions and are being implemented by *faculty* committees. Nevertheless, the convenient scapegoat myth that "administration" runs the promotion and tenure show persists. Faculty committees on several levels sometimes reach conclusions at variance with each other, some faculty committees are closely divided, and sometimes a faculty committee reaches a recommendation without full documentation or, perhaps swayed by a particularly eloquent member, evaluates the evidence in a lopsided manner, calling for dissent by an academic administrator. But overwhelmingly it is—and should be—the faculty that is in charge of these vital decisions; with an average of 130 promotion cases every year about 125 annual decisions were in line with the recommendations of the faculty committee at the highest level—that is, the one to whom the most complete evidence was available. Furthermore, academic administrators on the all-campus or all-university levels, at least in our university, tend to come from the ranks of outstanding teachers rather than outstanding scholars, thus making a bias in favor of research improbable. Finally, administrators are usually much aware of student, parent, and alumni interest in teaching via complaints coming in (no complaints ever about poor research!) and thus unlikely to slight it for that reason also.

Research turns out to be the culprit in promotion and tenure cases because it is extremely difficult to secure evidence from a department that teaching or service are "unsatisfactory." Several years ago, the late President Joseph L. Sutton of Indiana University, himself a great teacher, remarked that when there were, allegedly, so many good teachers there must also be some bad ones. One would never know from faculty dossiers, and while students may occasionally massacre an instructor in their evaluations, the majority of a class very rarely rates an instructor as less than "satisfactory." That is not what they *say,* but it is what they *write*. As to the third category, service, it is practically never unsatisfactory—at least not in dossiers. That leaves the area of published scholarship as, in effect, the only one in which it is difficult to circumvent verification—and therefore as the convenient whipping boy.

I have heard it said that the unsatisfactory teaching and service cases are eliminated, before promotion or tenure, by departmental decisions not to reappoint. My experience indicates that this is true for relatively few departments only. Unless it is a flagrant case, departments delay such unpleasant decisions as long as possible.

Assuming that "research" and "service" are adequate, "teaching," in line with our standards, must be more than adequate or even good, it must excel. Although the utilization of student evaluations of instruction in tenure and promotion cases has increased by leaps and bounds in the past several years, and while it can furnish evidence of considerable value, its effectiveness and final persuasiveness is open to doubt. First, student evaluation instruments are of very uneven quality, rather, of all too evenly poor quality. 80% of those relying on multiple choice, prefabricated questions, and computerized processing are, in my judgment, elaborate hoaxes: meaningless questions, trite and undifferentiated, and actually dangerous because they bedeck themselves with fake respectability by superimposing a highly "scientific" apparatus on flimsy, non-analytic, pseudo-intellectual foundations. I have found the articulated individual comments of students under a number of teaching categories to be by far the most revealing and reliable element in questionnaires if collected over a period of three years. Which brings me, secondly, to the necessity, given a good instrument, of monitoring carefully the frequency and manner of administrating it. Third, and most important, it is inconceivable that teachers of German, or any other professionals, should leave the evaluation of their work to young amateurs one, two, three, or fours years out of high school. We must have far more systematic and differentiated *peer* evaluation of teaching, some of which must be based on direct observation.

What would we say if the evaluation of our research were done without direct access to the texts? We would call that absurd. But when direct, repeated, systematic access to our teaching (which is, after all, the work for which we are being paid, not a private pastime) is suggested as a principal though by no means exclusive way of evaluating it, we find all kinds of reasons and subterfuges why this should not be permitted. One of the favorite terms used for this threatening activity is "spying." It is historically understandable why teachers might feel uncomfortable in the presence of a visitor—a superior—who might exercise some kind of thought control, and I am aware of the existence of some institutions that call themselves universities in which heads or chairmen and deans exercise a potential or actual kind of thought control. I have not taught in such institutions, and will not condemn teachers whose fears may not be entirely unreal.

But in the better universities of this country this objection is more likely to be a smokescreen protecting a "do nothing" predilection. Even if a risk is involved, as there is in any willingness to have one's quality judged, that risk must be taken, or else we ought to abandon the sham of claiming excellence without allowing its verification from various angles, including direct testimony.

No doubt it takes more time, effort, and ingenuity to collect information on teaching than to plunk one's publications on the table. But when there is a will there is a way—a number of ways, as a matter of fact. There are student evaluations, by current students as well as by those having the advantage of a more objective distance in time. There are student interviews by other students, unsolicited student testimony, regular interviews with graduating seniors, questionnaires sent to alumni, and student performance in subsequent courses. There are course outlines, sets of examinations, textbooks published or edited, audio-visual materials prepared. There are evaluations from apprentice teachers assessing the capacities of a teacher supervisor and coordinator. There must also be testimony by several colleagues who have visited the faculty member involved repeatedly, consecutively, singly, as unobtrusively as possible, by other colleagues who have team-taught courses with him or taught other sections of courses directed by him, or heard him lecture publicly. The bone of contention is direct visitation, and it requires tact and planning. If it is done hurriedly, like belated student evaluations, at the time when promotion or tenure are at stake, its credibility will be minimal. Rather, over a period of years a system or practice of intervisitation might be devised in which the entire department, junior and senior, tenured and untenured, participates. Intellectual pleasure, pedagogical profit, and increased collegiality are its primary, assessment in terms of promotion, tenure, etc. only its secondary though important purpose. The system could start out with members of small congenial groups of three visiting each other and discussing their ideas and methods, without notes or reports. Over the years, balancing good days with bad ones, and involving multiple experiences by multiple parties, some body of evidence accrues that does not make a mockery out of our present empty protestations about the pre-eminence of teaching.

This particular part of quality assessment, as is the entire idea of value differentiation, will undoubtedly be in trouble if unionization comes to colleges and universities. High school practices of early, semi-automatic tenure have already entered some college procedures: prohibition of elimination through professional assessment, except in flagrant cases, burden of proof on the administration, "satisfactory" rather than "excellent" as the requisite retainment factors. If the trend continues, teaching evaluation in depth and breadth is in trouble even before it starts. But then the entire quality concept of colleges and universities will be in jeopardy, a problem that transcends this chapter. With it may come the policy of some unions keeping any but a minimum of recruits from entering its ranks since they might threaten the livelihood or the income level of those already in it. Humanists worthy of the designation cannot be insensitive to the consideration of our *Nachwuchs:* our successors are entitled to reasonable job opportunities, and if we continue to strengthen job protection for those of us who sit pretty, we may be very unfair toward those whose only crime is that they were born in the wrong year. Chances for positions in our field will not be bountiful even *with* meaningful controls on faculty retention continuing to operate.

Imagine the rumpus that would be raised in a university if the promotion and tenure proceedings were entitled, "Reward and Punishment System." "Punishment" is an "in" word no longer, and it is not a nice word. But whatever we call the beast—and I favor humane euphemisms as long as the facts are recognized—remember that without screening on the job we will not earn proper recognition for the truly excellent teachers of German—and after thirty-five years of teaching I am willing to assert that German has more outstanding teachers in its ranks than any other foreign language. We have the data for this at my university where German faculty as well as teaching assistants have scored higher than any other department in the number of university-wide teaching awards granted. I have no statistics for the country, but a strong hunch that this is not a local phenomenon.

The service category is seldom the one that gains or denies Humanities professors advancement, except insofar as it may include personal compatibility, good colleagueship, congeniality, cooperativeness—qualities that must be taken into consideration in the American departmental organization system but that also represent delicate areas where the personal and the professional *Gestalt* tend to merge and "menschliche, allzumenschliche" factors complicate judgments. But since the teaching of a foreign language in an American university is missionary work, universities ought to recognize outstanding service to the institution, the state (particularly its high schools), or the country in designing and implementing foreign language curricula, techniques, and approaches, and assisting foreign language instruction in general, if such service goes clearly beyond what we all are—or should be—prepared to do in line of duty. William Riley Parker, the great late Executive Secretary of the Modern Language Association of America, made a compelling but largely unheeded plea sixteen years ago for the spotting and rewarding of such high-caliber professional service on a plane equivalent to teaching and research.[1] If that has not happened except rarely, the fault lies, as in teaching evaluation, in large part with departments: for in the category of "service" departmental write-ups of candidates for advancement are even less discriminating than in the area of teaching. The category is not really taken seriously. It often consists of a compilation of meetings

---

[1] "The Profession and George," Presidential address delivered at the 74th annual meeting of the Modern Language Association of America, in Chicago, December 28, 1959, published in PMLA, 75 (1960), 1–7, reprinted in Parker, *The Language Curtain,* (New York: Modern Language Association of America, 1966), 1–16.

attended, organizations to which the faculty member pays dues, committees on which he has served (no matter whether poorly or well) etc. As in teaching: if we do not make distinctions, there will be no distinction—and no reward.

Here is one example for exceptional service suitably rewarded because it was carefully documented. One of my colleagues designed a curriculum, composed learning materials, created audio-visual aids to teach German to disadvantaged, largely black, freshmen students who had typically never taken a foreign language, or, if so, had tended to fail, or had discontinued it at the first opportunity (and sometimes before). He created an intermediate language, Germlish, to facilitate transition between English and German, tested his design and media, criss-crossed the state recruiting minority students, counseled them in many ways when they were on campus, took them to Germany, Austria, and Switzerland as part of a carefully developed language training and civilization exposure plan—in short, has not only initiated and refined a significant departure in German language teaching but set the stage for the real emancipation of minority students. He recognized—and made them realize—that first-rate citizenship does not stop with job preparation but goes on to the mastery of less standardized skills and insights that often make the difference between a policy-making and a routine job, between a life rich in enjoyment of the "extra" things that constitute the cream of our existence, and making a living.

Because the foreign language profession tends toward isolation from the larger community, we should reserve special rewards for academic service on behalf of but outside the profession, e.g. for essays or books on German literature or culture or language published or accessible through non-professional media and of influence on the society-at-large.

As to research, I see little basic difference between what we expect of a foreign language teacher and any other humanist in a university. Someone who does not want to engage in research and, normally, invite peer feedback and assessment via publication should not *want* to come to a university with exceptional research facilities. If he does, whether it is his fault or the university's, it is a mismatch. There are many places in this country—the majority of institutions of higher learning—that, whatever they call themselves, are not really "universities," do not normally expect much research though they appreciate and reward it when encountered, and still fulfil their mission, some admirably. But my assignment deals with university teachers of German: the reward system for a teacher of German in a liberal arts college, a community college, a higher institution with limited research facilities is outside my subject and my competence. All I can say in the research category that bears specifically on the university teacher of German is that promotion and tenure committees on the various levels seem somewhat more willing to act favorably on a humanist whose strongest suit is teaching (but whose research is at least "satisfactory") than on a scientist (whose research is at least expected to be "good"), and that is as it should be, given the "missionary" context we have talked about.

A few major universities have tried to solve the question of reward for faculty heavily engaged in first and second-year teaching of German by setting aside a "Lecturer" or "Adjunct" track with good salaries, tenure, and fringe benefits, separate from the professorial faculty. Excellent teaching and service are expected, but not scholarly research. This is an attractive option, but not my preferred one. It perpetuates, rather than bridges, the gap between language teaching on the one hand, literature, culture, and linguistics teaching, on the other. It allows the latter to operate in an aristocratic alienation from the very sources whence their students must spring, to work in ignorance of the trials and tribulations (and occasional triumphs) of a young American who undertakes the formidable task of mastering a foreign language far from its natural environment, a foreign culture far from his own. However good the intentions, it sets up, psychologically if not in fact, two types of faculty citizenships, a first-rate and a second-rate one. Far better to involve, in principle, all faculty in work of all types on all levels. Not mechanically, of course: some distinguished faculty are not able to handle a first-year course with "ordinary" students, to hold their interest and zeal. On the basis of our experience of many years in a large department (presently 25 full-time faculty), there is practically no regular faculty member who, given good will and effort, cannot and should not teach from the second year on up, and there are quite a few *Honoratioren* who not only are teaching first-year now and then but are enjoying it, to boot. In a country where foreign language instruction is never secure, flexibility of faculty is a paramount professional obligation, and should be rewarded accordingly.

With my preference for a one-track faculty goes the plea that promotion, tenure, and salary committees cease their often indiscriminate labeling of text-books as being, *eo ipso*, unscholarly, commercial ventures not worthy of academic rewards, or, at best, belonging to the "teaching" rather than "research" category. Textbooks should be scrutinized, on their own merits, like any other publication. It is absurd to dismiss a publication as irrelevant to scholarship and education just because it benefits 5,000 students rather than 50 fellow scholars. Or because someone is willing to pay for it. The reverse could be argued more easily. Given—once again—the missionary context of foreign language instruction in this country, good textbooks are paramount to our endeavor. Like traditional scholarly articles they can be dull, drab, poorly structured, unoriginal, they can be satisfactory but not inspiring, they can be original, pioneering, they can have—and have had—profound effects on the teaching of German on the entire American continent. This *may* fit the research, as well as the teaching category. Editions of literary texts for American students vary all the way from "benign neglect" to ingenious, intelligent, scholarly but readable achievements. That research in language learning and teaching should also be evaluated on its merits rather than automatically treated as a footnote to teaching has, alas, still to be emphasized.

Even more complex is the question to what extent "research" and "publication" are synonymous. The common assumption in the reward system that they are identical is not tenable as such. Even in the case of research clearly destined for publication, time delays (sometimes enormous) between its acceptance and its publication, completely beyond the control of the author, prevent finished work from being printed. Book manuscripts must not infrequently wait for years before finding a publisher, even when their merit is uncontested. Research must precede publication in print, but does not necessarily lead to it. Scholarly teaching on every level presupposes research. Much more research goes into our teaching than reaches publication. To what extent should this non-published research be rewarded as research rather than assumed as an indispensable basis for first-rate teaching?

The arguments for *published* research are powerful. As we do our teaching for students (and because we like to teach), we do our research for an external audience, for the world of scholarship to which we also have a profound obligation (and because we like to write). Publication is the most practical form of dissemination. Furthermore, whoever wishes to publish takes considerable risks: risks of rejection, of criticism, of rebuttals by some of the most sophisticated members of the scholarly world, risks far greater than a teacher takes in teaching a more ephemeral class, students who may be very bright but hardly as knowledgeable as our peers elsewhere (or even here). Publication is still the most important and effective way of evaluating research. But not the only one. Research findings can also be disseminated by lectures, colloquia, other forms of written materials (in Linguistics, e.g., important findings are often circulated in manuscript throughout the country before publication), and there is no major university that does not have some scholars with a mental block against publication—or, for that matter, public lecturing—but with an intellectual acumen and originality going into teaching that by any name *must* be considered high-powered scholarship. So, while publication remains the first and most important manner of testing research, it is not the only one. However, in nonpublished research it is clearly the primary obligation of the teacher desiring proper reward to produce the evidence, otherwise difficult to get at.

If confidence in the reward process is to prevail, we must make sure that faculty or faculty committee judgments, representative and competent, be brought to bear on teaching, research, and service at every level of consideration. The better a university, the likelier the readiness of the faculty to assume the responsibility of quality judgment, the more subdued the role of the administration. The worse a university, the less ready and able the faculty to make quality assessments, the greater the power and willingness of the administration to step into the vacuum and make those judgments itself, for better or for worse.

Chances are that the average salary of the foreign language university teacher in America is lower than that of his comparable colleague in Business, Law, Medicine, some (but not all) sciences, Economics, and other subjects in demand by the "outside world." But there is little evidence that given a similar record and ability the foreign language teacher is paid less than other teachers in the Humanities (English, History, Philosophy, Fine Arts, Music, etc.). It is not possible to eliminate the supply and demand situation when a university must provide teachers for its students, but there should be deliberate internal catch-up plans to minimize the differences between these sectors.

Humanists, including foreign language teachers, tend to have much less clerical help than their colleagues in the social sciences and in the professional schools. The discrepancy is sometimes so great that the more service-oriented roles of these university components cannot account for it alone. The Humanist's underprivileged position in this respect is probably a result of tradition (the Humanist works for himself, does his own research, writes his own letters, is more subjective, tends to shy away from mechanization, works with individuals rather than with groups), but that tradition is changing and humanists are increasingly group-minded and action-oriented. The reluctance to press for more office support is perhaps somewhat anachronistic, but administrators are not likely to call their attention to this.

There is one more reward category very important to our teaching, research, and general morale: grants. Foundation support in the Humanities has dried up, partly because of reduced income, partly because some foundations have turned to the financing of socio-political-economically tinged projects, which in turn has exacerbated competition for the remaining Humanities grants. Scientists, themselves facing reduced support, have re-entered competition for general foundation help (e.g. Guggenheim), thus further narrowing down the chances of humanists. We must engage and persevere in persistent lobbying—I am not at all ashamed of the term—on all levels to increase present outside funding opportunities for Humanities research, and encourage our own institutions to keep in mind the tight external situation in making available internal research moneys. We have a long way to go before we really feel at home in this kind of game. We have no choice: more of us must get into it to get our fair share.

Fortunately, when we needed it most, Government support of pure Humanities projects, formerly almost non-existent, entered the scene. One cannot but be impressed with the intelligent dedication and imagination with which the National Endowment for the Humanities has operated, and we might well spare a word of thankful acknowledgment for the remarkable acceleration of NEH during the Nixon administration, which has not gotten exactly spoiled by gratitude from academia. Talking about gratitude, it is also in order to the government of the Federal Republic of Germany which has not only made available to the college and university teacher of German in America travel, training, and research opportunities in Germany when he needed it most—and he still does—but which has done so in good style: unobtrusively, without grandiloquence, tactfully, efficiently, effectively.

I find myself unable to end this analysis with a ringing clarion call. Even the most highly self-motivated university teacher of German needs reinforcement through rewards. They must be judiciously made and cannot be meaningful unless they correspond to "no rewards" or "less rewards" for those who do not rate—or not yet rate—them. We cannot expect others, whether students or higher-up faculty committees or administrators of external agencies, to make these distinctions competently unless at the departmental level and within our professional cadre in general we are willing to make them ourselves. We have got to take care of our interests, for no one else is likely to consider this *his* first priority, but we must do so as part of the main, not as sideliners booing the others. That is the gist of my observations.

THE PRESENT AND FUTURE SHAPE
OF GRADUATE PROGRAMS

FRANK G. RYDER
University of Virginia

Our present state and our prospects for the future are dominated by paradox. Considered in relationship to the "career goals" for which they have traditionally prepared, graduate programs in German are too numerous, too productive, and overstaffed. If, however, we were to redefine our goals in deference to educational and demographic change, we would be barely adequate in numbers of staff and kinds (if not discrete numbers) of programs, and there would be jobs for our graduates.

I have carried the burden of this argument in different forms from the ADFL meeting in June of 1975[1] to the October session of the project on German Studies in America—both in Madison, Wisconsin—and to the Atlanta meeting of SAMLA in November, specifically with directors of graduate study in German. Travel, they say, doesn't improve wines. It probably hasn't improved this paper, either, but it has tended to shake out some of the dunnage and permitted me to sense, from comments and reactions, what is of substantial importance, what needs emphasis, what the burden of the message really is. My conclusion is reflected in the proposition which occupies the first paragraph. I am convinced that it is true and urgent, and that it has survival value, but I think we will have to show enormous capacity for heterodox action in order to resolve the paradox.

As to the likelihood of change, one cannot be complacent. Is it irreverent to suggest that graduate training, in *whatever* field, is the most traditional part of the long years from grade school or high school to the tender maturity of the doctorate at 30 or 40 summers? Is it a false observation that any list of curricular reforms and experiments in *our* field, for example, is dominated by new undergraduate courses and unconventional college majors, by specialization of undergraduate "tracks" toward Grace in language and literature, by undergraduate interdisciplinary offerings? How much of the variety of academic and professional concern reflected elsewhere in this volume—Louis Helbig's paper (pp. 47–55) is only one example—has any objective correlative in existing graduate curricula? Is there not a great sameness, from place to place and, in

---

[1] See *ADFL Bulletin*, 7:1 (September 1975), 3–8, from which this essay derives.

time, from year to year in those curricula; indeed, couldn't one fall asleep in one program this year (scandalous thought!) and wake in another next year without suffering cultural shock or even much discomfort? In sum, is not graduate training a *monumentum aere perennius* to our own perception of our own particular syndrome of merits; are we not supremely self-perpetuating?

It is another matter to ask whether all this sameness is warranted, even on its own terms. The need for what we *have* been doing is simply not so great as we would like to think. And I'm not just concerned over falling enrollments at the college level or about the relative shortage of jobs. I sometimes think we derive a kind of protective consolation from being so meritoriously disturbed over these things, which are in a sense external to us. Worrying over problems at the level of "existence," about which for the moment we can do little, helps to keep us from thinking about problems of "essence," which are serious and truly ours.

Consider the following figures, which center on German but which would be almost interchangeably valid for other foreign languages:

●The last available statistics from the Office of Education (1971–72) showed 167 new Ph.D.'s in German that year, 1,591 in English. The numbers of B.A. majors (which must be some kind of measure of the clientele involved) were: German 2,477; English 56,094.[2] Or roughly: in German 1 for 15, in English 1 for 35. We know of course that many of our Ph.D.'s teach in the populous courses of the first year or two, but this is no answer, either absolutely or comparatively. I won't belabor the point.

●Nor do we need this large number of Ph.D.'s to "expand our horizons of knowledge." In the first place, most of our *doctores* don't do any expanding. I would allude to two studies of Ph.D.'s in the Humanities, duly noted in the *ADFL Bulletin* some years ago, the more charitable of which showed 70% never publishing a word after receiving their degrees.[3] In the second place, with 431 full or associate professors *in our doctoral departments alone,* we probably have enough person-power to match even the Germanists on home territory, witness the comparatively modest listing in *Germanistik an deutschen Hochschulen.*

●For traditional purposes, we also have too many programs. The Personalia issue of *Monatshefte* listed, for 1973–74, 45 departments which actually gave Ph.D.'s and, for 1974–75, 63 which offered the

    [2] Charles Anderson, Ed., *A Fact Book on Higher Education: Earned Degrees.* Fourth Issue for 1974 (Washington, American Council on Education, 1974). See also Volkmar Sander's contribution to this volume (pp. 24–32).
    [3] The less charitable says 85%! See M.J. Brennan, "A Cannibalistic View of Graduate Education," *ADFL Bulletin,* 2:1 (September 1970), 19–20, 26.

degree. It is hard to establish firm criteria for adequacy, but these numbers seem generous, especially given the small size of many faculties and the scope and complexity of a good doctoral program. To argue a fortiori, however: seven of the 63 doctoral departments list only two full professors, six list only one, and two have none at all. One assumes there is no inverse correlation between promotion to full professor and qualification for graduate instruction. Such departments (one-fourth of the total) are almost precluded, by their own testimony so to speak, from offering a full Ph.D. program.

In the light of our conventional goals—I use the limiting phrase once again—we appear overextended. We have too many marginal graduate programs, some of them kept alive by Herculean efforts on the part of understaffed faculties. (My travels reveal one case of a single professor responsible as director for over 15 current dissertations.) Others are kept alive by the admission of marginally qualified students—in this kind of market, where even the best may ultimately founder! Unhappily, with graduate programs as with national airlines, everybody seems to want one, though the price in both cases and many respects is too high.

Clearly, the interests and demands of doctoral education in foreign languages, in so far as they are directed toward the maintenance of the scholarly tradition, and the teaching that goes with it, would be well served if, by elimination or "merger," the number of programs were considerably reduced. Particularly in the latter avenue, in the combining of programs, I see the greatest advantage. Geographically isolated schools such as my own should tremble at the thought of the competition NYU and Columbia could offer if they joined forces, or Chicago and Chicago Circle, or USC and UCLA.

We should also fortify our criteria for admission. I am appalled when I view the standards applied to prospective graduate students—or the propensity to eschew selectivity and take things on faith. Is this a manifestation of our compulsion to get students, fill quotas, justify programs? Is it wrong to expect a GRE Verbal of 600 (or the equivalent, concretely demonstrated) when such a Verbal at the SAT level wouldn't make the 50th percentile at a selective undergraduate college? How many of us have hard evidence that candidates for graduate admission can write a persuasive essay in English or any other common language? How many of us have the remotest notion in advance what a new student's spoken German sounds like? Is there no way to recruit, review, and select so as to minimize future trauma or shame? Of course there is. But it's not the too familiar criterion of the warm body in ambulatory condition.

It would also seem incumbent on us to exercise more rigorous quality control en route: at the M.A. examination, after the qualifying exams (if any), at the Ph.D. written, indeed every time the progress of our students comes under review. But this is a more agonizing process and more cruel than saying no in the beginning. It would also seem necessary to be a good deal more selective in the distribution of A's, High Passes, Honors, or whatever badges of merit we bestow. Am I the only chairman or graduate faculty member who has sat through an evaluation session for all graduate students, after the M.A., for example, in extreme discomfort at others' or my own inconsistency of judgment? Do I or do you feel odd when it is seriously questioned whether X has the ability to proceed toward the degree and it turns out that he has never come close to a C in any single course, indeed averages B+? Or doesn't this ever happen?

We must also apply respectable standards of qualification for *teaching* our graduate students. We all realize that you have to start somewhere and that if experience in graduate teaching were the unmitigated prerequisite for graduate teaching all our problems would be solved because in a few years we would lose our faculties. But we can't be satisfied, and our students will soon wake up to the inequity, if for whatever reason—charity, empty slots, or leaves of absence— we allow other than serious and proven scholars to teach literature and linguistics, other than teachers of proven merit to teach teaching. And in these respects we can reasonably demand a successful apprenticeship: study and publication in the discipline, successful teaching of undergraduate literature courses, inventive supervision of multiple sections of German 1 and 2. Assignment to graduate teaching must reflect demonstrable merit, not the suspicion of it, mastery of subject *con amore,* not amateur ebullience.

Every consideration or proposal advanced thus far is in a sense retrospective and, though I would claim for each the merit of obvious logic, also in a sense restrictive and therefore uncomfortable. What now if we turn to the future and the statistical shape of things to come? We will not behold that most jejune of promised lands, the golden age restored by magic, with no effort or change on our part, a graduate program in every college and two jobs in every pot. We will, however, see a massive challenge, the meeting of which could transform and re-justify our mission as graduate instructors, rescuing us from desuetude.

These are the facts:

●The total college enrollment in 1972 was ca. 9,200,000. It is *now* 10,198,294, but it is projected to change so little that in 1982 it will probably be 10,416,000. As Volkmar Sander points out (see p. 25), of the relatively small growth foreseen between 1972 and 1982, 83% will take place in two-year colleges. Or: two-year schools will grow 37.4%, four-year ones only 3.1% over 1972. Or: the 1972 four-year college enrollments will grow, by 1982, from ca. 6,550,000 to 6,750,000, while those of junior and community colleges will rise from ca. 2,660,000 to 3,660,000! And the Costand Report predicts that by 1985 half the age group involved will be in two-year institutions.

I draw from this the simple moral: stick with the traditional training of our students for colleges and universities and face entrenchment, or reorder priorities and curricula and enjoy at least a chance of vigorous expansion.

•And we had better make up our minds before it is too late. Of the total enrollment in all sorts of colleges (over 10,000,000) we in German have a paltry 152,000; French 253,000, and Spanish 362,000. In the two-year colleges we have 18,763; French 34,330 and Spanish 87,060 (the latter being over 56% of the total foreign language enrollment in such schools). Further, although foreign language enrollments are still rising in the junior and community colleges of Florida, Texas, and California, they are down in New York. The tide, a modest one at best, may be turning.

I prefer to contemplate the situation in California, in hope that it contains some cheer for us. A leader in junior colleges, California now has almost as many foreign language enrollments there as in its four-year institutions (55,000 compared to 65,000) and even in that very Hispanic state the dominance of Spanish is less than one might think (32,000 or 58% of all FL enrollments). Clearly, languages *can* prosper in two-year colleges, and German has a fair chance. In other words, there is hope—but not without some action. And what precisely do any of our graduate departments do to serve that sole growing segment of our educational system? Isn't the answer: "Approximately nothing"?

Obviously if we are to meet this quite different demand—and if *we* don't, "they" will!—we shall have to be more practical, training our students for a radically different sort of teaching: more general and less specialized, more interdepartmental, in many cases closely integrated with the community, alert to everyday and pragmatic concerns.

Here, perhaps, one might interject that a degree of practicality in our conventional training might not hurt. It could even be argued that what a new Ph.D. does in his first job (if he is so blessed) should be something of a criterion for the way we train him. To gather from the way we actually train, all he does is teach 1 and 2, argue over Shklovsky versus Stanzel, compare Hebbel's concept of tragedy with that of Schiller, make out quizzes, and read a little Gothic. In point of fact what he does is some or all of that, plus teach Introduction to Literary Masterpieces, supervise the elementary course and the TA's in it (if any), order or help order books for the library, serve on the departmental committee on admissions or curricular policy, cooperate with colleagues from English in organizing a humanities course, try to decide what journal to send a thesis chapter to, and give a talk at SAMLA. This is a real-life composite of faculty members in their first two years of appointment in our department at Virginia. In some aspects their previous education did not give them much help.

Training for these broader tasks, for this greater professional awareness, would in many instances comport well with preparation for teaching in the two-year colleges, which must by the nature of those schools be interdisciplinary, functional, educationally and professionally "activist," and recognizably American. (This might be the place for a parenthetical note on the crippling ignorance of our students—and our colleagues—concerning present trends in American education and the once and future place of our discipline in the schools of this country. The present volume should be required reading for required discussion.)

For reasons implicit in the above, I do not subscribe to the concept of the D.A. as a substitute or replacement for the Ph.D. It would seem greatly preferable to contemplate what Richard Brod has proposed: the Ph.D. reformed in the direction of the D.A.[4] The worst of fates and most ominous for American education would in my opinion be division among institutions according to degree given, by some a scholar's Ph.D., by others a teacher's D.A. I should fear, in that event, the ultimate failure of communication between, on the one hand, the ever so competent academician who has forgotten what the relevance—yes, relevance—of his pursuit might be and where his *Nachwuchs* comes from and, on the other, the ever so dedicated teacher who has had no part in nor opportunity to observe the processes which enhance the body of knowledge he teaches, knowledge which therefore he cannot really understand or truly impart.

To visualize a graduate program that would serve both a logically extended traditionalism and the new missions of the future, we might ask what, concretely, TA training would look like. In varying mix for various students, experience would have to be provided *inter alia* in:

- —Teaching supervised sections of elementary language in the "home" university.
- —Supervising such work.
- —Teaching language, under internships, at the nearest 2-year college.
- —Utilizing the basic insights of theoretical and applied linguistics.
- —Teaching introductory literature in a 4-year college.
- —Teaching culture in the 4-year college.
- —Teaching literature, culture, and linguistics in appropriately general form in the 2-year college.
- —Explaining at every level the purposes and benefits of foreign language study.
- —Designing courses and organizing syllabi for every level.
- —Utilizing the principal ancillary sources (bibliographies, lists, services, etc.).
- —The use of audio-visual materials.
- —Evaluating and choosing textbooks, etc.
- —The preparation and delivery of lectures; the preparation and delivery of papers after the fashion of SAMLA or AATG meetings.
- —Development of techniques for encouraging students to talk the foreign language and to discuss its literature in the language.

[4] See "Reforming the Ph.D. on the Model of the D.A.," *ADFL Bulletin,* 6:4 (May 1975), 9–12.

- —Joint or team teaching.
- —Teaching literature in translation, at 2- and 4-year institutions.
- —The technique of working one's own materials into programs of Comparative Literature, World Literature, Humanities, at both 2- and 4-year schools.
- —Organizing and teaching service courses such as Spanish for business, German for engineering, French for travel.
- —Devising courses to meet the needs and interests of the community, notably for 2-year colleges with explicitly local base.
- —Bilingual programs, whether as participant or visitor, with discussion of the bearing of such programs on the future course of foreign language study in colleges.
- —Test design, measurement, evaluation, placement and (for universities) admission.
- —Assessing, on the national scene, professional and organization activities, journals, educational trends and issues; on the local scene, the place of one's department or subject in the policies and councils of the institution.

This is not a kind of "modest proposal" to make the task impossible. Such training could be offered—by larger and *fewer* graduate programs. And there is serious reason to believe that comprehensive, versatile departments, diversified but united faculties with a variety of specialities or emphases, one general curriculum with two or three different "tracks," perhaps even one degree with suffixes, would represent the kind of unity in diversity most appropriate to and healthy for the American scene, in preparing together all teachers who will guide the quest for competence and knowledge in the years after high school.

THE FUTURE OF GERMAN STUDIES:
A GRADUATE DEAN'S PERSPECTIVE*

GUY STERN
University of Cincinnati

To be tested by adversity is no new experience of the university. If the past is any guide at all, higher education, from the Middle Ages onward, has responded to challenge and crisis with inventiveness and creativity. Thus, while it would be folly to gloss difficulties by rhetoric, it would be equally ill-advised to overlook that the professions, including the teacher-scholars of German, have coped with difficulties as grievous as those that face us today: there are still in our midst those who have turned the desuetude of the Depression Years into a dramatic renewal of the spirit, who have provided intellectual, scholarly, and philosophical leadership during the war years and have come to grips with the unrest of the 1960's. As we, Janus-like, look backward and forward, we can take comfort from Nestroy who tells us that a realistic look at the unvarnished past will give us the strength to confront the present.

What is called for today is both a flexible credo for graduate studies in German and a plan for action. In seeking these, our talents, our ingenuity, our inventiveness, and our good-will for one another will be taxed as rarely before. In order to make a beginning in this harnessing of our own mental and spiritual energies, I should like to recommend that each German department in consort with other language-literature departments establish task-oriented action groups or other means of effective self-study. They should try to meet and anticipate a whole set of new and old problems.

Although many of the problems that confront us may be known by a majority among us, let me define them once again. The latest statistics reflect a dwindling enrollment in the graduate sector of German. This is particularly disheartening because the phenomenon is by no means global. In the countries of Europe, for example, the demand for education in languages and literature at the highest level is substantially increasing. While we may legitimately ask ourselves what has happened to the intellectual atmosphere in the United States, to the very zest for scholarship and learning, we should in addition look for self-help, when external leadership has palpably faltered.

We should, therefore, begin by asking some searching questions on recruitment:

*A revised version of the article published in *Unterrichtspraxis,* 7:2 (Fall 1974), 7–14.

1. Do we effectively transmit the excitement of our quest to the traditional degree-candidate seeking admission, i.e., the traditional undergraduate-senior? Something more than a supposedly dwindling job market may account for the lower percentage of college graduates seeking admission to graduate school in German. Each department, in its own way, must find ways to communicate this excitement.

2. Have we identified and eased admission for the part-time or special students of our graduate program? Do we know that population groups are emerging, eager as never before to continue their education? (Against all expectations, graduate enrollment in the U.S. increased by 6.6% in 1975–76.[1]) Have we, for example, eased renewed accessibility to graduate education for post-college age women? Have we recognized that they often seek enrollment in traditional programs, but need help, untraditional and imaginative, to achieve their purposes?

I should like to cite a plan, evolved by Ruth Angress, Helga Slessarev, and myself which offers one model for the recruitment of post-college age women. It takes the form of a memorandum to one of our university administrators:

> In discussing the predicted attrition in student enrollment, we explored various educationally sound channels for attracting new groups to language classes. One idea engendered in this mutual exchange appears to have particular appeal since it would serve, at one venture, three educational goals.
>
> In brief, we advocate making a concerted effort to enroll nonemployed women of post-college age, many of them mothers of preschool children, into our daytime language, literature, and culture classes. The department, in order to enable many of these women to participate, would establish a new type of child-care center, staffed by our undergraduate majors and minors. The new direction of this child-care center is a nursery school, conducted in a FL, with games and recreation in the same target language as their mothers'.
>
> We see the benefits as four-fold:
>
> 1) it would permit these women to continue their education,
>
> 2) it would provide in-service training for college students interested in FLES programs,
>
> 3) it would expose the children to a FL even prior to elementary school, and
>
> 4) it would win for our classes a population group that rarely participates in evening college classes.
>
> It should be added, parenthetically, that the fear of many past

[1] Garland G. Parker, "Collegiate Enrollments in the U.S., 1975–76: Statistics, Interpretation, and Trends in 4-Year and Related Institutions," *The American College Testing Program Special Report,* Forthcoming in March, 1976. I am grateful to Dr. Parker, Executive Director for the Office of Enrollment Policy and Education Research at the University of Cincinnati and Vice-Chairman of the Board of the American College Testing Program, for allowing me to quote from his article while still in MS form.

college age of not being able to keep pace with university students has to be dispelled in announcing such a program. Also we feel confident, though we have no data for this, that participating women would be willing to pay a small sum for such child-care service; these amounts would largely go to the in-service undergraduate instructors.

We might point out that this project is entirely in keeping with recent developments in education, such as the new stress of life-time education, exposing the very young to FLs, and the demand for a greater accommodation for women seeking careers and an increased recognition to the responsibility of child-care centers.

Other population groups, not greatly represented in our graduate classes, can likewise be attracted. We have learned from such perceptive studies as Simone de Beauvoir's *Coming of Age* that frequently the intellectual curiosity of retired people is undiminished, that advanced studies could, in fact, be the antidote to the tedium of retirement. Universities, and particularly their graduate divisions, are showing more and more their recognition of this potential "student market," using various incentives (for example, lowered tuition) to attract the elderly. One example comes to mind—this time from the perspective of a researcher of the fate of the exiles and a board member of the Leo-Baeck Institute, rather than from that of a graduate dean. I can attest to the fact that those immigrants who are enjoying some leisure are eager to revitalize their ties to their cultural past. The burgeoning attendance at the Leo-Baeck Lecture Series in New York, Chicago and San Francisco is a most revealing symptom. There is no question that many of these immigrants, though coming from all walks of life, are intellectually equipped to participate in our graduate classes. German graduate classes, especially those located in urban centers, may profit from their presence, both from their intellectual and numerical enhancement of our classes.

Finally, have we been imaginative enough in the recruitment and retention in German departments of qualified members from minority groups? Surely, the small number of black students in our programs argue otherwise. Again and again, recruitment has been desultory or has led to frustration, not because a student's potential, but his or her preparation was deficient and subsequently not compensated for by a graduate school program. Surely it is illusory to think that a deficient undergraduate program can be remedied by a few hours of compensatory education in the summer. To the best of my knowledge, no university, certainly no German department, has yet tried an intensive approach through peer teaching, in which more advanced graduate students could in small groups ready an educationally-deprived student for graduate school on an individual basis. We would furnish both a better model for the student and a better mode of preparing him. I think the rewards for our profession would be more far-reaching than any one of us can foresee. There are currently high schools and colleges in the South with a predominantly black student population and with negligible or non-existent German programs. If there were qualified black applicants for positions in such programs, often the only ones accepted under the currently prevailing racial sensitivities, we might well witness the emergence of new or expanded German programs.[2] Both idealism and self-interest argue for such an experiment.

Another focus of self-study should be financial self-help. It is a truism that traditional sources for outside support have dried up; NDEA, NEFH and other federal grants and traineeships have either dwindled or disappeared. To a minor extent, graduate programs can effect some economies by eliminating duplication between departments (why not combine the method courses of various language-literature departments?), by combining upper-division undergraduate courses with beginning graduate courses, by establishing consortia with sister institutions, or by rotating offerings, and the like. But these will most likely be mere strips of adhesive tape where sutures are needed. Also, not many graduate students will be able to or willing to finance their own education. Nor do I anticipate, in the foreseeable future, a stronger support of graduate studies from states.

Two avenues suggest themselves. We, as humanists, should take a far greater interest in the budget-making process of our institutions. All too often we leave the process—based on some premises disadvantageous to the humanities—to the experts who have the most experience but are not knowledgeable in the particular problems facing our discipline. To them it is far easier to comprehend that a scientist must be supplied with the latest equipment for his professional development, but they are less aware that a hidden cost for a language/literature teacher is a constant need to travel abroad for a renewal of his knowledge of language and culture. Analogously, representatives from business, industry, and government are fully prepared to pay for expert advice from consultants in the sciences and social sciences, but feel that expert knowledge from the language departments can be solicited free of charge. In a society which, rightly or wrongly, assesses the value of a service by its cost, it would not be at all remiss for language departments to establish a scale for services, such as translation or advice on foreign countries, in conformance with the practice of other professions.

We might also try, in a hitherto under-used approach, to gain new allies for our graduate programs in business, industry, the professions, religious organizations, Community Chest, health and welfare agencies. I think this is possible: we have found through our German Department at the University of Cincinnati that a specific request may gain a hearing where appeals by all-university fund raising drives have failed. We should seek not only new donors but also concerned

---

[2] The sudden burgeoning of the German program at Fisk University under the imaginative leadership of a black woman professor makes this suggestion more than a hypothesis.

citizens who would under the tentative title of "Friends of the German Department" help us solicit subsidies.

For example, in the development of such University of Cincinnati programs as FLES for Minorities, National Work-Study Program, and the Lessing Society, we benefitted not only from the largesse of such conventional sources as AATG, the Office of Education, and the Deutsche Forschungsgemeinschaft, but also from the Ohio Valley Foundation, the Greater Cincinnati Association, the Corbett Foundation—all of them local—and from interested private citizens, here and elsewhere. German-American firms in other parts of the country have similarly benefitted German departments in their regions. Drawing on local support or on donors anywhere who are interested in specific projects may be one escape route from our financial dilemma.

Of course, we need allies for more than fund raising purposes. All too often we have been our own spokesman on behalf of the merits of our discipline. I would like to propose that we collect and solicit "endorsements" from respected spokesmen who are members of the general public or from academic disciplines removed from our own—we avoid the appearance of being self-serving. Let two examples stand for many. The championing of a language requirement claims greater credence if it comes from Albert C. Bartlett, a respected astrophysicist; a plea for general education is more effective if issued by a Professor of Business Administration, such as James O'Toole.[3] The latter, together with his Task Force, argued, "A good general education . . . is probably the best career education a young person can receive." Perhaps we should publish, from time to time, these statements of support from unbiased advocates.

Realistically speaking, the students now entering our graduate schools will probably not enter our profession until 5–7 years from now. What will be the status of the profession at that time? What are the implications of our projections on the curricula of our various subject areas? What new interdisciplinary programs are needed to meet the demands posed by the frontiers of knowledge as they will stand five years from now? We should anticipate this need in our departments by founding interdisciplinary study commissions to anticipate the needs of the future. Beyond that, we should attempt to explore all areas where long-range curricular planning transcends traditional approaches. I suspect that we will find that the educational demands of the future will affect us in analogous ways. (As an aside, it is high time that we at the universities help shape the future of our society and not leave it to the levellers. To misquote, "for mediocrity to triumph, it is but necessary for competent people to remain

---

[3] James O'Toole (Chairman, Special Task Force to the Secretary of HEW) *Work in America* (Cambridge, Mass. and London, England: MIT Press, 1973). In an address at the University of Cincinnati, "Making Education Relevant for the World of Work" on May 28, 1974, Dr. O'Toole, Professor of Management at the University of Southern California, added: "We have devised as yet no better preparation for a career than a liberal arts education."

silent." Possibly we should not only be the scholars but the professors, advocates, and even popularizers of our fields of knowledge.) There are some aspects of the future, as it reveals itself even now, that will affect all of us. These range from greater leisure to a re-emergence of the individual, from the problems of the aging to the quest for racial equality, from international interdependence to ecology and the expanding field of services.

What might we do in our German departments by way of exploring "alternate approaches to graduate education"?[4] Here, each German department might emerge with different answers; it is, in fact, desirable that we spread widely in order to avoid unnecessary duplication and competition. The German Department at the University of Cincinnati, for example, has evolved a program in International Management in concert with our School of Business Administration and with Romance Languages. What future would a joint program with a Graduate Journalism department hold? Or what promise would there be in a joint effort with a Communications Division, one of the fastest growing and most future-oriented academic pursuits? Is there a need in an expanding communication industry for bilingual or even multilingual speakers rather than readers? What are the implications of such a need, if it is adjudged to be real, for elementary and high school education, such as the necessity for bilingual schools in monolingual settings?[5] These are merely "sample questions" for such action groups. Dozens more will come up when individual departments, each with its own predilections and capacities, start "brain-storming."

The next problem for our departments is placement. While ideally a student might hazard an uncertain employment market, even after being made aware of the risks, we glean from some early surveys that the diminution of enrollment in German is related to the dwindling job opportunities in our field. I personally am convinced that the so-called Ph.D. glut on the market is temporary and that a highly developed society will have increasing rather than decreasing demands for specialized knowledge in all areas. Nor am I convinced that hitherto unforeseen utilizations of many skills do not lie ahead. I am, therefore, not discouraged by the glum predictions of the Newman Report for those departments that essentially send their graduates back into the academic world. If we will but recall that not too long ago (meaning within a single lifetime) psychologists enjoyed little employability beyond the campus compared to today's expanding and diverse job possibilities, we might be far less given to despair. Again, we ourselves can suggest to tomorrow's society a better and more diversified use of the skills, knowledge, and insight we impart in our classes and language laboratories. What, for example, will be the implication of the expanding communication industry

[4] The phrase is borrowed from the name of the panel that produced the exciting and controversial brochure *Scholarship and Society* (Princeton, N.J.: Educational Testing Service, 1973).

[5] Such a bilingual school was recently started by Margith Stern and Larry Stevenson in the Cincinnati Public School System.

for such traditionally "academic" skills as languages? What effect will added leisure and hence added travel have on the study of national cultures, languages, and the like?

And even in the field of graduate teaching itself, entirely new possibilities may evolve, for example, a far more expansive program of off-campus teaching for agencies, clubs, community groups, and industries. The German Department at the University of Cincinnati, to cite a case in point, established a mini-campus at Proctor and Gamble, where the German language and Area Studies were taught. This may well be a harbinger of the growing realization on the part of international industry that language and cultural knowledge must accompany an executive abroad. With these future possibilities in mind, it becomes apparent that the conventional university placement service is inadequate, that departmental and personal help by faculty must be encouraged, and that a graduate school-wide approach can bring about a sharing of ideas and of resources. One should argue for putting parts of placement service and its funding into the hands of the graduate school and the departments. As a recent publication of the University of Michigan puts it, "we may raise these considerations without believing that all graduate education should be dominated by a manpower approach. To be sure, the graduate schools must keep their doors open to students who have no clear occupational motive for learning. We are likely to see the ideal of liberal studies strongly reasserted at the graduate levels."[6] Nonetheless, we must link our programs to manpower or rather to societal needs. "The effort to adapt the intellectual strength of the graduate university to changing needs can bring a new vitality to graduate education in the 1970's," says the Michigan report. As far as our own discipline is concerned, the future needs, spelled out above, may already be potentials for the present. An action group on placement, aided by the survey on employability in industry of language specialists[7] should fully explore this potential.

A further action group should try to facilitate the research activities in our departments. The incentives should be more summer grants for our younger faculty (where available), more recognition both in monetary terms and in reputation, and more released time through flexible scheduling at that critical period when a major research effort is launched. The measures, while feasible in some departments with a maximum of cooperation and goodwill, will sound illusory to others.

But one measure does not require funds: recognition is one of the ineffable, but important rewards that our profession can bestow. I believe that appreciation by our peers and by those who can indeed sympathize with the struggle and

[6] *Rackham Reports,* 1 (Fall 1973), 3.
[7] "Foreign Languages and Careers" by Lucille J. Honig and Richard Brod was published in the April 1974 issue of the *Modern Language Journal* and is available for purchase in pamphlet form from the MLA. Richard Brod informed me that a new study by Ernest

pain of scholarship and appreciate the successful completion of it is part of the satisfaction for which we strive. Recognition should be visible: Libraries should allow for departmental displays of their scholarly achievements; local news-papers should become more attuned to the achievements of our departments; and the media should give us a chance to air our accomplishments. We may have made far too little use of educational radio and television in bringing merit to the attention of a wider public.

In German departments, as in all other academic pursuits, the Research Encouragement Action Group should also concern itself with stimulating team research, a concept more practiced in the sciences than in the humanities. But departmental research efforts, for example, the editorship of a journal, a year-book, or an author's collected works; the publication of an imaginative text-book; the advocacy of new teaching methods; and the utilization of computers for linguistic or library studies are not new. In our field, they are underutilized, however.

These are some of the goals that I see as aspirations of our departments—each of these specifics is but a first step. There may be other vehicles; whatever these may be, they demand a close partnership between faculty and students. We may wish to sponsor faculty-student workshops, or we might ask the president of our German graduate student association to acquaint us with their most overriding concern in the course of a department meeting.

In this era of better student-faculty relations, we must not only alleviate the financial plight of graduate students, but also accord them greater dignity and recognition. Much of what we can do requires ingenuity but little or no budgetary outlay. Why not establish, through the university credit unions, health-care plans, group insurance, junior membership in faculty clubs, or child-care centers for the benefit of graduate assistants? Why not argue for the same discount privileges in book stores, at university events, etc. that only are accorded faculty? Why not accord them status by including them in appropriate directories or encourage them to read papers at departmental societies or professional meetings? These and many other ideas will surely come to the collective mind of concerned departments.

In closing, let me state a more basic philosophical perception of the future of graduate studies in our field. In the nation, in journals ranging from *Science* to the *ADFL Bulletin,* we hear of debates about the merits of pure and applied research, about the needs of new methodology versus the needs for new conquests at the frontiers of knowledge, and about the distinctive nature of the university versus its obligation to society. Many of these debates to my mind are

----

Wilkins "Languages for the World of Work" (Salt Lake City: Olympus Research Corpora-tion, forthcoming), sponsored by USOE, confirms the data of the earlier MLA survey, which Honig and Brod utilize. See also Barbara Elling's article in this volume, pp. 233–246.

artificial. The university has traditionally fulfilled all of these functions, and we can pursue every one as long as the achievement is genuine. Nothing may be more urgent in our field and at universities in general than to affirm the validity of all intellectual pursuits and to allow abundant room for experimentation, reform, and a variety of approaches. In the search for renewal, we would be ill-served by dogmas.

SHOULD THE CANON BE CANONIZED?
THE FUTURE OF GERMAN GRADUATE STUDIES IN AMERICA

BLAKE LEE SPAHR
University of California-Berkeley

Foreign language teachers in America are paranoid. Moreover, they wear their paranoia so prominently that it becomes a way of life and is accepted as a natural condition by their colleagues in the sciences and even in the humanities. Hence, paranoia, implying an *imagined* condition of persecution, is perhaps not the right word. We have become accustomed to playing the rôle of the persecuted so well that it is only natural for others to join in and *really* persecute us. No other discipline has been so self-critical, so apologetic for its existence, so diffident in its claims and so happy to consume the crumbs from the academic table. We examine minutely our methodology, justify self-consciously at periodic intervals our right to a place in the curriculum and are absolutely delighted if no one bothers to dispute our modest claims. This very publication is a proof of what I am saying, and the articles in it would cause raised eyebrows if they were to have been written by sociologists or physicists. In the 1940's, when I entered the profession, it was always an easy matter to locate the German department on any campus. One simply searched for the oldest building on campus, found the furnace room, and there beside it in the basement was the departmental office. And we were delighted that we were not relegated to the coal bin.

In the 1960's our worst fears were realized. Students, rebelling often for the sake of rebellion, wisely chose the most vulnerable area for attack—the dread language requirement, a requirement rendered all the more vulnerable by the fact that we, lacking the courage of convictions that we hadn't even dared admit, had permitted our "requirement" to dwindle to a level that we all realized was a mere token—who of us thought that two years or four quarters were sufficient to master even the rudiments of a foreign language? So we were loath to defend what was obviously an inadequacy (an argument which on a higher level is also even now being used against Latin—to that later), besides, we always knew we were unnecessary, perhaps even undesirable. So we put our tail between our legs and ran, accelerated even by some colleagues within our own discipline, when we should have been *demanding* that the language requirement be increased to a good four years in college after adequate foundations had been laid in high school. (Ironically, the rallying-cries of our opponents provided us with the very ammunition that we were too timorous to use—cultural imperialism, inability to understand our neighbors, isolationism, racism, nationalism, etc., etc., in all of which causes the knowledge of a foreign language would have been a most valuable adjunct.) Particularly, we failed to realize that the spirit of the times was anti-authoritarian, against any requirement, but *not* against a structured curriculum. Rather than taking upon ourselves the difficult task of restructuring the curriculum responsibly, providing the proper tools, while freeing the use of them, we capitulated ignominiously—but who could blame us, as paranoid as we were—and admitted that perhaps the opponents of the language requirement were right (we had secretly suspected it all along). We are *now*, a decade later, treated to the edifying spectacle of having our students suggest (gently, for they realize the delicacy of our psyche) that we might perhaps assume the responsibility inherent in our position, but which we have long since abrogated, and venture to present a structured curriculum. And students are so right in suggesting (they should *demand*) that we draw upon our experience and knowledge to respond to the *real* needs of our students, not to the vagaries and modishly determined whims parading under the cloak of "relevance" to which we acceded in our preoccupation with our real or imagined persecution.

Fearful lest someone discover how dispensable we are, we have hacked away at our programs, graduate and undergraduate, eliminating prerequisites, dispensing with necessary tools, streamlining our courses, offering Mickey Mouse lectures to draw enrollment, all this with no sense of responsibility for our total programs[1] or their effects upon the educational needs of our students, patting ourselves on the back withal, saying that we were simply "going with the times." (Indeed, we will be going *out* with the times, if we keep this up!) No one has had the courage to say: "We are offering herewith a well-rounded program, designed to meet our firmly stated goals. It may be tough, require real work, but we are confident that the results will justify it!" Instead, working upon the principle that educational institutions and the dentist are two examples where one does not mind paying for as little as possible, we have repeated again and again: "Come take our courses. We will make them interesting and fun. You won't have to work much, we'll all have a good time together." And we imply thereby: "You may not have much to show for your time and effort, but at the same time you won't suffer much." I find this insulting to our students, and I have too much faith in them to suppose that they have fallen or will fall for such an approach. By this I do not wish to imply that one should not keep up with the times, but I should like to regard this as a duty, not a concession. If there happens to be a current interest in an author (such as Hermann Hesse), a literary trend or an aspect of culture, it is our duty to provide courses to inform our

---

[1] As Frank Ryder puts it: "Worrying over problems at the level of 'existence,' . . . helps to keep us from thinking about problems of 'essence,' which are serious and truly ours." See "The Present and Future Shape of Graduate Programs," p. 122.

students about such things as a part of their general orientation to the world they live in. But they should be regarded as the icing on the cake, a public service function, if you like, and have little to do with preparing our students to meet the goals of our program, other than in the peripheral sense of having them become well-informed about all sides of our subject matter, however trivial.

It is time that we take a step backward, to gain perspective, look at our goals in an objective way, realistically, from the point of view of our place in humanistic studies, and apart from the pragmatic, timorous considerations of how we may increase our enrollment, how we may attract students and how we may sugar-coat the pill of learning. If we are really a valid part of the curriculum and if we really believe in our discipline and in its contribution to the humanities, the two purposes will fall into one, and a solid realistically conceived curriculum will indeed attract students and give them the benefit of that to which we have dedicated our own lives. It is also time that someone should stick his neck out, state his convictions, and have enough confidence in his discipline to believe that its pursuit will result in a rich humanistic experience, a foundation for the fuller enjoyment of the human accomplishment, as it is reflected in the creative arts.

"Should the Canon be Canonized?" In order to analyze this question, we should, in traditional German style, have a look at the foundations of the canon and the presuppositions from which it emerged in order to determine whether it is still valid today.

Traditionally, the graduate professor was, by definition, a "great man," thinking great thoughts about his significant research, and his students, sometimes carefully selected by him, could be privileged to listen to the great man thinking aloud and could learn from his great thoughts—learn about the mysteries of his research, which were not to be found in any textbook, but which were being developed before the very eyes or ears of those sitting at his feet. He would frequently call upon them to help him in the more pedestrian tasks involved in his research and, if he were so inclined and his students sufficiently advanced, he might even question them as to their ideas of the solution of the problems with which he was dealing, feeling perfectly free, of course, to take possession of *their* ideas as his own—completely justified, since his students would do the same thing to their students some day. There was obviously no question of *teaching*. Students on this level were expected to acquire the fundamental knowledge necessary on their own, develop their own methodology, and, again some day, think their own great thoughts aloud. The professor's "classroom" function was solely to *think* (moreover, about what he pleased) and to *profess* his thoughts. This ideal professor would have been completely puzzled by the phrase "Publish or perish!" and even more so by student evaluations of his "teaching." His very *raison d'être* was research, and a great deal of it was "published" only via the notes of his students.

While this ideal situation regrettably no longer exists (and perhaps never did exist in a pure form), a surprisingly large number of details of our canon are postulated directly upon this concept: "After the master's degree there are no specific course requirements (for the Ph.D.)." "Students are expected to present themselves for an oral and written examination which will test not only the knowledge acquired, but also their ability to think abstractly and to put their knowledge to work in an original fashion." "The dissertation will test their ability to do original research and to present that research in a well-organized, understandable way," etc. The professor will be rewarded primarily upon the basis of his research. "Requirements," when they exist, are simply a codification of the obvious necessary tools for the student's independent research. In fact, virtually our whole canon has its roots in the above-depicted utopian professor-student relationship.

Obviously, in today's mass education, such a situation is untenable. Alas, we must admit that not all graduate professors are great men, and sometimes their thoughts are not exactly great thoughts. By the same token, not all candidates for the Ph.D. are capable of developing into great men thinking great thoughts. Moreover, the situation in America is further complicated by the amalgamation of the German and the English tradition of higher education—a condition which inserts incongruent factors into even that utopia depicted. A canon built upon an ideal situation which no longer exists and which does not fit into the present day educational system anyway is obviously not valid. Or is it? Leaving that question open for the moment, I should like to make the point that the canon has not been revised in accordance with the modern needs of the student or even in congruence with the institutional demands superimposed upon it.

For example, most graduate German programs have given up the Latin requirement, many as a result of student pressure, justifying the action upon the basis that the modern-day student no longer has the foundations of a humanistic education from which the Latin "requirement" emerged. Besides, if the student's interest is in modern literature, he no longer needs it. In addition, a smattering of the language will do him no good, and the requirement was only an out-moded token anyway. No one raises the question whether Latin is still a necessary tool or not.

But the Ph.D., whether we like it or not, is still a professional degree. The bases upon which it is granted are postulated upon this assumption. However, since it has become a necessity for employment in any large university, it can no longer be reserved for its pristine original purpose. But, rather than face this paradox, we have streamlined the degree in such a way that it now serves *neither* the original research demands *nor* the teaching-undergraduates-and-graduates-on-any-level purpose. We expect excellent teachers to produce significant research, and we expect truly great scholars to be able to teach dynamically. Both expectations are unjustified and not even necessary. Some of the most lasting impressions I have, which indeed changed the course of my own life, were made by execrable teachers, who could not explain clearly how to get out of the building in which they were teaching, but who, on a much higher level, had something to say, however badly they said it. On the other hand, when I look back through the haze of time to my own graduate days, I cannot, with the best of intentions, bring to mind a single thought that has remained with me from absolutely superb teachers who had nothing to teach. I do not mean the fundaments, the hard facts that one must "know," but rather the abstract projection of those facts, the productive combination of knowledge and wisdom which is the essence of graduate study. Facts can be mastered by anyone, but they are most efficiently passed on by a good teacher who can present them clearly and interestingly. Wisdom is invaluable, however badly it is transmitted. It is time that we recognize these basic truths and stop trying to make a professional research degree serve two disparate purposes which may, but need not, correspond. A great deal of the modern crisis in graduate education is caused by students with true insight who want to be teachers, but who protest the necessity of learning branches of knowledge which they feel they will never need or use; while, on the other hand, there is another group, fundamentally interested in scholarship, who are discontent because *they* feel *themselves* ill-equipped to meet the demands which research places upon them. Both groups are right.

While I do not like the solution for a single moment, I can see no other way than to further the development of two different degrees, one to serve each purpose. The result is perhaps monstrous—two categories each of students and teachers, divided probably on the basis of undergraduate and graduate teaching. But we cannot serve God and Mammon. We cannot continue to turn out scholars who are not equipped to do real research and teachers who have been soured by learning great bodies of unnecessary material while, at the same time, never having been taught the rudiments of pedagogy or the methodology of, say, teaching a foreign language.

I shall leave the development of the proposed teaching degree to those more capable of designing it. Since it has no canon as yet, it does not fit into the framework of this paper. I shall restrict myself to the Ph.D. as a research degree. Moreoever, as one whose primary interest is literature, I shall not attempt to examine the curriculum of Germanic linguists, except to the extent that their discipline also forms a part of the program of the literature student.

Traditionally, in addition to the requirements of a certain number of seminars and lectures, usually measured by "units," the Ph.D. candidate had to show a reading knowledge of Latin and of French (often at the M.A. level), pass an examination or its equivalent in course work in linguistics, including an earlier state of the language or a history of the language, and perhaps an outside related field such as history, French literature, etc. (Perhaps no one institution had exactly these requirements, but most had some sort of equivalent before it was watered down.) In addition, the candidate had to write a dissertation which would give evidence of his ability to do original research. Recently, some institutions have included a requirement in teaching methodology, but this is a concession to the new function of the Ph.D. and does not belong to the traditional canon.

I would submit that, *for a research degree*, the traditional canon, in spite of its utopian origins, should, for the most part, not only be canonized, but should be expanded to encompass other desiderata which have never been a traditional part of the canon and yet are congruent to present day research. Reactionary heresy! But remember, this statement is postulated upon a *research* degree—and I am optimistic enough about the future of graduate studies to believe that we can afford this luxury.

The defense of a research degree is based upon a few axioms. If these axioms are regarded as invalid, then the reader may spare himself the tedium of further reading. (1) The reading of literature is a true humanistic experience and one which will continue to endure. (2) Literary works are "open," that is, we, the readers, contribute to them as we bring our own spheres of experience into contact with the creative work. (3) The purpose of the literary critic (read *Literarhistoriker*, or Professor of Literature) is to make manifest the whole compass of the literary work to the reader—an idealistic purpose, since "the whole compass" of no literary work can be "made manifest." (4) The more one knows about any given literary work, both internally and externally, including *all* aspects from style to the author's mood at the time of composition, the closer one may come to the unreachable goal of the "whole compass." (5) Literary research is the tool for the acquisition of such knowledge. (6) It is a valid endeavor which may provide immense benefit to all who are capable of responding—it will enrich their spiritual life and render them, cumulatively, more capable of self-fulfillment.

The stuff of our research is man's creativity, primarily for us in the realm of literature, but also including (especially nowadays) the relationship of literature to others of the fine arts or to man in his sociological, political or historical framework. The canon was canonized at a time when these other dimensions were unknown. But, rather than take a position on this problem of our modern age, I would rather say that if a student be attracted to such aspects of research, the best we can do is to design our curriculum flexibly enough to permit him to venture into those areas and to pursue his interests. Since there is not as yet either a canon or a methodology for such ventures, our students will have to form their own and will have to assume the responsibility—some day—of demonstrating their efficacy. However, I do wonder if any of us, without the benefit of the canon of the fine arts, sociology, political science, history, or psychology, can do justice to this expanded area of investigation—would not group research be a better answer to this modern dimension?[2] But see below, the "horizontal approach."

[2] Cf. Peter Heller's cogent remarks concerning "humanists dabbling in a psychology for literarians," etc. in "Beyond Intermediate Proficiency: A Look at our Basic Problems," pp. 95f.

Let us now look at the canon of the Ph.D., item by item.

1. *The Latin requirement.* Now almost extinct, this requirement was at one time almost unnecessary to state, for everyone studying for the Ph.D. had had a humanistic education of which the backbone was Latin. In our discipline it had two functions. First, it was a tool for reading that material written by Germans in Germany but in Latin—*true* research from the beginnings to at least 1700 was (and is!) impossible without it. (I am frequently painfully reminded of its most trivial necessity by my students, who find to their horror that the catalogue divisions in greater European libraries, put together in the 18th and 19th centuries, for the convenience also of foreigners, are in Latin!) In addition to its function as a tool, Latin served (and serves!) another purpose. If we have to find a common denominator for a formative factor in the thought of those authors whom we study—even in the 20th century (including that magister ludi, Hermann Hesse, and Bert Brecht, who wrote poetry in Latin), then it must be the classical heritage which formed the foundation of their education. To exclude this heritage means that we are excluding the most common constituent part of those authors whose works reflect their own background. (Let us study medicine, but exclude the heart.) Latin must be reestablished in the canon and not as a mere token—although however little a student may have is better than nothing. (A summer Latin workshop is an excellent springboard.)

Yet we have dropped this requirement, frequently at the pressure of students protesting a difficult examination—who of us, had we been given the choice, would not have preferred, if anything, *no* examination to *an* examination—it is invalid, even naive, to take a poll of student opinion on a point such as this. I protested the Latin examination in my own day, but thank God no one listened to me. Surely it should not be necessary to develop the justification any further. I sincerely believe that none of us could have been so blind as to have believed that Latin is not necessary for real research in German literature. We yielded to pressures—an understandable weakness—but now it is time that we reassume our responsibility.

While we are at the matter of constituent parts of the educational background, the "culture" of our authors, I would expand the canon by insisting upon an examination in the Bible, make Grimm's *Kinder- und Hausmärchen* a must on every reading list, and include a thorough course in Germany's greatest dramatist, Shakespeare, as a sine qua non for every Ph.D. in German. And, if for no other reason than to permit students to use German libraries, they should be able to read German handwriting in German script, Sütterlin and before. (I recently had to help a student, engaged in a study of women's literature, to read the catalogue entries in the Göttingen library as well as those in Wolfenbüttel.)

Moreoover, still on the same subject, a thorough course in bibliography is a necessary tool—bibliography, not only in the usual sense, but also as "the study of books as material objects."[3] Both McKerrow and the modern supplement by

[3] Philip Gaskell, *A New Introduction to Bibliography* (Oxford, 1972), p. 1.

Gaskell would have to appear on every reading list. How many of our students know what it means when an author claims his work "runs to three alphabets," or who could define the difference between impression, issue and state? Yet, at this very moment, more than 50 *Neudrucke* of 17th-century books are being produced by American scholars, many of whom hold their Ph.D. less than five years, and who will be expected to deal with the most complicated questions of bibliography in an expert way, without ever having had a single word uttered to them about the making of a book. (Ask your best students for a definition of: *Custode, Druckvermerk, Signatur*, or even octavo, incunabulum, or galley). I was appalled to hear, at a recent international conference, an established American scholar of some repute, demonstrate convincingly that he had no idea of the difference between a catalogue and a bibliography—my chagrin was not relieved by the fact that few among his audience seemed also to be aware of his lack.

And, above all, while we are speaking of the expansion of the canon, a thorough *periodic* knowledge of the German language should be required. In the last two months, I have seen at least four examples of errors, made by reputable Germanists, who had suddenly discovered that baroque poetry is indeed worthy of interpretation and who tried their hand at the analysis of a poem without realizing that 17th-century German has its own denotative and connotative framework, that *lebendig* is accented on the first syllable, that *künstlich* is a positive term, and that a pious author might pray that her soul be *niederträchtig*. While such errors would not be avoided by a reading examination, nonetheless, students should be given enough practice in reading the older stages of the language to be *aware* of the possibility that there may be semantic differences.

By the same token, I have often given my MHG class Pfaff's diplomatic rendition of a poem from *Minnesangs Frühling* and Lachmann's normalized edition thereof, solely for the shock value and to impress upon them that a normalized text is often a far cry from the MS. How many of our students, if they were suddenly to find, as backing for the spine of an ancient tome, a scrap of parchment containing the lost ending of the *Hildebrandslied* would know what to do with it? One student, whom I asked this very question in an oral examination, replied honestly that he would burn it quickly so as not to be embarrassed by it! How many students could edit, even *read* a medieval MS? And we speak of "streamlining" the canon! Especially in this day and age, few colleges or universities can afford on any level the luxury of a specialist who can teach only German literature of the 20th century. Yet we blandly eliminate the necessary tools that would enable them to cover even a modest range. American scholarship in German studies has just begun to acquire a modicum of the respect due it in Germany. Now, when the erosion of the Ph.D. is worldwide, we in America have a golden opportunity to rescue it and at the same time to acquire the respect and admiration of our German colleagues and to enable our students to compete upon a superior basis to that of the German Dr. phil. (At one reputable German university, students, when questioned in their exams upon the field of medieval German literature, declined to answer, stating boldly:

"Das haben wir nicht gelernt." Instead of being failed and sent back to their books, they received the answer: "Das schenken wir Euch.") It is time to call a halt to our concessions and reform the Ph.D. to its former respectable position, and if another degree is necessary to meet the exigencies of the modern age, then fiat!

2. *The French requirement.* A scholar in German studies who does not read French is semi-illiterate, and if you do not believe this, then ask any of your French colleagues. While the bland French attitude that *everyone* speaks French can be somewhat irritating, nonetheless we cannot escape the fact that French *was* the cultural language of Europe for more than two centuries. Every important German author whom we study read it, and French literature, in spite of Lessing, exerted an enormous influence upon Germany. If we wish to give any perspective at all to our teaching and research, such a basic knowledge is obvious. In America, we have the further advantage of English, which is also rather desirable for German studies. But I shall not mention that fact that French is not only a tool but also represents a part of the background of every *Literarhistoriker*. Nor shall I bore you with repeating what we all know, namely that the cultural movement even in the Middle Ages is from west to east, and that France has been the spawning ground for so many literary-cultural origins which have then been taken up by Germany to be brought to their extreme development. We are all aware that we must know the French genesis in order to understand the German development. I would be embarrassed to write such obvious statements, but remembering recent arguments about replacing French with Swahili and/or computer "language," I wouldn't apologize. We are constantly faced by the objections of our students to this and that requirement, objections which are frequently logically developed and cogently presented. But our dilemma is such that one cannot convince a student that French (or Latin) is necessary until he has learned it and seen its value first hand—by that time there is no longer a necessity to convince him. A very real assistance in both requirements would be to demonstrate their value by giving assignments in both primary and secondary sources in those languages.

3. *The linguistics requirement.* Only here do we have a real point of discussion within the framework of our canonical question. For when our canon was originally canonized linguistics meant something else from what it does today. At that time there was no such thing as descriptive linguistics, not to mention generative grammar or any of the myriad of other developments which have come into being within the last half century, and the question arises as to how much of this tremendous body of literature, this full field in itself, should we require of our students. As the requirement was originally conceived, it killed two birds with one stone. The stuff of the requirement was the older stages of the language (MHG, OHG, etc.), including closely related branches (ON, Go, etc.), and the approach was that of historical linguistics, so that the student would learn both the discipline of the approach and the stuff of the material studied. If one was fortunate enough to have a real philologist as a teacher (and I

am thinking with nostalgia of my own old teacher, Konstantin Reichardt, the news of whose death reached me while I was writing this diatribe), then one gained also a number of fringe benefits, such as some literary insight into the material studied as well as into the cultural framework within which the older literature was produced. In most cases, however, the material was treated as merely a basis for the illustration of linguistic principles for translation and explication of phonological/morphological/syntactical examples. (This tradition, by the way, may explain why we still, after more than 150 years of *Altgermanistik,* have no literary-stylistic analysis of MHG and OHG literature. Does anyone today dare to postulate what constituted stylistic excellence at the beginning of the 13th century?) If the luxury of a *literary* treatment of the older monuments could be afforded, then it was only in a few of the larger universities and available only to the highest level of graduate students who had already "mastered" the rudiments of the language.

Now the question arises, should we canonize that which, in retrospect, seems to have been an unfortunate compromise? And, should we insist that our students venture into the new field of structural linguistics? Here, we may open a real discussion. I may make bold only to advance what seem to me to be a few cogent pros and cons. But in this area, as well as in the "horizontal approach," discussed below, we should, perhaps, maintain a certain flexibility of the canon.

Few universities can afford to employ a specialist who, in his teaching and research, will never venture outside the area of his greatest competence. Which does not mean to say that specialists in Hermann Hesse will have to teach the *Nibelungenlied.* But I do mean to say that a specialist in Hermann Hesse should be *equipped* to teach the *Nibelungenlied* even though he be never called upon to do so. In virtually all graduate programs, he *will* be called upon, at the very least, to evaluate students' examinations of which a part may well be devoted to the *Nibelungenlied.* A certain basic competence *is* necessary. Moreover, even on the level of pure language teaching, we are all asked from time to time about the etymology of peculiar words, or how a particular syntactical construction came into being, or what *Umlaut* means, etc. Here, even a basic knowledge of the development of the language we are teaching is indispensable. Then too, what should we do with Thomas Mann's *Der Erwählte*, Hauptmann's *Der arme Heinrich* or *Kaiser Karls Geisel* (or *Florian Geyer*, for that matter), Goethe's *Götz,* Hebbel's *Nibelungen,* etc., etc. without a knowledge of their sources. (I hesitate to mention Wagner!) Certainly, on virtually any practical level, a rudimentary mastery of the earlier stages of the language is an asset.

The argument obviously needs no bolstering for those students whose interests lie in the Middle Ages, but just as I am arguing that some knowledge of linguistics is necessary for those whose interest centers in literature, so also would I argue that linguists should not only have a basic knowledge of literary history, but should also pass on to their students something of the literary merit of the models which they are using as reading texts. Moreover, few linguists, even at the larger universities, will be able to devote themselves purely to linguistics. They will also be dealing with literature, which necessitates them, willy nilly, to become philologists in the old sense of the word. None of the great men who founded our discipline ignored the literary or cultural merits of the monuments which they brought before the public eye for the first time. Literature has been and will continue to be the final justification for foreign language study, although, of course, not the only one. But just as one cannot study the older literature without the earlier stages of the language, so also can one not study the earlier stages of the language without the literary monuments, and to allow these works to pass before the student's eye as mere illustrations of the development of *Umlaut* or the second sound shift cannot be justified. This may be sour wine for linguists, but if they drink it, they will find their classes better populated and will be adding a new and exciting dimension to their materials.

As to the question of whether our students should be introduced to descriptive or generative grammar, I would again argue "yes," insofar as this aspect of our discipline can contribute to their future teaching of the language. It is manifestly impossible for them all to become capable structural linguists, or even to have an insight into the vast literature which has mushroomed in this area. But it *is* possible for them to form a concept of the methods and techniques of the descriptive linguist to the point that they can make use of these techniques in their own teaching. In my own classes, I teach the MHG noun via a synthetic scheme which uses a structural approach and my students learn in a single classroom hour what took me weeks to master. The stuff of linguistics is language, which happens also to be the concern of language departments. I think it is a mistake to separate the two, when an amalgamation and cooperation could benefit both directions. I have seen this separation in my own university, with the unfortunate result that colleagues in the German department are often not even aware of the courses having to do with the German language in the Department of Linguistics.

A case could also be made for cultural or political history, but in any profession the real "professionals" gather in the slack on their own. A certain foundation is necessary, however, and many necessary building blocks can be gathered so much more easily via a good teacher who will also show how to put them together. Further stones can be acquired as they are needed, but the foundation must be solid if the building is to stand.

I wish I could consider it unnecessary to advance argumentation for the staples of the canon beyond those "requirements" outside of the immediate area of German literature. Today especially, when our younger generation is impatiently seeking new approaches, new methods (some of which may be immensely productive), it is difficult not to wash the baby out with the bath. In the welter of interdisciplinary studies, the sociology of literature, the politicization of the university, it is not easy to resist the argument that there is too much on the modern scene which must be studied and comprehended to leave time for the old chestnuts of the traditional graduate curriculum. Besides, they are no longer relevant. But aside from the arguments on the primary level (i.e. the instrinsic value of Goethe, Schiller, et al.), we may also argue on a secondary level: It is important to understand the constituent parts of the modern scene. Handke and h.c. artmann have read their Goethe; so did Brecht, and the theater sensation out of the *DDR* this past year in Germany has been *Die neuen Leiden des jungen W*. Schiller and Kleist are currently being played and transmitted by German television. Grimmelshausen's *Simplicissimus* occupied eight hours of prime TV time in four 2-hour episodes this past year. Günther Grass and Martin Walser are both engaged with (Grass, working title, *Acht Nonnen und mehr*) or have just finished (Walser, *Das Sauspiel*) works that presuppose a knowledge of 16th and 17th century German literature. Yes, I am afraid Goethe and Schiller must remain a part of the canon. It is ironic that with the present sharp critique of specialization, we should be constantly compromising the curriculum to permit, even encourage such specialization. With the excuse that students want to design their own education, we have failed to provide them with a structure *within which* they can pursue their interests. Students of today want *carte blanche* as little as they want iron-clad rigidity. They want structure, but freedom within that structure; they want guidance, but free will to develop along the lines of their interests and talents; they want help, not coercion. But, regardless of what they want, they will look back upon us with bitterness if we do not provide them with even the basic tools of their trade.

A basic knowledge of the developmental process of German literature from its beginnings to the present day *is* such a tool. Literature (culture) is organic, dynamic, and cumulative. It has its roots in yesterday, though it be ever in flux. It builds upon and assimilates the accomplishments of the past. Without the past there can be no real understanding of the present. Traditions *do* exist. Every literature has a heritage from which it grows and upon which it draws. We may scorn that heritage in our own *Weltanschauung*, but if we are to teach a literature embedded in that heritage, if we are to show its meaning, yes "relevance," to our students, or even if we want to show the limitations of that literature, we must be aware of the consistency of the soil in which it grows. If we consider the literature *and* the heritage to be worthless, then we should not be teaching it.

I shall not discuss the merits of the dissertation. They are obvious, and it should be kept. It represents the only opportunity which a graduate student has to do a larger project (a book!) on his own, but with the benefit of a mentor who will guide him, correct his errors or extravagances. Here is the golden opportunity to show his originality, to be independent, yet not to have to assume the complete responsibility of his independence, not to have to be thrown upon the cruel world of book reviewers who will pounce upon his first commercial book.

Dissertations should *never* be published. Perhaps a few articles may be derived from the dissertation, but any graduate student who takes advantage of a vanity press will regret it twenty years later.

All of the foregoing discussion does not mean that we are to condemn out-of-hand any new approach, any attitude which does not emerge from the canon. Our insights deepen, and we are aware of some things today that were not known as our canon developed. Interdisciplinary studies can be extremely valuable, especially among the arts where, however, the heritage from which they develop may form the common denominator and thus even gain in importance. And this leads us to an attitude which is in keeping with our times and which may indeed prove to be, at least for the immediate future, *the* direction for literary studies. It is what I should like to call the "horizontal approach," and it has reached its most overt form in the "new" discipline called Comparative Literature. I shall not discuss its implications for German studies in detail, for that has been done most capably elsewhere in this collection. But I should like to quote one sentence from Gerald Gillespie's essay, which seems to me to be extremely important. He writes: " . . . a strong German program should ally itself in advance with Comparative Literature as a constructive, reliable partner" (see p. 164).

The basic thesis of Comparative Literature is that one cannot understand, say, Romanticism on a national basis. Not only does it have its roots in its own national heritage (vertical), but it is also a reflection of a much larger phenomenon (horizontal) whose reflexes are to be observed in many different countries which, in turn, reflect their own national traditions as well. I have often been asked: "What *is* Comparative Literature?" and we are constantly plagued by the confusion, still fostered at many universities, with the pseudo-discipline of World Literature. World Literature is a dilettante, undergraduate course, taught usually by non-specialists who try in one easy lesson to acquaint the student, in English, with a smattering of great masterpieces produced all over the world from the beginnings to the present day. Its only unity is the epithet of greatness bestowed upon the examples read either by the past or present. In spite of this, it often has excellent results, especially when taught by an inspired teacher, in that it shows the students masterpieces which they might not otherwise have encountered and frequently kindles a spark which will later flame. The comparatist, on the other hand, seeks unity in diversity, attempts to understand an organic whole. *Comparative* is not a good word for his endeavors, for it gives rise to the unjust accusation that all he does is compare. (As the Harvard *Lampoon* cartoon had it: "Madame, the men are here to compare the literature.") The comparatist does not have an easy task, for he must be aware of the national (and/or classical!) heritage and the extent to which it conditions the integral parts of a horizontal phenomenon. Therefore, he must master the canons of each national literature which he studies. Fortunately, these canons overlap. Moreover, in view of the "horizontal" nature of his discipline, he may concentrate upon that part of the canon which is most relevant to his area of concentration—which does not mean that he may neglect the rest, for again, for purely pragmatic reasons, he will scarcely be permitted the luxury of complete specialization. But a medievalist, for example, will obviously be more interested in the older stages of the national languages than he will be in the contemporary scene. One may counter with the argument: "Then why should one interested in the contemporary scene be forced to look to the Middle Ages?" The cumulative aspect of literature is the obvious answer.

But by the very horizontal nature of the comparatist's outlook, this is the field in which interdisciplinary studies can best be housed. Comparative Literature *is* interdisciplinary study, and split appointments or committee assignments facilitate cooperative work by specialists offering together their own contributions. Comparative Literature departments should be urged to share courses with historians, classicists, sociologists, etc. The result of such communal work could be phenomenal.

However, if our modern insights are valid and the horizontal approach does indeed represent the direction of the future, then we must be all the more careful to provide students entering upon this vast area with the proper tools to cope with it. A comparative student must be equipped with the entire development of his major literature and all that it implies. Moreover, he must be in command of that part of the canon in his other literary interests which applies to his horizontal area. As the situation is now (and probably will be for the foreseeable future), such a student will be a member of a given language department with a "split appointment" in comparative literature, or a member of a committee which administers the comparative literature program. Hence, he must have a complete vertical command of his main field. He must be able to compete upon equal footing with his colleagues in his "home" department; yet he must also have covered that part of the canon in other departments which pertains to his field. This is a demanding task, but I see no other way to avoid letting the comparative discipline sink into the dilettantism of World Literature. And, it can be done![4] Our colleagues must only remember that a comparative student has a most extensive task which requires him to expend his energies both vertically and horizontally. Moreover, the more modern his field, the more of the canon in his outside field(s) (within reasonable limits) he must have mastered, since obviously growth takes place within time and for the purpose of analysis it is more important to look to the past than to predict the future. Thus the roots of a modern work may go back to the Middle Ages, which may be an important factor in the analysis of that work, but the fact that a medieval genre will decline in future years may play no rôle whatever in the analysis of a work of that genre.

I feel very strongly that all of us who have split appointments with

---

[4] For such a program, consult the University of California-Berkeley catalogue.

comparative literature should extend all efforts to insure a professional attitude in that discipline. With the rapid expansion of comparative literature departments and programs, there is sure to be pressure for compromise, yet it is extremely important for comparative literature to gain and maintain respect. There is an ingrown prejudice against it; and one constantly hears the accusation of superficial dilettantism. The heritage of World Literature remains. To give the lie to such accusations means that we must be sure that our students meet the most severe demands of a given department, yet be able to extend their teaching and scholarship to other areas. The discipline will prove itself, but our students must be prepared to cope with it.

Let us turn now to the M.A. in German. The M.A. is essentially two things: (1) a stepping stone of the Ph.D. or (2) a terminal teaching degree. The ideal canon for the M.A. must include both possibilities. Here I would not insist upon a necessary division into two degrees. If the two ends are regarded as options, then their divergent curricula must be flexible enough to permit shifting from one to the other. The M.A. as a teaching degree for high schools, junior colleges, etc., must also be loose enough to permit students to fulfill educational requirements for the teaching credential. I would strongly favor the M.A.T. programs to meet this end. That is a separate question, just as the D.A. is, and I should like to limit my discussion here to those M.A. programs which must serve both ends.

The study for the M.A. represents most students' first brush with graduate study, but all too often they are thrust into seminars on an advanced level where they are intimidated by advanced graduate students and professors who do not differentiate between the levels of their graduate students. One summer's vacation does not make a graduate out of an undergraduate, no matter how talented he may be. As Cecil Wood demonstrated in his excellent, witty, but unfortunately still unpublished "A Survival Kit for Graduate Students," such a sink-or-swim method has decided advantages. Still, the shock effect can be severe and can lead to a discontented attitude, based upon a lack of realization of the nature of graduate studies and the why and wherefore of the courses offered. The malaise can last throughout the student's entire graduate study. While not all graduate programs are extensive enough to permit the convenience of first-year graduate classes or pro-seminars, still certain courses can be devised which will serve as an introduction or explanation of graduate study.

Such an introductory course, which would also provide a basic tool, could be a graduate course in bibliography, which encompasses both meanings of the word. It could easily avoid the tedium of such courses, first by presenting the book as a material object, then by coordinating the material in such a way that it could be tied into other courses the student is taking by devising bibliographical projects supplemental to the other courses, thus putting the material into practical use. For example, if a student is also enrolled in a Hölderlin seminar, a bibliographical project could be a survey of the waves of interest in Hölderlin as measured by the number of books and articles written about him throughout a given period of years. Such projects, easily devised, provide practice in the use of bibliographical tools and methods as well as a more thorough foundation for the other course. With all of the modern bibliographical tools available today, the course could easily encompass also discussion and illustration of methods of literary analysis, as well as a presentation of the goals and aims of German studies, and I have enough confidence in our discipline to believe that if students were made aware of what we are doing and why we are doing it early in their graduate career, much later discontent could be avoided. Most graduate students have some sort of a crisis during their career. While they were obviously motivated to *enter* graduate study, sooner or later they ask themselves: "What am I doing here? What is the purpose of it all?" If these questions could be anticipated and frankly discussed, graduate student life would be simplified. So the first item on my canon for the M.A. would be a bibliography course which would serve its own ends, be supplemental to other courses, and act as an introduction to graduate studies.

While I would keep the French examination on the M.A. level, I would also draw the attention of students to the fact that Latin is also essential for the Ph.D. The modern graduate student, lacking a humanistic education, has a lot of "catching up" to do. Obviously he will not be able to do it all during his graduate career. However, he can and should lay the foundations as thoroughly as humanly possible and reconcile himself to the fact that he has a lot to do on his own.

A survey course, or a series of them, is a desideratum for a German undergraduate major, but if a student enters graduate school without having had this background, he should be given the opportunity to acquire it. He should be aware of the whole scope of his chosen field of study. If such courses prove to be impractical on the graduate level, students should at least be required during their first graduate year to read through an extensive history of German literature. There *are* graduate students, Ph.D.'s in hand, who have never done this!

One of the older stages of the language, preferably MHG (because of its literature) should be another first-year course, and it should be designed in such a way as not only to provide a knowledge of the methods of historical linguistics and the language itself, but also to give some insight, however small, into the literature written in that stage of the language.

The term paper or seminar report has also become an entrenched part of our canon. While such papers are extremely valuable on the Ph.D. level, since they represent an occupation in which the student will be engaged throughout his life, there is no necessity to consider them as an absolute must in all graduate courses. So many seminars are structured around the monotonous reading, week after week, of mediocre term papers that would kill the interest of even the most dedicated student. It is time to reintroduce our "great man" (if he can be found!), who will work with his students on a research project and will show them method and thought, and who will inspire them to work on their own. If seminar papers are a must, then they should be no longer than a half hour (or 15 pages), so that both professor and students have the opportunity to add critique and assistance to the person reporting. The paper should be a springboard, not an end in itself. Group projects can be both valuable and valid, although not as they are conceived in Germany today where in some universities, as a Marxist cop-out, separate evaluations of individual participants are taboo. (Students will not be getting jobs as a group, nor will they probably ever again find a congenial group with which to do communal projects.) But students must also be taught how to write papers. A single glance into any of our journals will demonstrate adequately that it is an art which many of our colleagues have never acquired. The failure of English teachers in high schools and colleges is nowhere more apparent. So we must do their job for them.

The "reading list" for either M.A. or Ph.D. is still valuable, especially if it is devised by the student, for here he can be eclectic and show his own concept of what he should read. He should however have the benefit of guidance if he wants it. One may save a student many hours of his precious time which he might have spent reading peripheral *Epigonen* or in turn, suggest essentials which he may have neglected or forgotten. Such a list should not attempt to be all-inclusive, but should rather represent the core of the student's reading, works which *he* feels to be significant and upon which he is prepared to be examined in depth. Which does not mean to say that his examination(s) should be limited to the works listed. The list is again a springboard from which to jump (or be launched).

So much for the M.A. as a foundation for the Ph.D. Fortunately, however, most of the details described will also contribute toward the M.A. as a terminal teaching degree. For the preparation of teaching skills (if, indeed, teaching skill can be taught), the schools (departments) of education are all too ready to spring in. The M.A.T. is much to be preferred. But where the M.A.T. does not exist, the M.A. must continue to serve a double function and hence must be left flexible. But what will a teacher on the secondary level need? Certainly a command of the language and some insight into its history. He should also know the cultural framework within which the literature developed. He should have a foundation in pedagogy and the rudiments of bibliography. He will probably not need Latin (although it certainly will not hurt him), nor will he need to know the techniques of higher research. His ends may readily be met by preserving flexibility.

While the gospel which I have been preaching seemingly advocates a proliferation of degrees (D.A., M.A.T.), it would also restore the integrity to the Ph.D. and M.A. It is not fair to those students who have worked hard for their degree in the older sense to allow these higher degrees to degenerate into a "union card" for admission into the professions. The older degrees endowed professors with *caracteres indelibiles*, they were almost ordained—hence the veneration in which they were once held. But when their canon is reduced to a clump of pliable clay, molded into a different shape by every passing mode, fad, or interest, then it is evident that *not only* the canon is clay. And if the priests of the profession do not believe in their own canonical scriptures sufficiently to defend them, then they deserve the fate of all heretics!

GERMAN AND COMPARATIVE LITERATURE

GERALD GILLESPIE
Stanford University

I wish to speak here from a distinctly personal vantage as an American who has been involved in the Comparative Literature movement and taught under several official arrangements—in a full-fledged Department of Comparative Literature, in a Department of Germanic Languages and Literatures, with a "split" appointment, and collaborating in a Comparative Literature Program through an all-University committee. In these notes I will be taking for granted what eminent scholars such as Wellek, Rüdiger, et al. have said about the evolution and contemporary situation of Comparative Literature. It scarcely needs repeating that exact knowledge of German pathways—e.g., the immense contribution of the age of Goethe to later comparative theory, but the relatively delayed establishment of the discipline in German universities—is essential information for a comparatist attached to a German Studies program in America, the Netherlands, France, Hungary, Japan, or any other nation where both fields flourish. Ulrich Weisstein has chronicled the German story of Comparative Literature in the broader context of other national tendencies in his valuable *Einführung in die Vergleichende Literaturwissenschaft.*[1] I begin, then, as an American observer and experiencer of German literary culture, among several other rather closely related European heritages. That is, I bring into or discover at work in my own native sphere—whose language happens to be the dominant medium of the twentieth century—certain understandings formed elsewhere.[2]

If the original formulations are in German, they must compete for attention with materials in the virtual Babel of other national languages, be evaluated from one or more of the variety of competing viewpoints influenced by the life of

[1] Ulrich Weisstein, *Einführung in die Vergleichende Literaturwissenschaft* (Stuttgart, 1968). For the perspective of an important German pioneer in CL regarding the development and current scope of the discipline, also consult Horst Rüdiger's article "Vergleichende Literaturwissenschaft," in *Handlexikon zur Literaturwissenschaft,* ed. by Diether Krywalski (München, 1974), pp. 493–498.

[2] Among such understandings formed elsewhere is the picture of America generated by German literature in the German-speaking lands, the subject of the Wolfgang Paulsen Festschrift: *Amerika in der deutschen Literatur* (Stuttgart, 1975), ed. by Sigrid Bauschinger, Horst Denkler, and Wilfried Malsch. Ideally, American Germanists would be in a position to match this comprehensive set of studies with a volume on the representation of German-speaking people and Germany in American literature.

those other languages, and finally, be explained to students who by and large have in common the Anglo-American tradition or, though of diverse origins, generally become acculturated Anglo-American cosmopolitans. Some of my students even belong to a future wave of American comparatists who will venture to bring elements of several entire civilizations (i.e. European, Indic, Chinese, etc.) into meaningful relationship with the only one I can hope to treat on familiar terms. It is therefore not surprising that, in order to communicate with me at all, many of this more recent breed of American *literati* may pursue abstract methodologies which make literary studies sound more and more like a branch of anthropology. To many of us this is an Alexandrian age of increasingly bloodless constructions, but to others it is a future—the post-Joycean rather than post-Rabelaisian—opportunity to luxuriate eclectically, probe syncretistically, and discover systems hidden just over today's own "pre-Columbian" horizon.

Fortunately for us American comparatists with a primary interest in German letters, German exiles have forged strong links between their inherited and adopted culture. We can attach German literature to the moorings of European literature with fewer preliminaries because so many distinguished migrants have shored up that entity while the storm of history was crashing over it toward mid-century. For example, the German-speaking Romanists Walter Naumann (who returned to establish a Comparative Literature institute in Germany) and the late Leo Spitzer helped maintain the sense of the whole European enterprise, without losing sight of its dynamic diversity; E.H. Gombrich and Erwin Panofsky taught us to see better the structures in art both synchronically and diachronically; and the late Sigurd Burckhardt elaborated a German analogy to New Criticism, as well as demonstrated its applicability to English literary works. Let these few names and illustrations suffice to represent a long, revered German honor roll in the English-speaking nations. But barring another catastrophe like World War II, the unique impetus imparted by the presence of major German authors on our soil such as Thomas Mann and Bert Brecht—not to speak of the thousands of scholars, philosophers, theater and movie people, et al.—will continue to wane with the century. Progressively, American Germanists will move into an internationalist future at least at first dominated linguistically by English. The fact that, outside Europe, German probably will not gain even the tenuous lingering position of French as an international medium of second rank in our lifetime intensifies the problematic conjuncture of "negative" forces for the study of foreign vernaculars in America as regards German, too, even though it is now one of the esteemed "major" languages in our universities.

If I read my contemporaries correctly, Comparative Literature is striving to furnish a general, positive response on a world plane to a paradoxical crisis whose symptoms we all detect in ourselves. On the one hand, we recognize the unrelenting technological revolution in transportation and communication which accelerates the process of "imitation" and "assimilation" (with startling shifts above all in the highly developed nations) and leads to an eventual underlying "uniformity" in cultural patterns despite local flavor. On the one hand, the comparatist, like his or her counterpart in a national literature department, feels he or she is helping to rescue as well as communicate the authentic, original characteristics and values of the separate language groups. They are threatened by pressures which seem likely to turn some subject areas into "parochial" enclaves; yet, objectively, mere size is no merit, and the tyranny of a majority trend may be just as oppressively parochial, so that minimally the comparatist wants to preserve as part of the human record, and thus sometimes as a latent potential, treasured "foreign" literary utterances. On the other hand, the comparatist suspects less humbly that he too is a factor in the shrinking of our globe and that his complicity thrusts on him the standard Western role of acting as responsible museum-keeper for those living forms which his omnivorous civilization slowly overwhelms or inevitably alters. Yet, as he industriously jells certain matters in intellectual aspic, he knows that the cultural barriers which he bridges as a specialist serving an elite minority are often still effective enough to tribalize the world and permit most of its denizens to commit outrages on others with only rare displays of pangs of conscience. The American comparatist is instinctively a disguised, if not an overt, humanist; he actually believes that the human race constitutes a single species even though its tribes coexist on different planes of time (from the Stone Age to the Space Age) and are locked, with varying fastness, into a welter of dialects. Nonetheless, everywhere—and most certainly in the libertarian Anglo-American territories of the globe—the mentioned historical pressures portend further erosion of whichever mere *modus vivendi* any of us have been able to establish in our work for the incongruous elements of competing "world views." The more traditional humanists keep hoping that all the turbulence does not mask an underlying collapse of the complex process by which, for all its regional variations, we manage to revise the "Western" heritage. We have piously enshrined a number of such temporizations in our general humanities offerings, even while we ponder whether we are hurtling toward a collision, rather than fruitful coexistence with other civilizations and people whom four centuries of European expansion and invention since the Renaissance have profoundly affected.

Into a corner of this picture, then, we insert those few brush strokes attempting to represent German literature for Americans. Just as there is no consensus about what constitutes a canon of world literature today, or shall in a few decades, so too within the framework of American culture there is no guaranteed permanence for the overall status of German literature alongside other national literatures, let alone for our particular versions of a German canon relevant to students in North America.[3] This unpredictability reflects the awe-

---

[3] Though from a German-and-Continental perspective, Horst Rüdiger arrives at an analogous conclusion regarding the relationship of external elements to the enormous complexity of European tradition and the constant revision of our mutable literary canons

some proliferation of choices available to the American as to other audiences in developed countries. We specialists choose whether to revel in an instability of manifold delights or to interpret the shifting of attention and taste as a disaster, but how many students are really listening to our opinion in the first place? Numerous professional observers have been disturbed by the way in which, as they judge, both "greater" (Kafka) and "lesser" (Hesse) writers are "indiscriminately" adopted by American studentdom and promoted in survey courses, courses to a large extent offered by English departments and quite frequently staffed by colleagues who cannot read the originals or indeed know little about their German context. By the time German departments have grown suspicious and mounted their own courses in translation to any significant degree, the directions may once again have altered. More and more, however, they do feel constrained to play the game of catching up with the vagaries of the "host" country.

For students seem ("far too often" in the eyes of those who are no longer or have never been tastemakers) to acquire their first contact with the German mind through already internationalized clichés in puzzling strings and clusters— the "newest" combinations such as Herbert Marcuse's fashionable fusion of Marxism and Freudianism. German departments weigh the relative merits of committing expensive talent to satisfy perhaps ephemeral vogues, but also feel obligated to provide important linkages, for example, advanced theory courses presenting German phenomenological and linguistic-model approaches in relation to contemporary Anglo-American, French, and Russian contrasts or analogues. American departments of German can, in fact, take some pride in having contributed to broader changes—e.g., the Hölderlin and Kleist renascence, rise of Baroque studies, etc.—which have characterized the protean Germany literary canon after Positivism. The backwash of exiles and sojourners has left some marks on contemporary German criticism and scholarship, too, but they are probably no deeper and no less general in their impact than the ready-packaged importation of concepts such as "Agitprop" by some American Germanists and theater people since World War II. Doubtless the statistics show that a far higher ratio of current writing gets translated from English into German than the other way around, and Volkmar Sander has discussed in detail the enormously complicated question of the filtered and retarded reception of German literature in America both past and present.[4] The dominance of certain major American

in his introduction "Ein Versuch über Weltliteratur," to *Meisterwerke der Weltliteratur,* ed. by H. Rüdiger (München, 1974); however, he posits the methodological and cultural need to reconstitute a "classical" guide in every age through the creative engagement of the trendsetting readers with literature, with the consequence that this drive itself brings about the liberation of great works from purely historical contexts and endows certain ones with effective stature ("classical" rank untrammeled by norms and rules).

[4] Volkmar Sander, "Die *New York Times Book Review:* Zur Rezeption deutscher Literatur in den USA," *Basis,* 4 (1973), 86–97.

literary organs and papers, the inordinate gaps, delays, and accidents of translation or review, and other vagaries can and do cause gross distortions. The probabilities are great that the contemporary blur will not be resolved until long after the moments when the new directions taken by traumatized postwar German writers, the rising of critical schools such as the Frankfurt group, and so forth, are past as immediately close events. It remains to be seen, of course, whether certain of the "neglected" workings of current German literature will yet make a real mark here or even earn some retrospective distinction in American eyes as minor or major florations.

I readily agree that it is worth investigating how tastemakers enable any considerable shifting of the horizon of sensibilities and expectations, and why under particular circumstances they may or may not appear on the scene to champion certain things. That task pertains to Comparative Literature as much as to sociology and cultural history. But when Sander polemicizes against the supposed hegemony of established attitudes in American literary studies as these affect the American treatment of German literature, a deeper issue comes to the surface. Implicitly the nature of American society—at least, initially of Academia within it—would need to undergo sweeping alteration so as to promote a readier understanding or indeed sympathy for the "neglected" insights. The complainers against the American obtuseness would have to win over a significant phalanx of Americans capable of acting as channels for "improved" receptivity. That entails the gargantuan achievement of somehow reversing the relative strength of the native versus the foreign culture and making American teaching a coordinate to the latest German thinking. Such situations have existed and will again exist; however, the outside cultural center must radiate powerful and attractive ideas. For example, Italy in the early Renaissance, Britain and France in the Enlightment, Germany in the Romantic age—to name random examples—have exhibited the requisite literary energies which permanently pierce national armor. It is entirely possible that those who attack what they deem to be a "moribund" canon of German literature abroad will demolish the American, among other, "anachronistic" outposts—a serious effort is underway, at least, in several reputable American German departments.

The failure to topple all the idols or introduce some new ones as their peers can, however, all too conveniently be attributed to the perverse reinforcement of bad habits (*negative Rückkoppelung*). That is simply another way of admitting that America does have its own culture and interests which, in specific and not inalterable combinations, may indeed prove impervious to the blandishments of various choruses of "improvers." And it may turn out that the American receptivity to German literature at some earlier point in time and subsequent lack of will to reject that prior interest or radically modify it reflect just one more case of a familiar pattern in the annals of European literature. As a civilization with multiple centers, now extended on a global scale, the vitality of the European "system" as a whole has depended on its capacity to generate and nurture alternate pathways, yet preserve fundamental achievements, too. The American treatment of foreign literatures as an instance of the activity of a major segment in that total community plays no more or less perverse a role than, let us say, the French treatment of English literature, the Swedish treatment of Spanish literature, etc.

Naturally, we will be swayed eventually by this or that siren's song, and it will be integrated into the American cacaphony. Yet the point must be asserted that, while an American department should present as much contemporary German literature as possible (which means inviting "believers" and "participants" in the events to visit or work), it also has a duty to itself to subject the new, as well as the old, matter to the same traditionally governing disrespectful scrutiny—that is, to rigorous scrutiny. An American department should, in short, place contemporary German writing in "difficult" frames of reference (i.e., other frames than the original German ones) and not grant it any privileged status. At least, from a Comparative Literature perspective, it possesses no greater a priori validation than post-liberation Hindi poetry, medieval Coptic romance, or Goethean drama. Definitely, it would be folly to ignore the reality of the American literary world (whether the American inclination appears hostile or friendly in any particular case) when taking the measurements of a foreign creation. To start with, one might miss those dimensions which reveal that a particular work belongs to some generic revolutionary fashion among the staples of international commerce, rather than being specifically German. So much current writing does have its unwitting analogues in America herself that all parties might be salubriously embarrassed, or delighted, to end the mystique of novelty.

My purpose is not to inveigh against any particular doctrinaire enthusiasm for some recent view of literature directly imported from overseas, so much as to caution against facile presumptions of righteousness which can so quickly usurp actual thinking about the nature of literature and of literary experience in the United States,—hence commit the same dereliction imputed to those whose only fault may be that they too have a point of view and care enough about some chapter in the German tradition to teach it for the values they recognize in that act. Proposals to reform the American literary mind land in the midst of that "free market" which many assiduously argue does not exist or is actually phony—a conclusion buttressed sometimes by the argument that their self-evident truths have not been acclaimed. I myself know how painful such rejection is. It vastly complicates my own coping with the persistent central problem of shaping any viable German syllabus at all in the face of increasing internationalization of literary themes and forms while German is being relegated to lower status (but English, as the American medium, maintains its dominant role with all the attendant cultural habits). Yet I do not accept that, because we are not electrified each time some colleague solemnly pronounces the truism that our choices in the universities on this continent involve philosophic as well as pragmatic decisions, we must be jaded.

Swamped, yes; bailing water, yes; compromising, I hope so. If German literary studies are to remain vital in America, German departments must, for example, share Dürrenmatt with Theater (or English, or French, or any group sponsoring a course on those ambiguous interests termed "destruction of illusion" and "absurdity"), Nietzsche with Philosophy (even if far too few philosophers in the States can read German), and so forth. In fact, as often as not, these figures were introduced widely in America by scholars in fields other than German literature. Whereas the traditional sharing of Old Norse with English has involved largely good diplomacy, to interact with the serpentine progression of tastemakers requires an educated sensitivity for American intellectual values— whether one endorses, despises, or is indifferent to particular sets. We could more properly expect such awareness from the professed comparatists, rather than the national specialist. Thus, whether through formal training, later research, or amateur dedication, the comparatist who serves in a German department in the United States ought to know English and American literature *thoroughly*. Naturally, the same holds with regard to French literature for a French comparatist who serves in a German department in France.

Before turning to some special considerations touching the American scholar, I would like to distinguish the pedagogical levels with which a comparatist must cope appropriately. There are at most only some two dozen "genuine" undergraduate Comparative Literature programs in the United States, by their very nature if not in name, virtually all honors programs.[5] Most comparative education of substance at the traditional elitist schools takes place on the graduate level, to which selected undergraduates are admitted for specific interests, because the complexity and needed preparation for the work simply does not permit otherwise. To public view, however, the situation may look different, because when the term "comparative" gained such vogue with Administrations in the sixties, a lamentably large number of institutions tacitly let the older distinction between General and Comparative Literature lapse—at least with respect to undergraduate training. In the older terminology, the bulk of undergraduate offerings in America are still taught as General Literature, that is, with

[5] My estimate derived from application of the severer standards described in the findings just published in the comprehensive report on "Undergraduate Comparative Literature: Profile 1974," *ACLAN*, 8:2 (Winter 1975), 1–32. The report upholds the distinction I make below between Comparative Literature courses, requiring ability to read one or more foreign languages, and General or World Literature, taught in translation (p. 3f.). Interestingly, the statistics show that "Comparative Literature programs actually contribute to an increased enrollment in precisely those advanced foreign language literature courses which traditionally have been low enrollment courses" (p. 5). I also point to the problem noted in the report (p. 17f.), that though introductory synthetic courses in Western classics do act as feeders for both CL and FL, they tend to blur recognition of CL as a distinct, demanding discipline in the minds of casual undergraduate participants and of poorly informed administrators who promote "service" courses. But it is precisely to offset such ignorance of the foreign language component in a Comparative Literature major that FL and CL people *must* involve themselves in general offerings given in translation.

readings in translation rather than in the original languages. Essentially, General Literature programs have tended to be dominated by English departments because the latter have larger staffs, allowing considerable flexibility, are committed to teaching the "whole" heritage from the viewpoint of its relevance to Anglo-American letters, and in the past have been able to operate with scant competition from the foreign language groups. More enlightened faculties have, however, long shared General Literature as a separate program to which numerous departments contribute, as at the University of Pennsylvania under the cosmopolitan aegis of the late Adolf Klarmann. Yielding to unmistakable pressure, many foreign language departments have increasingly been giving courses in translation, and from the welter of such nationally segregated offerings there have emerged, in a second step, broader offerings staffed now by one, now by another foreign language segment and qualifying as General Literature.

It is precisely at this juncture that a German department can derive maximal benefits if it manages to budget enough time for its comparatist(s) to participate in undergraduate teaching on the all-university level in General Literature or other basic Humanities courses, as well as German literature in translation.

Most German departments are very tight ships and will, therefore, find it hard to assign their comparatist for undergraduate work because he or she is rather regularly booked out for "internal" or "external" graduate offerings. But the added importance of undergraduate contact in the university at large is that it means productive departmental exposure to other faculty groups. Given the pivotal position of English, English departments must sometimes assign a teaching assistant, inexperienced junior member, or old-fashioned monoglot senior member to staff a more broadly titled course (e.g., "European Romanticism") and, out of lassitude or lack of resources, frequently enough stage what is merely a disguised English offering.[6] In the past, the German or French specialist in Romanticism would ordinarily defer out of recognition of his own limited familiarity with the English materials, even though he might be highly dissatisfied with a perhaps poor treatment of the crucial German or French materials, and would accede to the notion that English department membership automatically outfitted a colleague better for General Literature. A competent specialist in Comparative Literature, however, clearly "outranks" the dilettante generalist and is more readily accepted as a peer by counterparts in English and other groups. To follow my illustration: the comparatist who can offer German Romanticism within a German department can also easily assert his natural prerogative to offer or collaborate in offering either generalized or specialized courses on Romanticism on the graduate level, too, for wider audiences. Such a person can establish strong ties with his counterparts in other departments, and

---

[6] To avoid invidious comparisons, I have deliberately chosen for sake of illustration an area in which exemplary interdepartmental sharing and sympathetic mutual interest prevail at my own university.

each area of such contact not only enhances the prestige of the German group as a whole, but also legitimizes in the eyes of the university all interrelated honest attempts to bring German literature and culture into the larger picture of the Humanities.

If an older misconception of the way in which undergraduate General or Comparative Literature courses relate to "language" departments no longer lingers in any quarters, the following corollary remark will be superrogatory. Historically, American foreign language departments have tended to concentrate on snaring majors through attractive language learning—certainly an essential function they perform. The underlying assumption has been that a major language will spellbind its share of adherents even though, obviously, it is a cultivated oasis, an alien enclave. (In contrast, the introduction to older sacred or classical languages such as Greek, Latin, and Sanskrit no longer emphasizes speaking and writing skills.) To promote the aura of that enclave, some departments radically seal the environment from outside influences. The foreign language "house" at a college is a good example of this technique which is valuable in specific forms. But even if the department supports direct immersion (overseas campus), enclave residence (language house), and related inducements, these efforts are not necessarily incompatible with comparativistic openness (e.g., an elective, general introduction to German "culture" conducted in English for all undergraduates). Since the natural pathway of approach for the vast majority of new students is over basic survey courses on major Western works *to* particular national cultures in which the masterpieces were originally conceived, the generalist contact is probably the single most important *initial* instance for suggesting to undergraduates the interconnection of their own and "foreign" cultures, but also for exciting curiosity about a distinctly "other" people. Many of us have observed that, when colleges drop their language requirements, German literature in translation and comparativistic courses perforce evolve into a significant watershed gathering potential majors. What matters is that this "indirect" access to departmental subjects can ultimately bring late-starting majors together with those majors who derive from the language courses. Experimenting with programs which allow students to switch voluntarily and smoothly from track to track—and induce some to gravitate toward "hard core" German Studies—can test the will and resources of a department formidably. Good universities are likely to perceive positively such determination to take stock and revitalize. Rather than offer one sample description of multiple options for B.A. students, I refer readers to Walter Lohnes' discussion of the Stanford model (pages 78–87).

Though the integrative role of Comparative Literature on the graduate level has gained widespread recognition, certain problematic realities still inhibit the flow of students from undergraduate backgrounds into a graduate German or combined German and Comparative Literature concentration in many universities. The perennial attempt by some one or other of the national literature departments to hoard or restrict their own students, or unfounded refusal to accomodate outsiders who might profitably do relevant work, can thwart the more ambitious graduate majors. Defection of graduate students to Comparative Literature or English as an escape from oppression, which departments regret too late, can be embarrassing. Less embarrassing, yet perhaps more significant for longterm health, are the silent decisions a priori to avoid entanglement in the "smaller" outfits.

But if a university administration habitually penalizes the separate smaller literature groups because they *are* enlightened and do risk occasional enrollment gaps for the sake of producing truly humanistic graduates, one can scarcely blame French, German, Spanish, etc. for assuming a defensive posture. "Clever" administrative analysts regularly rediscover that playing the numbers game is a convenient way to cannibalize faculty positions and/or implement a policy of curriculum change which, rightly or wrongly, the faculty may or does resist. In some unfortunate precincts, the smaller literature groups are kept divided, with a marginal rather than critical mass of faculty and students. They can thus more easily be picked off one by one as they "break down" (that is, when any variation of small magnitude in their fortunes occurs at a moment coincidental with a move dictated by the extraneous planning of social engineers). Such apparently benign neglect allows administrators to wash their hands in public, even if, in the worst case, they have decided "philosophically" to kill off an entire viable department, because—in certain circumstances—its continued exis-tence, despite its grave burdens, can impede completion of policy or cast doubt on the competence of those who earlier predicted the inevitable death. I believe that a good deal of pious waiting for the decease of "sick" Humanities groups was practiced in the late sixties. In contrast to logical, comprehensive planning, a standard manoeuvre in institutions whose administration has tolerated or pro-moted the malaise is to create an omnibus foreign languages department out of the remaining fragments, or to propose a "rational" division into two "buses," a linguistics ensemble, with subcompartments for each language in demand, and a matching literature ensemble. In such an eventuality, a genuine Comparative Literature program ordinarily steels itself to resist the call to "manage" the literature mess. Rather than risk waiting for any symptoms of administrative perplexity, a strong German program should ally itself in advance with Compara-tive Literature as a constructive, reliable partner.

This latter relationship may well entail some serious restructuring to serve students better. Older members of many a German department probably recall the time when, in addition to philology, the principal fields were medieval literature and literature of the mid-eighteenth to early twentieth centuries. Whereas English departments offered a full range of literary periods as well as of authors, themes, genres, etc., corresponding to that in a full-fledged French or Spanish department, German graduate programs showed enormous gaps. Besides, to a considerable extent, students from "outside" departments could not participate effectively in, let us say, a seminar on E.T.A. Hoffman unless they spoke and wrote German (and reciprocally, a German doctoral candidate sometimes could not take Victor Hugo on the minimal basis of reading French with fluency). Now that the twentieth century and literature before Lessing have come more into their right, more comparativistically minded students who read German are likely to venture across the frontier from English, Romance, and other areas, following the trace mainly of the medievalists and romanticists. They will not remain if they are immediately resisted as foreign bodies because the study of German literature is treated not as subject matter of international interest, but as national matter cleverly converted into a private preserve of native or trained German speakers. The comparatist in a German group can help create a better climate by giving some highly specialized German subjects in English, opening them to ambitious outsiders, and introducing and comparing the thereto pertaining key critical terms (German versus English and other sets).[7] These courses can run mixed with courses given in German in which the non-major may discuss or submit writings in English, and so on.

The point is to end the role of German as a shibboleth for other members of the academic community—naturally I refer exclusively to serious, initial curiosity. With the demise of language requirements we simply no longer can rely on the proposition that a serious student will already have made great headway in German skills; indeed, the attraction to German letters may first begin on the threshold of graduate studies. During the next decade, it may prove necessary to look above all for intellect and literary sensitivity, even at the price of lesser preliminary training in the language, in order to maintain and rebuild German Studies as a humanistic discipline. To help preserve the critical level which, inevitably, has suffered and must suffer in the interim after a massive national repudiation of language training in general, German departments may be well advised to recruit heavily from English, French, Philosophy, History, General Literature, and other B.A.'s who have made a start in German as a minor and profess interest in Comparative Literature.

The levelling which occurred in American higher education during the sixties has, among other things, caused numerous gifted American students not

[7] The "Report of the Committee on Graduate Programs in Comparative Literature in the U.S.A. and Canada" published in *ACLAN*, 7, no. 6 (Winter 1974), 15–22, shows that about 30% of the typical combinations of languages for the M.A. and Ph.D. programs actually being undertaken by CL students included German. However, the "Statistics from *Vitae* in ACLA Listing November 1974" (p. 42) show English and American at the top with 109, French second with 101, and German a much lower third with 64 persons who opted for it as the major language and/or speciality. Spanish with 34 and Italian with 29 are next; a good number of this set, in combination with the French concentrators, probably lends reinforcement to Romance departments. The strength of the French school of CL is undoubtedly reflected here in the territory of the American school. No comparable movement exists within the German-speaking countries as yet, so that the American Germanist must fill the gap himself.

of foreign background to be handicapped through no fault of their own by a late start in learning languages. Many foreign literature departments, understandably, have reacted with fatalism to the fact that the cream of the good literary talent will go into English by default—other language channels were never opened to them in due time. Strong departments of German, French, etc., can choose the heroic path of splendid isolation and bar the door forever, after some particular undergraduate semester, to the "tardy" aspirant. Comparative Literature students—precisely that segment of the student population who have bucked the trend against linguistic isolationism—will be penalized, too, by this kind of German department insofar as individually they happened to begin with Classics, or French, or Russian as undergraduates. Thus, in the long run, that sort of "elitism" leads to further decline and fragmentation and pits parts of the humanities community against one another as rivals in a shrinking enterprise.

The current picture is, in fact, not especially rosy for the Comparative Literature Ph.D.'s who ordinarily have qualified as peers in graduate courses in several major departments and trained so extensively in one as to match other regular doctoral candidates in whole fields. In addition they have passed stringent scrutiny with respect to comparative theory. According to ACLA research on the status of new Ph.D.'s, the hiring national language departments—English, French, German, or whatever—care mainly about suitability for departmental teaching and exploit their Comparative Literature credentials to justify the position to the university "philosophically." The Comparative Literature newcomer has a far heavier burden of preparations and committees. He must also balance claims on him by the national literature versus generalist faction in the university as a whole, simply in order to survive. Utility saves this high-level "slave" from being rejected by *one* of these masters or factions. But sometimes he is a ready target and quick casualty, caught in no-man's-land between the trenches upon the sudden eruption of hostilities.

For this reason alone Comparative Literature students often regard foreign language programs at large with a degree of suspicion or resentment. After all, it would be much easier to stay in the confines of the English program proper and not court the risks and misunderstandings, as well as assume the burdens, in pursuing other literatures "officially." Whereas the foreign language departments view themselves as providing a complicated service to the university, many Comparative Literature students look on them, with regret and frustration, as monopolists who control this or that significant literature.[8] Such resentment is

---

[8] The problematic situation for newly hired CL specialists who must survive in national language and literature departments is strikingly evident from the compilation of reports, "The Employment Picture for Ph.D.'s in Comparative Literature: Individual Views," *ACLAN*, 7, no. 1 (Spring 1975), 13–17. Through the responses of recent Ph.D.'s runs a theme of bitterness over exploitation by departments who are manoeuvring vis-à-vis the pressures exerted by their university Administration, yet who often fundamentally resist CL as a discipline.

not necessarily going to be aimed only against an "old-fashioned" German faculty that, for instance, spends almost all of its best energies laying offerings on the Goethe altar in the departmental inner sanctum (a cult I, for one, fully comprehend). It can be directed just as readily at a department which pursues some other newer party-line, such as Marxist "social relevance," rather than representing larger and global concerns. The modest size of the best intentioned foreign language department can make it appear less flexible than the English group in which, for instance, there may well be several romanticists of different views or temper, and which hence exudes the aura of that free market of ideas of which I have spoken. Some colleagues may bristle at my repeated use of a cliché from classic-liberal economics; the theory of a free exchange may be regarded as inoperative a priori by those critics of American higher education who deem it to be bound and fettered to some "Establishment." But my sense of the complaints from a majority of American students is that they certainly want to test the possibilities of intellectual liberty, but are disturbed by the seeming irreconcilability of the structural rigidity of specializations on the one hand and the vastness of knowledge on the other.

In fact, the British comparatist Henry Gifford argues that, as a result of special factors, after two centuries of maturation, American literary development tends epochally toward comparativistic assimilation of diverse elements—even to the point of a chaos and fragmentation which mocks the effort.[9] For better or for worse, Comparative Literature has evolved in America as a means to satisfy the more pressing dilemma of organizing the diverse subjects which might otherwise evade all control. Until and unless something superior is hammered out in the critical smithy, the traditional German department can pursue the investigation of literary interchange on a larger scale through Comparative Literature. Comparative Literature represents one immediate remedy to satisfy that most natural craving of many American students who study German: the craving for a non-dogmatic, larger frame of reference for their chief interest. Realistically, the "chief" interest of today may become a minor area in several years. But the openness to two-way and eventually a multidirectional traffic exhibits that kind of participation in the creative life of our age which, I submit, can appeal to certain of the keener young minds from whom alone the study of any literature will continue to draw its hope.

[9] In ch. 6, "American literature—the special case," in his *Comparative Literature* (London and New York, 1969), Henry Gifford nonetheless stresses that "the pattern of American literature over the three centuries in which it has struggled from small beginnings to world stature takes on almost a diagrammatic quality"; that "American literature presses the student to form his own conception of the whole Western inheritance, and to invoke, as Eliot did, 'the mind of Europe'"; and "thus the study of American literature, as dominant partner in . . . [English as an emerging world] language, would seem to prepare us for the reception of world literature" (pp. 84ff.).

THE GERMANIST AS EDUCATOR IN THE FIRST
TWO YEARS OF COLLEGE TEACHING

ROBERT SPAETHLING
University of Massachusetts at Boston

The National Defense Education Act of 1958 provided foreign language departments with an opportunity to grow that was unparalleled in the history of American higher education. The decade of expansion that followed, however, was not always based on sound pedagogical planning but, more often than not, was euphoric in character rather than realistic. The last five years have changed all that. As the wellsprings of government subsidies for language studies dried up and student demand dropped to a disconcerting low, foreign language departments, along with many other humanities programs, found themselves not only in a quandary but actually fighting for survival. And the crisis is by no means over.

The expansion in the 1960's on the one hand and the sobering recognition of our limited role in American education on the other, have compelled us to begin a review of our tasks as humanists and language teachers, to reassess some of our cherished educational assumptions and, above all, our own professional attitudes. No one can offer any quick and easy solutions to the dilemma facing us; it is difficult enough to venture a prediction. But being forced by urgent circumstances to reflect and reexamine provides its own therapeutic effects and may indeed start the necessary process for a cure.

Let me assume, for the purposes of this discussion, that the teaching of foreign languages and literatures proceeds in three major steps: the introductory level (roughly comprising freshman and sophomore courses in college as well as Advanced Placement courses in high schools), the advanced stage in college (junior and senior courses), and the graduate programs. Each of these levels generates its own programmatic and pedagogical questions and, particularly today, its own human needs and problems. I will focus here primarily on the introductory level, and at the same time widen my perspective towards the non-major, the student who requires our services without expecting to get a degree in our field.

Let me say at the outset: there is no dearth of exciting and attractive material in German for the introductory level, nor is there any lack of interest in it as far as I can judge. Modern German authors, particularly Thomas Mann, Rilke, Hesse, Brecht, Kafka, Böll, Grass, etc. enjoy an excellent reputation and even a kind of popularity among young Americans, and it is no secret that many an English literature course is studded with these very German names. Numerous students (and faculty from contiguous departments) are also becoming increasingly aware of East Germany as a potential source for literary, political, and sociological studies—and Germanists, too, are beginning to recognize that forgotten country as a culturally significant area. In addition one finds currently considerable fascination with German intellectuals of the late nineteenth and early twentieth centuries (I include Austrian and German Swiss names in this description), men who have so decisively shaped the intellectual and spiritual climate of our own time: Marx, Nietzsche, Freud, Jung, Weber, Heidegger, Tillich, Marcuse, Bloch, et al. But while there is, as most of us will agree, no problem with materials, inspiration and interest, there may well be reluctance in some departments to organize their efforts (more accurately perhaps: their sparse resources) toward exploration of such a vast and undelineated realm of German cultural heritage. Clearly (and I can hear the chorus of affirming voices) we cannot be everything to everybody, we must not dilute our principal obligation which is, after all, the teaching of the German language and its literature and, in fact, most of us are simply not qualified to deal with sociological, psychological, or scientific texts in any depth. These objections are valid and I agree with them. Yet I submit—and this proposition leads me *medias in res*—that there is much we *can* do if we are at all serious about reaching a broader spectrum of students at our universities: we can add flexibility to our existing curricula (including courses in translation), we can involve ourselves in administration and governance, and we can participate in university-wide teaching programs. But whatever the methods and the means, there is a distinct and basic need for single language departments to break out of their sometimes cultivated isolation and become more visible to the rest of the university. I wish to make clear, however, that I am not recommending a merger with other foreign language departments to solve the problems we are facing. For one thing, it would not increase our visibility; for another, it would only relocate the existing problems. It may be hard to accept this fact, but the truth is that foreign language departments do not have a great deal of political clout and influence—at times for good reasons. Even our well disposed colleagues in neighboring departments, such as English, are not always fully aware of where we stand and what we do—especially in the area of scholarship. It is a fact that some of our best scholars direct their research efforts toward Germany rather than toward their own university, many publications are aimed at a distant reading public while our own colleagues and students have only a faint idea of our intellectual positions. Students not knowing German often have to go to the English department to learn about Mann and Kafka. I am not saying that there is no place for *deutsche Literaturwissenschaft* or *Literaturwissenschaftler;* their indispensability in American *Germanistik* and graduate education is obvious. I am even less advocating that we challenge our friends in English and French into combat over the interpretation rights on Mann and Kafka. Quite the contrary! It can only benefit us if German literary thought circulates outside our own province. But I *am* saying that we must participate as vigorously as we possibly can in the affairs of our colleges and universities and broaden our intellectual and pedagogical commitments to include our own colleagues down the hall. It furthermore behooves us to take note of whatever German interest exists and is being engendered in our colleges and to nurture it and cultivate it to our best ability.

Of the various possibilities for branching out, for getting involved, probably none is more personally rewarding than teaching in tandem with a member of another department. This practice has blossomed in the last several years and is one of those genuine learning devices from which all participants profit, faculty as well as students. To teach together with a historian in a course on German culture and civilization, to team up with an English scholar in a common exploration of Dr. Fausti literary history or of "What is Enlightenment?", to collaborate with a musicologist on German texts and music from Haydn's oratorio *The Creation* to Benjamin Britten's *Death in Venice* means not only to expand one's own mind and learn anew, but to expose oneself and one's department to a greater number and variety of students and to the university in general. Team-teaching with a psychologist or a sociologist is no longer a rarity, and an engagement in such widening perspectives often means that old and staid acquaintances, such as Werther, Tonio Kröger, Gregor Samsa, along with one's own shopworn interpretations take on some new and fascinating dimensions.

There is one potential problem with team-teaching of interdisciplinary courses that might be mentioned here. The problem often is where to locate such courses. Generally they are taught in English, and foreign language departments must take care not to crowd their own regular offerings with a plethora of so-called translation courses. It seems to me that the best programmatic home for this type of course can be found in Humanities Sequences, Great Books Courses, Programs in Literature etc. In other words, we should put our strength where it belongs: German courses within the department, courses in translation in suitable university-wide programs. Naturally each department will have to have some courses in translation, especially if they satisfy a language or distribution requirement.

Of special value and significance is a two-semester course on German culture and civilization taught in English and using translated texts. Large departments might offer a culture course in German as well, but the majority will have to be content with one, and in my experience such a course will be of greatest advantage to the department as well as the university if it is given in English on the freshman-sophomore level. It frequently provides the students with their first conscious contact with German classical music, German art, German customs etc.; and it can be the beginning of a lasting experience—some of our best graduate students got their start in this unsuspecting manner. Beyond such immediate effects lies yet another, a more fundamental charge and obligation, and that is to convey a touch of German culture to the general, non-German speaking public in and outside the university. We *are,* after all, the representatives of German culture in America and it is part of our profession as teachers of German to make people aware of both our function and the culture we represent. Let me summarize: we should have courses in English or in German wherever they will do the most good. Participating in courses and programs outside the department is important for our work, for our intellectual lives, and for our survival in the university.

There are various other forms of programmatic involvement. A perennial headache, at least in urban schools, is the inability of students to write a well-formulated and logical paper. I think we can and should help to alleviate this problem, even though the task calls for instructors of writing skills and foundation courses rather than Germanists. Often one member of a language department offers writing workshops (concentrating on style, structure, vocabulary) in conjunction with German literature courses in translation; in this manner the department helps address not only one of the university's most persistent problems but again provides another fruitful way to enhance the image and reputation, and thereby the indispensability, of a foreign language department. Programs in literature, aiming to teach literature as a phenomenon of art unbound by linguistic ties, translation programs, aspiring to teach practical knowledge of the language as a useful adjunct to the regular liberal arts major—all such undertakings present possibilities for involvement. In general, it seems to me, efforts leading to a greater awareness of our own scholastic positions vis-à-vis the actual needs of our students as well as the needs of higher education in America should be supported. We can ill afford to sit on the sidelines while the fate of our professional speciality is being decided in mid-field—by people who barely know us.

I would argue that the most productive time for curricular innovations comes in the first two years of college. The junior and senior classes and especially the graduate schools have to take, by necessity, a narrower focus with respect to subject matter and field coverage; once students have found their way into German and decided to remain a while, they must naturally be subjected to more rigorous training in both the language and in literary thought. But on the introductory level the large and central issue remains how to productively harness and, if need be, activate student interest in things German and channel it toward an educational or even professional goal. These are questions serious enough to warrant consideration in our hiring policies. Since we cannot be everything to everybody, yet are facing rather diverse curricular demands, we may have to meet such demands by creating diversified departments; and this means, in part, tenure and promotion for good teaching and educational planning as well as for scholarship.

The second major issue I should like to raise in this paper relates to the familiar question: who and what should be read in freshman and sophomore classes, what should be covered in German, what can fruitfully be done in translation courses? Let me say at the beginning: I am in principle opposed to sacred cows and canonized literature. I would argue instead that the works presented to students in their early college years possess a high enough literary quality so that they will stand comparison with literature the students read in English and perhaps other foreign language classes. Obviously the works must be linguistically approachable: a wide choice of poems and edited texts exists for the first year level, there are plays and texts for the second year (e.g. *Die Physiker, Siddhartha, Die Verwandlung, Bahnwärter Thiel*) and there is an even greater selection for the junior year (e.g. *Tonio Kröger, Woyzeck, Der kaukasische Kreidekreis,* and let us not forget the recent edition of *German Literature: Texts and Contexts* by Bernhard Blume). In translation courses approximately the same criteria apply: the works must be thematically and culturally approachable and interesting. It is difficult at best to send a literary novice into rapture over an ode by Klopstock or a prose piece by Uwe Johnson. This implies no value judgment; but clearly some authors require, for full comprehension, a linguistic and literary experience that cannot be expected from a student at the introductory level. The freshman and sophomore courses need strong literary profiles and accessible issues. Naturally, as students move along in reading skill and literary sophistication they will have to become more and more knowledgeable about works of a more subtle and complex nature.

Another point I should like to emphasize: literature must be introduced into language courses as early as possible. We are all aware of the different pedagogical views in this matter stemming from the controversy as to whether language is first and foremost oral communication or, in fact, written art. Jack Stein has characterized the concomitant problems of this argument as they relate to the classroom situation: "Where the study of literature is indiscriminately forced on all foreign language pupils regardless of their interests and abilities, this is an abuse. But so is it an abuse . . . to withhold this step perilously long from the more gifted student whose interest in the foreign language may well be greatly increased by his contacts with its literature."[1] In general I am persuaded that carefully selected literature is meaningful at any level, in high school or in college (even to students who want to learn only the language), and good literature, if taught properly, communicates its own joy and reward. It is even feasible to offer (on the beginning as well as on the intermediate level) a German language course featuring poems and texts set to music—there are numerous attractive choices ranging from Eichendorff/Schumann's "Mondnacht" to Brecht/Weill's *Dreigroschenoper.* Such a course furthers learning processes in several media at once and it comes with the unexpected bonus of a built-in rationale for language requirements. Programmatic experiments are important

[1] Jack Stein, "Language Teaching and Literature," *German Quarterly,* 38 (1965), 437.

for the vitality of a department and should be carried out, even if only one section of the new program can be offered on a given level. Obviously the scope and range of these curricular ventures increase with each successive step, the higher one reaches the more intriguing become the possibilities: sections on contrastive analysis of bilingual texts, culture courses in the native tongue, a science reading course, a section of English-to-German, German-to-English translation, a program in total language immersion. There is enormous potential and great variety and we must not be afraid to use our imagination. At the same time freshmen and sophomores must be given opportunity and encouragement to expand their minds and roam as far afield as their intellectual curiosity will take them—and if that means letting them read *Faust* or *The Magic Mountain* in English, then so be it. Whatever we do, especially on the introductory level, we must not stifle intellectual interests and growth by insisting that the reading has to be done in German. That goes for classroom discussions as well. We all work hard to attain a modicum of literary education within the foreign language; but it is unproductive for the educational benefit of the student if both teacher and student come to a standstill because they cannot reach each other linguistically. Here, as in all other concerns, the education of the mind is more important than the imparting of a language skill.

The obligatory reading list presents still another item for discussion. While I have certain (limited) regard for coverage, I am not convinced that much education takes place when a student concentrates primarily on checking off a list of required authors. A systematic introduction to the technique of reading literature is by far preferable to a "must-list" of literary works. We must pay more attention to the teaching of what literature is and concentrate less on what or how much should be read. Recent steps taken in this direction by the College Board's German Advanced Placement Committee are of interest and significance. The Committee has abandoned the (by now almost sacrosanct) idea of a prescribed reading list and testing for specific content. Instead it has begun to test literature as literature on the basis of reading ability and literary perception. This makes for a more complex examination procedure as well as for greater difficulty in preparing the students—the absence of a specific syllabus tends to be unsettling. But the positive aspects of the new approach clearly outweigh such relatively minor drawbacks, for now the test seeks out ability and in-depth knowledge, it searches for true intellectual acumen and literary sensitivity; and that change in emphasis must be applauded. English classes have used such methods of inquiry for years and indeed the new Advanced Placement Test may well be inspired by the English example. On the college level we, too, should follow suit and train our students for technique and not only for coverage. Again this applies especially to introductory courses where students need to be exposed repeatedly to methodological systems which not only illuminate a literary work but sharpen the student's thinking. Several years ago, Frank Ryder outlined an excellent instructional model which leads the student in a step-by-step analysis from a simple appreciation of the text to a highly sophisticated level of abstract thought. The model was originally proposed for Advanced Placement students in high schools, but it applies to college level work as well and is particularly appropriate to freshman and sophomore courses. Ryder's major structural points: (1) Simple reading level, appreciation of language or text. (2) Characterological criticism, hero, antagonist, das Ich. (3) Extrinsic concerns, pertinent biographical notes. (4) Themes, motifs, concepts, images. (5) Figurative language, symbolism. (6) Structural analysis, point of view, irony. (7) Differing outside perspectives. (8) Literary history. (9) Historicity, changing meanings.[2]

Ryder's methodological suggestions and my own concerns point in the same direction: we must educate for reading ability and analytical skills. No one, of course, will be unhappy about a student who is well-read, especially if he or she is majoring in the field. But it is without doubt more important that the student has received training in how to approach a literary text, what to look for, and how to read the evidence, than how many works he has crossed off his obligatory list. It is up to us to guide the students in the right direction; underneath our Germanist cloaks there must be, available and accessible, the educator.

This brings me to my final point: the educator as humanist. I mean humanist in the full sense of the word, as a teacher of humanities courses and even more as a humane individual. I have often reflected on this subject, but never found the appropriate forum to express my thoughts about it—until now. Inasmuch as we are attempting to understand and improve our professional situation and take a critically constructive view of ourselves and the future of German Studies, we also need to realize (or remind ourselves) that nothing persuades and attracts the present generation of students more than clarity and honesty in our own behavior. I am indeed implying that our attitudes toward students, or, in fact, toward our own colleagues, are often rather different from the themes of beauty and human dignity which we espouse with such *Einfühlungsvermögen* in the classroom. So often we deal with human frailty and despair as a classroom exercise and then thoroughly confuse our students when they find that we do not necessarily practice what we teach. Of all the errors and failings that we may carry into our profession, none is less palatable than the presumption that there is only one truth and that we possess exclusive rights to it. I once was present in a graduate seminar where the professor asked a question to which no one knew the answer. The students took turns trying to gain entrance into the professor's mind as if it were the gate of truth. But each timid attempt was met with a decisive shaking of the professorial head. Half of the seminar session was taken up with this guessing game which ended, as one might suspect,

[2] Frank Ryder, "Literature in High School—A College Point of View," *German Quarterly,* 38 (1965), 469–479.

in a bewildering anticlimax. This can happen on any level, and wherever it happens it spells doom for education. Learning must proceed by exchange and dialogue, especially in the humanities, and students have a right to be part of the process by which we search for meaningful answers; they need us, to be sure, but we need them as well. The greatest sin imaginable to me is the sin of manipulating minds. It is our job to train students to think for themselves and not to become extensions of ourselves.

This is not a sermon in moral behavior, but rather a sincere argument in favor of reviewing not only our curricular affairs but also our own pedagogical practices and human attitudes. I am not advocating a hand-holding operation and I am especially not recommending any avoidance of discipline and rigor in intellectual training. Quite the contrary! But to be humane and generous does not mean to lower standards; strictness is by no means synonymous with rigidity. I am proposing simply that we be as flexible in our programs, particularly in the first two years, and as involved in the university as we possible can and that we take an interest in our students both as specialists and as educators. I firmly believe that to the degree that we can fruitfully combine these various tasks and charges, we will enhance, to that same degree, our image, role and function as Germanists.

GERMAN LANGUAGE TEACHING
IN AMERICAN HIGHER EDUCATION

WILLIAM C. CROSSGROVE
Brown University

People who identify themselves as German teachers, or professors of German, are likely to be thought of as people who teach others how to use the German language.[1] High school teachers seemingly have no difficulty accepting this characterization of their chief professional activity, but colleagues in higher education are rather uncomfortable with it. Yet it would seem to be the most accurate *single* description of what we do in higher education as well as in high school. German teachers existed before Germanists in North America, and the number of language courses continues until today to exceed the number of literature courses at all but a handful of institutions. Nonetheless, we have remained remarkably ambivalent towards language teaching at the college and university level. In this paper, I propose to examine several areas in which greater clarity of purpose about language teaching might aid us in formulating goals for the last quarter of the twentieth century. On the one hand we seem reluctant to transform our theories of why we teach the German language into practice, and on the other hand we have difficulty in defining our professional status as language teachers.

Reasons for Teaching German.

The very first issue of *Die Unterrichtspraxis* includes a report on the "National Symposium on the Advancement of the Teaching of German in the U.S." which begins with a detailed statement about how to develop "motivation and rationale" for the study of German.[2] The next item in the same issue is a reprint of a pamphlet prepared by the California AATG Chapter entitled "Which Foreign Language Should I Study?"[3] Neither statement contains more than a cursory reference to German literature, nor do most similar statements from at

[1] I am grateful to the editors and to the participants in the editorial conference held at the Goethe House in New York on 9 May 1975 for their helpful advice and criticisms and to Jonathan B. Conant and Hannelore Crossgrove for their suggestions.

[2] Volume 1, No. 1 (Spring 1968), 132–6.

[3] Pp. 136–8.

least the last 30 years. Nonetheless, in the words of A. Peter Foulkes, many departments continue to see language instruction "solely as a preliminary stage to the reading of literary works in German."[4] We are capable of producing ringing statements decrying the monolingual chauvinism of Americans who deny themselves access to all sorts of putative benefits, but when we devise our college and university curricula we act as if the only real benefit to result from studying German is the ability to read German literature.

We were not as a group forced to confront our own inconsistency in recent times until language requirements began to be dropped at many institutions in the late sixties and early seventies. Severely declining enrollments have elicited a great variety of responses from language teachers: renewed efforts to increase our classroom effectiveness, innovative courses designed to stimulate student interest, discovery of uses of German other than as a prerequisite for studying literature, and many others. Nearly every issue of the *Bulletin of the Association of Departments of Foreign Languages,* or *Die Unterrichtspraxis* contains one or more descriptions of courses or programs designed to increase interest in language study. The proposals cover the full range from the sublime to the ridiculous, but for the most part it would appear that the quality of language teaching has been enhanced by the need to compete for student interest.

In particular, the growth of joint programs with another discipline or interdisciplinary programs in, e.g., German Studies has been notable in the past five to ten years. In part these programs may have been a response to the decline in interest in literature which was perceived in the climate of political activism in the late sixties, in part they may reflect the increasingly interdisciplinary orientation of literary studies, and in part Marxist and Neo-Hegelian views on the essential unity of all disciplines which study culture and society may have contributed a stimulus. In any case, we as German teachers are presented with a formidable challenge in adapting our techniques of teaching German to the needs of other disciplines.

There is no doubt about our ability to teach German literature relatively early in language courses. Discussion of plot, characterization, and style is a natural outgrowth of close reading of a text and provides a good basis for moving beyond narrow textual analysis to related issues. But texts which convey factual information at least partially unfamiliar to students do not readily lend themselves to discussion except at a level of linguistic sophistication beyond the capabilities of all but the most advanced undergraduates.[5] It is thus common for courses which lead into other disciplines to drop all pretense of being language

[4] "Some Speculations on the Future of German Departments in the United States," *The German Quarterly,* 47 (1974), 525–43, here p. 531. Foulkes' article should be required reading for all American Germanists.

[5] My initial wrestlings with this problem were reported in a note jointly written with Duncan Smith in *Die Unterrichtspraxis,* 4:1 (Spring 1971), 47–51.

courses and work in English, or to use materials so trivial as to dull the interest of the students.

In contrast to the situation in literary studies, there is not a comparably urgent need for Germanists to inform students in other disciplines. Historians, political scientists, sociologists, and geographers have been studying German society for many years, and there is no evidence that the specialists in these fields are incompetent to do their jobs—though of course there may be too few of them interested in German-speaking countries to suit us. Our goal as language teachers ought to be to focus on the notion that language studies are also organically related to disciplines other than literature. No single structural reform is likely to achieve the desired goal. It can hardly be our aim, for example, to see the establishment of a Department of German History with historians who also teach language. If, on the other hand, there are historians with the competence and the interest to teach language courses, universities should be encouraged to make joint appointments which will enable them to teach both history and German.

Large universities can, and to some extent do, further the goal of language courses leading to work in other disciplines by offering courses taught in a particular foreign language for students in fields such as history, where there might be large enough groups of students with the necessary linguistic skills. Given the increasing pressure to maximize class size in the face of budget squeezes, this solution is severely limited in its applicability. The greatest contribution of language teachers towards cooperation with other disciplines would seem to lie in developing new materials which are suitable for introduction in beginning and intermediate language courses but which also present intellectual challenges to the students. This will be no easy task, to be sure, but the difficulties should not discourage us from continuing our attempts.

A particular challenge is presented by the interdisciplinary German Studies program which attempts to integrate language learning with a number of disciplines in the humanities or social sciences. The language teacher can play a central role in such a program because the focus on a particular culture is perhaps most clearly articulated in the common language, the most pervasive of cultural phenomena. The pedagogical problems are at least as severe as in attempting to integrate language learning with a specific discipline, but the language teacher is not faced with the same intellectual disadvantage of collaborating as the junior partner of the "real" specialist. The language learning component is at least potentially the unifying element which links the various disciplines into a common effort to understand a particular culture. The German Studies program will benefit from some courses offered in English. These courses should serve to inform the academic community at large about German affairs as viewed from an American perspective, to generate interest among some students in learning the language to pursue advanced work in the interdisciplinary program, and to deal with complex issues early in the program. The language learning component must, however, continue to form the core of the program if it is to be of interest to language teachers.

In practice, it seems inevitable that some interdisciplinary programs are going to tend to emphasize a particular approach or period, and the participating language teachers are apt to become a new kind of specialist in a particular endeavor such as analysis of contemporary German society or nineteenth century aesthetic perceptions. There is nothing inherently wrong with this, but there is probably a real danger that the language learning component can be progressively neglected to the point of being meaningless. If this prediction turns out to be true, then the German Studies program will merely have served as an escape hatch for a Germanist into another field, a laudable endeavor given the present job market but hardly an appealing vision for the future of our profession.

Paradoxically enough, while the dominance of literary studies in German has hindered the growth of language study as a prerequisite for other activities, the dominance of the language learning component in our literature programs has diminished our influence in the American academic community. We have tended to guard the secrets of German literature against invaders from other fields as if anyone who did not first learn the German language was unworthy of initiation into our arcane subject. Instead of seeing ourselves as interpreters of German literature to the American literary world, we have been content to establish an overseas branch of *Germanistik*. The effects of these attitudes are amply documented elsewhere in this volume. Suffice it so say, just as we need greater flexibility in offering language programs which lead to fields other than literature, we need literature programs which enable us to make fruitful contacts with literary scholars and students who do not know German.

Literature in translation courses have flourished in recent years in the context of vanishing language requirements and declining enrollments.[6] To the extent that these courses are used only as a way of increasing enrollments, they may be a transitory phenomenon. But the growing influence of comparative literature programs makes it unlikely that we will be able to return to the exclusive use of German in all our literature courses if we want to be in the mainstream of literary studies in America. Specialists in German literature must of course continue to have a complete mastery of the language, but we need to recognize that interpreting German literature for those who do not know German is an integral part of our professional task rather than a way of increasing enrollment. As language teachers we should welcome more literature in translation courses. It is inherently improbable that there are large numbers of American students so interested in German literature that they struggle through language courses in order to take literature courses. It is at least possible,

---

[6] See, e.g., the survey by Marie-Luise Caputo-Mayr, "German Literature and Culture Courses in English: Trends in Pennsylvania," *ADFL Bulletin*, 6:2 (November 1974), 47–50.

however, that students exposed to stimulating courses in translation will be motivated to enroll in language courses so as to be able to read the original texts.

The Status of Language Teachers in Higher Education.

The problem can be stated bluntly: language teaching is not a respectable profession in large segments of American higher education. The language teacher can normally attain status only as the junior partner in an internal union with a literary scholar, a linguist, or even an analyst of contemporary German culture, as the lesser of "zwei Seelen in einer Brust." Graduate students are trained to be literary scholars, often while supporting themselves by teaching beginning language courses with varying degrees of supervision. In many institutions they have no formal training for work as language teachers, and the kind of work done in large language courses, especially audio-lingual ones, seems particularly unintellectual compared to the sophisticated analyses carried out in graduate seminars. Then, when the students become junior faculty members, they have to continue to "pay their dues" by teaching language courses and, at large institutions, by coordinating teaching assistants who are being trained as literary scholars by senior colleagues. Eventually the faculty members may achieve status and professional satisfaction by becoming full-time literature teachers and passing the drudge work on to new junior colleagues, or at least as much of it as possible in smaller colleges.

In short, there are cogent reasons why we should be uneasy about our role as language teachers: graduate work leading to the Ph.D. is largely irrelevant to language teaching; language learning is primarily skill acquisition and therefore seems low in intellectual content compared to most of the traditional academic disciplines; and professional recognition is not usually achieved through excellence in language teaching. Yet we as Germanists have avoided facing these issues squarely because of our persistent belief that we have to teach languages as a necessary evil brought on by some failure of secondary schools to do their job. This belief is misguided on at least two counts.

For one thing, the often cited German model, according to which language teaching is not done at the university, is accepted all too uncritically. The students who arrive at the German university with nine years of English behind them are widely assumed to have mastered the language and to be prepared for advanced study of literature. A closer look reveals a rather different picture. Language laboratories, language teachers, and an entire range of language courses suggest that the language learning process in the secondary schools does not turn out finished products.[7] We conveniently overlook the existence of many *Lek-*

---

[7] See also the comments by Kurt Otten in the North American edition of *Die Zeit,* April 26, 1974, p. 8 as cited by Jeffrey L. Sammons in *Die Unterrichtspraxis,* 7:2 (Fall 1974), 21.

toren, Studienräte im Hochschuldienst, etc. who enjoy permanent positions with respectable salaries as language teachers.

We also forget our own experience which suggests that a good, intensive one year college language course followed by an intensive summer program is capable of imparting as much language skill as four or more years in the schools. The point is not that high school teachers are ineffective—good students sometimes emerge with outstanding preparation—, but rather that the speed with which a foreign language is learned probably depends far more on motivation than on the age at which learning commences.

An even more grievous misconception, however, is the assumption that in the best of all possible worlds the high schools would teach a lot more *German,* perhaps at the expense of other languages. In fact, however, the appropriate analogy can again be found in the West German university system if we focus our attention on fields such as Slavic studies rather than English. Relatively few West German secondary schools offer language courses in Russian. The university program consists of a few research scholars who give advanced courses in Russian literature and a larger number of language teachers who offer courses to those who wish, for whatever reason, to learn the Russian language. Surely it cannot be our professional goal to see German be the most taught language in our secondary schools if we are to have a sense of national priorities derived from our perceptions as members of American society. We need to work wherever possible to encourage the offering of German as a high school elective, but the need for language teaching at the college level will, and should, continue.

The crux of the problem, therefore, does not lie in any failure of the secondary school system. The problem is in defining the role of language teaching in higher education. A partial solution might seem to be the redesigning of our graduate training in order to place more emphasis on language teaching. Certainly we should expect, as a minimum, close supervision of teaching assistants by experienced, and committed, language teachers. Some exposure to the results of pedagogical research on language teaching also ought to be a minimal requirement of all graduate programs. A more radical step is the Doctor or Arts program which places more emphasis on teaching.[8] But such evidence as is available indicates that the D.A. is not being accepted as a genuine alternative to the Ph.D. in most four year institutions.[9] Graduate training will not be effectively reformed until ability in language teaching becomes a demonstrably marketable skill beyond the usual "native or near-native proficiency and teaching experience" so familiar from job descriptions.

---

[8] For a brief description of the program at the University of Washington, see H.M. Rabura, "The D.A. Program," *Die Unterrichtspraxis,* 5:1 (Spring 1972), 127–30.

[9] See A.M. Hardee, "The Doctor of Arts in FLs—A Survey of Attitudes in the Southeastern U.S.," *ADFL Bulletin,* 4:2 (December 1972), 27–30 and Jean-Charles Seigneuret and David P. Benseler, "The Doctor of Arts at Washington State University: Results of a Preliminary Survey," *ADFL Bulletin,* 5:3 (March 1974), 44–8.

For all its diversity, the American educational system has been remarkably rigid in its reliance on a traditional definition of scholarship as the primary criterion for bestowing status on faculty members. There are of course many institutions which place less emphasis on scholarship than others, but if they wish to "upgrade" themselves to higher status, they resort to the same set of criteria as have always been followed. Here we face the central dilemma of the language teacher: language teaching appears to be "merely" the imparting of a skill readily acquired by millions of native speakers; publications related to language teaching are not likely to be recognized at prestigious universities and colleges; and some gifted language teachers do not engage in scholarship at all.

It is obvious, of course, that the reference to native language acquisition is a straw man and that the task of teaching foreign languages to adult learners is exceedingly difficult. It is also, however, true that a foreign language is a skill, however complex, to be acquired for some purpose other than as an end in itself. Analogies to other skill courses, such as calculus for chemists and physicists, are incomplete since mathematicians who teach beginning calculus are also, at least potentially, involved in expanding the language of mathematics through their research.

One solution would be to recognize the special status of the language teacher as a specialist employed by an institution for the specific purpose of language teaching with no expectation of regular participation in scholarly activities. Some institutions have adopted a policy of this type, but then usually by employing teachers with special titles, such as Lecturer, "outside the tenure stream." It is not clear to me why the language teaching specialist merits less protection from arbitrary dismissal than colleagues who carry the title Professor. The introduction of language teaching specialists into colleges and universities is perfectly appropriate, and special titles and increased teaching loads are appropriate in exchange for non-participation in scholarship provided that the language teacher is defined as an essential part of the institution with the expectation of permanent employment as the reward for excellence.

A second solution is to entrust the language program to scholars who specialize in developing better techniques for language teaching. There is no reason why a specialist in language pedagogy should not receive the same kind of evaluation as a scholar as is accorded to literary scholars. A number of universities have language teaching specialists on their faculties, and here the only serious stumbling block would seem to be the continued unwillingness on the part of some literary scholars, and university administrators, to give proper recognition to pedagogical scholarship. A cautionary note: excellence in pedagogical research is no more of a guarantee of excellence in language teaching than is excellence in literary scholarship a guarantee of excellence in teaching literature. The point is that an excellent language teacher who chooses to exercise scholarly talent in the field of language pedagogy should be evaluated in terms of the quality of the scholarship, not in terms of an arbitrary decision that some scholarship is by nature more "scholarly" than others.

The majority of the German departments in America, however, are probably too small to have the kind of specialization presupposed by the two models discussed above. They will continue to need language teachers who are also active in another discipline, most typically literature, but also linguistics, interdisciplinary studies, or any other appropriate field. In no case, though, should language teaching be related to status so that it is done primarily by younger faculty members only as long as they absolutely have to. *All members of a multi-purpose faculty should participate equally in language teaching.* Only if it is an expected part of the entire career of the average American Germanist will it be regarded as a serious profession and neither as a training ground for people who want to do something else nor as a dumping ground for those who are not good at other things.

If, however, a department chooses to specialize its functions following a model similar to the two discussed previously, then language teachers should be hired as language teachers, evaluated as language teachers, and released or given tenure as language teachers. The literary scholars should be treated similarly. New Ph.D.'s hired to teach literature should be put to work teaching literature. If there are not enough literature courses to keep an incipient literary scholar occupied, then a language teacher should be hired instead. The fact is that in German, as in several of the other traditional national literatures, we have more literature teachers than we need. Furthermore, most of us are not trained to be part of a broadly conceived discipline of literary studies which is somehow related to national educational priorities. Instead we are pale imitations of German *Ordinarien* of a preceding generation with neither the time nor the training nor the resources to do the kind of research we expect of ourselves. The need for language teachers, on the other hand, remains comparatively strong—until, that is, the fateful moment of the tenure decision. Then the language teacher is apt to be recycled into the job market to make room for a potential literary scholar who is then put to work teaching language.

To be fair to our junior colleagues and to build a strong future for our profession we must clarify our individual and departmental priorities and give appropriate professional recognition to achievements in language teaching. There are various models which are more or less appropriate to a particular institution, but none of them should be used to establish an inappropriately large number of alleged literary scholars by disguising the fact that some of them are, or ought to be, language teachers.[10] We ought to consider establishing a national committee to project our actual personnel needs as a discipline for the next decades using the best evidence available and to follow up with an evaluation of existing graduate programs. The report of this committee should include specific recom-

---

[10] I have excluded consideration of departmental reorganizations, such as establishment of separate departments of literature and language teaching, on two grounds: administrative fiat will be successful only to the degree that attitudes also change, and the current departmental system is too firmly entrenched to expect major changes at a significant number of institutions in the near future. I have also not considered the option of entrusting

mendations as to which programs should be dropped, how large the continuing ones should be, and what kinds of changes should be made in the training being done. No one would be obliged to carry out these recommendations, but the moral authority of our profession would surely have some influence on colleagues and administrators.

language teaching to linguists because the same arguments which apply to the relationship between language teachers and literary scholars apply virtually unchanged to the relationship between language teachers and linguists. Naturally I recognize that linguists have generated significant insights for language teachers, and I firmly believe that language teachers should be well acquainted with basic linguistic concepts.

THE CASE FOR LINGUISTICS IN THE GERMAN DEPARTMENT

JÜRGEN EICHHOFF
University of Wisconsin-Madison

Language is around us every day, every hour. We use language to communicate to others our desires, our feelings, and our ideas. By the same means the desires, feelings and ideas of others are communicated to us. We speak language, we hear language, we write and read it. We even use it when we think. Language is a genuinely human quality. No animal has it. In view of all this, should it not be one of the most noble occupations of the human mind to study language?

The field of scholarship devoted to the study of language is known as *linguistics*. Linguistics is concerned with language in its various aspects, such as its nature, its units, its structure, its history, its change, its role in communication, to name a few. The term *German linguistics* will be applied here to mean linguistics whose object of investigation is the German language.

Frequently, the term *philology* is used instead of, or synonymously with, linguistics. However, the two ought to be distinguished. Philology has come to mean the study of medieval texts. Though both the linguist and the philologist may sometimes work with the same materials, the philologist is concerned with a text's message while the linguist is interested in its language as such. This is not to mean that the distinction between linguistics and philology should be built into an artificially high barrier between the linguist and the philologist. The linguist has in recent years come to see his role within the scholarly community in a somewhat different light than at the time when he still had to struggle for the recognition of his specialization as a reputable field of scholarship. If he has not totally lost contact with what language study is all about, at least the specialist in the older stages of the language will agree with Paul Valentin's statement that a scholar who takes his profession seriously "has to be a philologist before he can be a linguist."[1] Likewise, the philologist will have to concern himself frequently and extensively with linguistic problems of the texts he is investigating. Should it come as a surprise that many of the best scholars in the two fields wear both hats, the linguist's and the philologist's?

In the majority of German departments, instruction in linguistics plays an ancillary role at best. There are departments which confer Ph.D.'s in German without offering a single course in German linguistics.[2] Linguistics courses on

---

[1] P. Valentin, *Phonologie de l'Allemand Ancien* (Paris, 1969), p. 297.

[2] According to a survey undertaken by this author for *Monatshefte*. Published as *German Linguistics in the United States and Canada* ([Madison, Wisconsin], 1976).

the undergraduate level are offered by few departments, and in only a small minority of such departments is the student offered German linguistics as a possible area of concentration.

There are at least three major factors which have contributed to this rather dismal situation. The first is strictly historical. When German departments were first founded in this country, literature was by many considered the epitome of German *Kultur* and the ultimate blessing for this seemingly barbarous nation. Secondly, there is no doubt that written and, particularly, published texts were (and still are) much easier to obtain than many of the source materials with which linguists work. And thirdly, the tremendous advances in general and theoretical linguistics in this country fostered the establishment of separate departments of linguistics. In the hope of gaining more status as linguists, many deserted the language departments, leaving literature and philology behind. Only recently have linguists begun to return to language departments.

I suggest that it is time to recognize linguistics as an integral component of the German department. I shall argue my case on two major considerations: first, that the objectives of an education in German linguistics are in total accord with the overall objectives of an education within the German department, and second, that the study of language as language plays an essential role in any meaningful training of future teachers of German.

Before we enter into our discussion, a word seems to be in order about the relationship between linguistics and literature. Not long ago Peter Foulkes upset the professional strudelcart by claiming, "there is no firmly established grounds for insisting that foreign language study should lead inevitably to the study of literary texts."[3] Walter F.W. Lohnes reports that the "vast majority" of the students in Stanford's beginning classes have "no interest" in German literature.[4] Both scholars are certainly correct. Neither of their statements need be taken to mean though that our students should not at some early point in their careers be confronted with literary texts. Every responsible linguist will agree that while the study of literature will "necessarily yield (. . .) ground to linguistics, culture and other related fields in which candidates will want and need to develop professional expertise," it "will constitute the core of most doctoral programs."[5] After all, as William Moulton put it, "as part of a liberal education we must be interested not only in teaching our students to speak, but also in teaching them to say something worth listening to."[6]

[3] A.P. Foulkes, "Some Speculations on the Future of German Departments in the United States," *German Quarterly* 47 (1974), 535.

[4] W.F.W. Lohnes, "Conversion and Expansion of a Department of German Studies," *ADFL Bulletin* 5:3 (1974), 30.

[5] "Doctoral Training for the Expanded Undergraduate Curriculum: Resolutions of the 1975 ADFL Summer Seminar," *ADFL Bulletin* 7:1 (1975), 18.

[6] W.G. Moulton, "Linguistics and Language Teaching in the United States 1940–1960," *Trends in European and American Linguistics 1930–1960*, ed. Chr. Mohrmann, A. Sommerfelt and J. Whatmough (Utrecht and Antwerp, 1970), p. 90 [first published in 1961].

Beyond these reasons based on educational policy it should not be over-looked that a number of important interdisciplinary studies have recently resulted in findings that render it imperative for the serious scholar of literature to acquaint himself with linguistic knowledge as it applies to his discipline. The perennial problem of style in language is only one of those to benefit from an interdisciplinary approach.

2

Generally speaking, the objectives of an education within the German depart-ment are the same as in other departments committed to the concept of humanistic study. We strive for a program which prepares a student for work in the profession of his choice. At the same time, we want to help him see the facts and experiences of everyday life from an intellectual position which allows him to evaluate their significance, and to help him find his own place both as an individual and as a member of the socially and historically determined frame-work in which he lives.

Surely, it is one of our tasks to teach our students to understand, speak, read, and write the German language. We ought to fulfill this task efficiently and unequivocally. No, this will not make us a Berlitz School. But for the students who come to us to learn the language (and the majority never get much more out of us than just that) we have to do at least as good a job as a Berlitz School could do, and if possible a better one. While this may seem to have little to do with linguistics in the German department, I will later argue that there is in fact a very close relationship.

What are the benefits to be reaped from an education in (German) lin-guistics?

One is simply to get acquainted with a variety of interesting facts. Now, it is not very popular these days to profess an inclination for empiricism. The truth remains that facts, or data, are the basis of language study. It remains for us to put the facts into a meaningful frame, and to evaluate their significance. It is here that we have to answer the students' call for relevancy, insisting, however, that relevancy is not altogether determined by the immediate needs of here and now.

Language is a means of communication which functions within a society or group. This is one of the fundamental insights we want the student to gain. It is an insight which will prevent him from denigrating languages he may not know well enough to appreciate, whether it be German, Swahili, or Black English. We do not wish to prevent him from admiring the utility or even the beauty of those languages he knows, but he should admire them without arrogance.

Language as a means of communication is subject to abuse as well as use. Abuses proliferate all around us: the subtle distortions of the hidden or not so hidden persuaders; the semantic twistings and machinations of the politicians; the seemingly objective technicalities of legal language which trap the uninitiated but leave a loophole for the expert, are just a few of them. The student of language gains an ability to recognize abuses and stand up to them.

Language is a system. The system's tendency to be in equilibrium reflects the human drive for order. At the same time, "the irregularities that constantly leaven and threaten the system reflect the balancing love of innovation and tolerance of the exception."[7] In this respect it is reasonable to maintain that since "language is so much a reflection of the human mind (. . .) much can be learned from it about ourselves."[8] Of course, we must be careful not to carry the analogies too far. For while in a system the position or shift of position of any element is determined by the elements around it, we educate people to find and establish their own place. Here we can learn about the difference between a system and a society.

An important dimension of language study has been and remains the study of its history. Studying the history of the language will make the student aware of the fact that a language develops in such a way that texts from earlier periods will become unintelligible to later generations. The students will develop a feeling that there is no natural law which requires a language to be what it is at any given time. However, it will also become obvious that language development is not altogether arbitrary. It closely reflects the cultural development of the society which speaks it, as well as the cultural and linguistic exchanges of this society with other societies. Again, this awareness will result in an attitude of understanding and tolerance for other languages and cultures.

Studying linguistics in a foreign language department (rather than in the Department of English or the Department of Linguistics) carries with it the enormous advantage of necessitating a rigorously confrontative/contrastive approach. The age-old observation, often quoted for the wrong reasons, is certainly valid here: He who learns a foreign language will gain a deeper understanding of his own. Once the student understands that case does in German what word order does in English, namely indicates the relationships between subjects and objects in the sentence, not only will many of the "peculiarities" in the German language appear in a new light but some in the English language as well.

The line of argumentation could be carried on almost endlessly. But it seems to me it has already become obvious that the study of language as language is a legitimate vehicle to introduce a student to what has been termed a humanistic education. Some of the insights I believe are peculiar to a study of any language, some to the study of the German language; others, probably the majority, could

---

[7] R. d'Alquen, "On the Humanistic Value of Philology," paper read at the Annual Meeting of the Modern Language Association of America, San Francisco, Dec. 26–29, 1975 (Session of the Pedagogical Seminar for Germanic Philology). Printed in the session program, pp. 10–15. Quote p. 13.

[8] R. d'Alquen, p. 13.

also be gained by studying the message of written texts ("literature," including "philology") or by studying German culture. To be sure, I neither intend, nor would I be able to claim humanistic value in any and all developments of general and theoretical linguistics, where theories often seem to run away from the facts, or where facts merely serve to prove or disprove a theory. But the truth remains that linguistic theory has offered valuable insights which can help us to understand language better, its structure and its functioning, and which can help us to teach it more effectively and more meaningfully. It would be foolish, indeed unhumanistic, of the profession not to learn about and use such insights and apply them wherever possible.

3

My second argument in support of recognizing linguistics as an integral component of the German department curriculum is intimately connected with what will be the chief professional concern for many of our students: the teaching of the German language. We have to prepare these future teachers as best we can. For it is in their classrooms, during the first years of language instruction, that it is decided whether we will have students in our advanced courses or not.

The notion that all a foreign language teacher needs to have is a thorough command of the language and a good textbook is outmoded and altogether self-serving. If we do not wish future members of the profession to be uninformed about the methods and merits of applied linguistics, and if on the other hand we do wish them to be able to "make judicious selection and use of approaches, methods, techniques, aids, material, and equipment for language teaching,"[9] then our students must definitely have a thorough training in linguistics, especially applied linguistics. Superficial training will not do because

> Applied Linguistics [...] is [...] not a finite body of knowledge that can be acquired in a course entitled "Applied Linguistics" or be communicated in a "definite textbook." The rapid evolution of knowledge which is characteristic of linguistics, just as of many other domains of inquiry, precludes the possibility that Applied Linguistics can be a static subject. "Applied Linguistics" is ultimately a habit, a way of using linguistic conceptualization to define and solve pedagogical problems.[10]

[9] "Guidelines for Teacher Education Programs in Modern Foreign Languages," *PMLA* 81:2 (1966), A2

[10] R. Politzer, *Linguistics and Applied Linguistics: Aims and Methods* (Philadelphia, 1972), p. 5.

Responsible teachers and administrators have for some time emphasized the importance of a thorough training in linguistics.[11] To quote a few:

> Within the limits of common sense, we can say that linguistics is now one of the three necessary competences of the foreign language teacher, along with pedagogical skill and an adequate practical command of the language.[12]

> The specialist in language instruction can no longer be permitted to remain in ignorance of what is now to be known about the nature of his subject matter. There is no better remedy for this than a sustained exposure to the descriptive linguist's analysis of language.[13]

> A good FLES program requires the services of a teacher with near native competence, and understanding of the nature of the language, and an acquaintance with linguistic principles.[14]

That the profession is aware of linguistics as an essential part of the foreign language teacher's education is reflected in the policy statements issued by the professional organizations. As early as 1955 the Modern Language Association of America, in a statement on the *Qualifications of Secondary School Teachers of Modern Foreign Languages*, emphasized language analysis as one of seven qualifications which a teacher should possess. A "good" secondary school teacher, according to this statement, should have acquired "a basic knowledge of the historical development and present characteristics of the foreign language, and an awareness of the difference between the language as spoken and written." In order to be rated "superior" he would also be expected to possess "an ability to apply knowledge of descriptive, comparative, and historical linguistics to the language-teaching situation."[15] This statement was endorsed by sixteen national and regional organizations, including the American Council of Learned Societies and the American Association of Teachers of German.

In 1966, the MLA's *Guidelines for Teacher Education Programs in Modern Foreign Languages* stressed once again that institutions preparing teachers of

---

[11] As is well known, none other than Noam Chomsky, in his address to the Northeast Conference in 1966 (N. Chomsky, "Linguistic Theory," *Language Teaching: Broader Contexts* [=Northeast Conference. Reports of the Working Committees, 1966, pp. 43–49]) disputed the significance of linguistics for the foreign language teacher. What he says though (after confessing that he was speaking "not as an expert on any aspect of the teaching of languages") is only with regard to a "*technology*" of language teaching" (p. 43). There have been attempts to prove the master wrong, e.g. K.C. Diller, *Generative Grammar, Structural Linguistics and Language Teaching* (Rowley, Mass., 1971), but scholars in generative linguistics are still divided on the issue.

[12] F.W. Twaddell, in *The Teaching of German. Problems and Methods*, ed. E. Reichmann (Philadelphia, 1970), p. 61.

[13] N. Brooks, in *The Teaching of German*, p. 453.

[14] M.S. Kirch, "FLES. Introduction," *The Teaching of German*, p. 357.

[15] *The Teaching of German*, pp. 454–55.

modern foreign languages in American schools should offer instruction in "language analysis, including a study of the phonology, morphology, and syntax of the modern foreign language and comparison of these elements with those of American English."[16]

While these statements are directed at foreign language departments in general, departments of German in particular have good reason to heed them. For, as has been stated before, it is in the early stages of language instruction that the German department has most to lose or gain.

It is a well-known fact that of the foreign languages which commonly compete for the favor of students, German has the reputation of being both tough and dull. It is hard to change this image, but if we are worth our salt we had better start trying. Unfortunately, German grammar is pretty much as difficult as it was fifty or a hundred years ago. But we aggravate the difficulties by sending inexperienced or poorly trained teachers into the battle. Should we be surprised that we start losing students in the first semester?

Among the foreign languages commonly taught in our schools and universities the early predicament of difficult grammar applies particularly to German. We consequently have to tackle the problem in a manner which the other foreign languages may forego. If we do not want to lose our students before they ever reach the ability to handle the language with some ease or read an average text, we will have to train our teachers so that they can judiciously guide the students' first steps into the foreign language. It should even be possible to make those steps an interesting experience. A thorough education in linguistics and its application to the teaching of German will go a long way towards the achievement of this goal.

In accordance with the experts quoted, but contrary to a widespread misconception, the linguist will insist that the foreign language teacher on the elementary and high school level ought to be just as well prepared for his job as the teacher at the college level. Part of the failure of the FLES program may very well be due to the shameful neglect of FLES teacher training, including training in linguistics.

With such an overwhelming case for linguistics as part of teacher training, why is remedial action to include it not taken immediately? Part of the answer, of course, is money. The other part seems to be the natural inclination in some quarters to cling to traditional structures, not to say sinecures. There is no immediate solution. But in the long run, as André Paquette put it, "the profession must (. . .) assume some responsibility for persuading *its own members* to offer an educational opportunity which will produce effective members of the profession."[17]

[16] "Guidelines for Teacher Education Programs [. . .]," (note 9), p. A3.
[17] F.A. Paquette, "Developing Guidelines for Teacher Education Programs in Modern Foreign Languages," *PMLA* 81:2 (1966), 3 (italics mine).

4

On the basis of the foregoing discussion it seems reasonable to suggest that courses in linguistics should be offered in every reputable department of German. For the future teacher, irrespective of his chosen area of concentration and irrespective of the level of school at which he intends to teach, a thorough education in linguistics, especially confrontative/contrastive and applied linguistics, ought to be a *conditio sine qua non*.

In closing, two questions need to be discussed briefly: How about the students' interest in linguistics? And: At what levels should linguistics be offered in the German department?

To answer the second question first: Courses in German linguistics should be offered by all departments on both the undergraduate and the graduate levels. Wherever their number warrants it, students should be offered the choice of a concentration in German linguistics. The Stanford Model, discussed elsewhere in this volume (pp. 78–87), in my opinion provides a convincing example of what a well-balanced program might look like.

Are students interested in a specialization in German linguistics? At Stanford, which is one of the few schools now offering a viable alternative program on the undergraduate level,[18] roughly 12 per cent of the German majors took this option in 1973/75.[19] On the graduate level, close to 25 per cent of the students at the University of Michigan are concentrating in German linguistics.[20] It would seem then that wherever a viable program in linguistics is offered, the number of students opting for it is substantial indeed.

---

[18] According to our survey (note 2), other schools allowing the undergraduate to concentrate in German linguistics are Brigham Young, Brown, Illinois-Urbana, SUNY-Buffalo.

[19] Information kindly supplied by W.F.W. Lohnes. The figures for German Cultural Studies and Literature are about 50 and 25 per cent, respectively.

[20] T.L. Markey, "Malice in Wonderland: The Linguist's Future in the German Department," Report prepared for presentation at the Annual Meeting of the Modern Language Association of America, San Francisco, Dec. 26–29, 1975 (Section German I: Germanic Philology), p. 3.

TRAINING GERMAN TEACHERS IN THE LATE SEVENTIES

ROBERT L. POLITZER
Stanford University

The purpose of this article is not to deal with specific and detailed suggestions concerning the training of German teachers. Such specific proposals—most of them applicable to the training of foreign language teachers in general—appear in the pedagogical journals and are summarized in the useful and informative yearly *Reviews of Foreign Language Education* compiled under the auspices of ACTFL. My intention is rather to look at a very general broad trend that affects the educational systems of the United States as well as of many other countries of the Western world and to offer some general conclusions as to how this trend influences foreign language teaching in general. Finally, I shall make some specific suggestions concerning German-American collaboration in the training of German teachers in response to trends present in the current educational climate.

Today, one of the most frequently asked questions concerning not only the foreign language course but many other parts of the school curriculum is *why*? We are taking for granted that this question is both legitimate and natural. Education must be "relevant." Nevertheless, the intensive questioning of the relevance of the educational experience is a relatively recent phenomenon. When I recall my own experiences in secondary school (a *Realgymnasium* in Austria in the thirties) or in college (U.S.A., 1939–42), I cannot remember that either I or my classmates were overly concerned with the relevance of what we were studying. Evidently, a dramatic shift in the attitude toward relevance has occurred during the past twenty or thirty years. Why?

Any experience can be relevant only in relation to another. Keeping in mind this relational nature of relevance, we can distinguish between two types of relevance for which I would like to suggest the labels "intrinsic" on the one hand and "*de facto*" or "extrinsic" on the other. There is probably a continuum leading from one type of relevance to the other—but the distinction between the the two types can be easily made in extreme cases. Thus learning to take out an appendix is an obviously intrinsically relevant experience in the education of a future surgeon, just as learning to adjust a carburator is intrinsically relevant in the preparation of an automobile mechanic. Extrinsic or *de facto* relevance exists if as the result of some societal rule or decision, an experience is made prerequisite for another. In many cases, it is brought about by a social convention which represents what classical sociologists called "a social fact": a societal rule or restraint tacitly accepted without questioning by members of a cultural group.

Except for the basic skills (reading, writing, simple computation, etc.) and obvious vocational or professional training experience (e.g., photography for future photographers, anatomy for future doctors, etc.) most of the subjects included in the school curriculum have varying and debatable kinds of predictable intrinsic relevance. Many subjects are relevant in the sense that they teach transferable skills. However, all subjects have high extrinsic relevance if they are part of a selection procedure. Assumptions of extrinsic relevance underlie statements like: "high school is the prerequisite for going to college," "college education is the prerequisite for professional education and a better paying job."

However, the extrinsic relevance of first high school and now also college education has been declining steadily during the past decade. One of the main reasons for this decline seems obvious: As larger percentages of the population attend high school, attendance of high school or even graduation become less useful as tools for distributing individuals on a socio-economic scale. As the number of students entering college increases, even colleges are becoming increasingly incapable of serving the same function. The obvious or *de facto* relevance of first high school and now college education is slowly eroding as the result of the increasing democratization of first high school and now college education. If the majority of the population graduates from college, graduation from college will no longer assure the graduate of entry to an upper socio-economic class. In a socially stratified society, the very democratization of education tends to erode the main basis of its extrinsic relevance.

Foreign language education in the United States is presently influenced by the rapid democratization of higher education and the resulting rapid erosion of extrinsic relevance. The problems created by the rapid disappearance of perceived extrinsic relevance are aggravated by other circumstances, e.g., declining population growth, reaching of saturation levels of enrollments in high school and college. All of these factors have resulted in a situation in which high school and college subjects "compete" against each other in a no longer expanding market, primarily in terms of demonstrating their intrinsic relevance to students who are becoming uncertain about extrinsic relevance of the educational experience as a whole. Many recent trends in foreign language education can be accounted for by this new "competitive" situation. The heavy emphasis on individualization of instruction which has characterized thinking foreign language education during the past three or four years is at least partly motivated by the necessity of competing for student enrollments (a fact which does not necessarily detract from the intrinsic value of individualization). The very strong trend toward linking foreign languages with vocational education[1] is an obvious attempt to demonstrate intrinsic relevance.

[1] For an example of the latter trend see K. A. Lester and T. Tamarkin "Career Education," *ACTFL Review of Foreign Language Education*, 5 (1974), 161–168 or L.I.

I do not see any reason why foreign language in general and German in particular should not do well in competition with other subjects. However, we must train teachers in such a way that they can respond realistically to the present concern with relevance. Above all, all foreign language teachers must clearly realize that the days in which we could rely on a perception of *de facto* or extrinsic relevance of (and thus, extrinsic motivation for) foreign language study are over.

New teachers must be trained specifically to be able to establish the relevance of their subjects. By this, I do not mean that relevance be necessarily defined only in an extremely narrow and utilitarian way. To mention a few aspects of the relevance of foreign language training:

1. Like the study of music or art appreciation, foreign language study can be relevant to an experience of enjoyment.
2. Foreign language study can be relevant to the acquisition of certain qualities (e.g., reduction of ethnocentricity, better understanding of other cultures) which are desirable and transferable to other experiences.
3. Foreign language study is obviously relevant to many experiences in which foreign language skills are required (e.g., enjoyment of foreign travel, or vocations like interpreter, bilingual secretary, salesman, or representative of U.S. firms abroad, etc.).

But whatever claim of intrinsic relevance we may make, we will have to train teachers who can make good on those claims: If we advocate foreign language study for enjoyment, we better train teachers who can make language study enjoyable. If we claim that foreign language study creates better understanding of other cultural groups, we must train teachers who can demonstrate an increase in intercultural understanding. And if we stress the utilitarian value of language study, we must produce teachers who are not only acquainted with the best methodology but who are themselves highly proficient in the foreign language.

There is, of course, no doubt that the most modern trends and concerns of foreign language education, e.g., individualization, affective education, etc., should be reflected in the training of the German teacher in the late seventies and that all the lessons learned from the NDEA experience of the late fifties and early sixties should be utilized. At the same time, however, I should like to suggest that some needed improvements may not necessarily involve new and radical ideas, but rather the wide and general application of principles that have been asserted for some time—among other occasions also in connection with the NDEA training or retraining of teachers. The NDEA institutes followed generally a pattern of courses dealing with (1) increasing the language proficiency of teachers, (2) improving knowledge of applied linguistics, (3) furnishing cultural

Honig and R.I. Brod, "Foreign Languages and Careers," *The Modern Language Journal,* 58 (1974), 157–185. See also Barbara Elling's article in this volume, pp. 233–246.

insights, (4) acquainting teachers with the most recent methodology. In some instances, the retraining institutes were conducted in the foreign country, because there was agreement that effective teacher training implied some kind of direct linguistic and cultural contact with the country of the teachers' "target language."

The NDEA institutes are past history—and so are perhaps some of the teaching methodologies advocated in them. But the overall structure of teacher training applied in the organization of the institutes, the emphasis on language skills, methodological proficiency, cultural knowledge, and direct contact with the German speaking countries are *not* past history. To what extent are these elements of teacher training reflected in the education of German teachers today? What is the relative amount of time allotted to these aspects of teacher training? Is this kind of training carried out as an integral part of the education of the German teacher within the departments of German or by the department of German in collaboration with Schools of Education? Or do many German departments still feel or act as if teacher training were not part of their concern and should be left to Schools of Education as a sort of icing to be put on the cake prepared according to old but perhaps no longer appropriate recipes?

I have no precise statistics to offer in response to the questions asked above. But I cannot help but feel concerned if my colleague Frank Grittner (p. 205 of this volume) feels compelled to make the suggestion that "German departments could allocate more of their resources to teacher education" and to convince German professors that "education is an old and respected field."

I believe that the educational era characterized by intrinsic relevance and intrinsic motivation on the part of the student will require the training of highly skilled "language teaching professionals." The traditionally trained German major who has received some additional courses in pedagogy, educational psychology, and student teaching, is not necessarily such a highly skilled professional. Training such professionals might be brought about by a very close and continuous collaboration of German departments with educational methodologists, psycholinguists, cultural anthropologists, or it may necessitate a restructuring of the organization of language teaching and teacher training at the university and college level.

The last comment leads to a final and specific consideration: During the past decade, the intrinsic motivation for foreign language study has been increasing as the result of more intense international contacts. The very same trends have been present in many European countries including Germany. I have found among many of my colleagues a belief that intrinsically motivated foreign language study has been for a long time part of the Western European educational tradition. I doubt that this is true. Until relatively recently, foreign language study within the context of the major educational systems of Western Europe was based almost entirely on extrinsic or *de facto* relevance and motivation. If foreign language study in some major West European countries seems to be in a much more solid position than in the United States, the main reasons appear to be the following: (1) Democratization of secondary and especially higher education, and with it the erosion of *de facto* extrinsic relevance, have not advanced to the point reached in the United States. (2) Intrinsic relevance and motivation, above all the kind based on utilitarian consideration, is ahead of the levels reached in the United States because of various interrelated reasons like the rapid increase in tourist travel, influx of large numbers of foreign workers in the industrialized countries, the common market, the concept of Western European unity. In other words, in a trend accounting for decline in motivation for foreign language study, a country like West Germany lags behind the United States, in a trend associated with increased motivation for foreign language study, it is ahead.

One of the relatively rapid responses to the increase in intrinsic (utilitarian) motivation for foreign language in Western Europe has been the creation of the language centers.[2] Such centers (*Sprachzentren*) dealing with the teaching of foreign languages, the training of foreign language teachers, and in some instances, also with the teaching of German as a foreign language, are becoming an integral part of most major German universities.[3] Intensive cooperation and exchange of personnel with those language centers could be of considerable mutual benefit: Unlike departments of *Germanistik* in Germany, the language centers are concerned with foreign language teaching. If the foreign language is German, the experience gained by them is, of course, directly relevant to our teacher training (in a way paralleling the obvious importance of such organizations as the Goethe Institutes).

In most of the language centers, there is a heavy stress on the teaching of English as a foreign language. An exchange of teacher trainees between German Departments in the United States and language centers in Germany could provide most valuable practical experience for both parties involved. Such an exchange would be particularly valuable if the language centers could give their prospective English teachers some training in the teaching of German as a foreign language, while our German departments and/or Schools of Education could prepare our trainees for their experience in Germany by including some training in English as a second language in their program. Regular exchange programs of the type envisaged here may go a long way toward increasing the number of German teachers who have the requisite language skills, widened methodological

[2] For a more detailed description of the rationale for the language centers, see K. Kelz, "Zur Errichtung von Sprachzentren an den Hochschulen der Bundesrepublik Deutschland," *Die Unterrichtspraxis,* 5:2 (Fall 1972), 53–57.

[3] For a brief summary of the history of the language centers, see Eric W. Bauer, "The New German University Language Centers and their Programs in Foreign Language," in Reinhold Grimm, Peter Demetz, Eberhard Reichmann, Walter Sokel, eds., *Proceedings of the 42nd Annual Meeting, Bonn Germany June 24– July 2, 1974* (Philadelphia: AATG, 1975), pp. 116–118.

horizons, and last but not least, a direct personal knowledge of German culture.

Most importantly, as a response to a trend toward intrinsically relevant education, the language centers and their ultimate fate should be closely observed by the language teaching profession in the United States. The centers may not become immediately part of the dominant pattern of teacher education in Germany, just as the patterns suggested by the NDEA institutes did not become generally institutionalized in the Unites States. However, in the long run, a stable institutional response to a continued demand for more professionalized types of language teaching is almost certain to occur in Germany as well as here. The German *Sprachzentren* may not be the wave of the future, but they are most probably at least one of the sign posts pointing to it.

TOWARD A SOLUTION OF THE ARTICULATION PROBLEM BETWEEN HIGH SCHOOL AND COLLEGE

FRANK M. GRITTNER
Wisconsin Department of Public Instruction

Approximately a century ago the American public high school began to emerge as the major agency for providing secondary education to American young people. The problem of program articulation has been with us since that time and has intensified in direct proportion to the success of public schools in drawing ever larger numbers of students from all socio-economic levels. Part of the problem lies in the fact that a large number of people in higher education have from the very outset misconstrued the purpose of the public high school. It originally was not (and to a large extent still is not) primarily a college preparatory institution. There is a bit of misinformation, which even appears in print from time to time, to the effect that the high school started out as a college preparatory institution and that it has gradually deteriorated into an institution devoted to general education. In reality, the opposite happened. Until fairly recently the high school was predominantly a terminal institution. The economic value of a high school diploma until well after World War I was somewhat comparable to the bachelors degree today. Thus, almost no one who was in high school in the 1890's and early 1900's was there for the purpose of college preparation. Paradoxically, that was the era in which as many as 80% of the students in high school were enrolled in the study of foreign languages. In the pre-World War I era the main language was Latin, but in a good year as many as 25% of all students were enrolled in German. There were lesser numbers of French and almost no Spanish students in that period.[1]

Various reasons have been given to explain why languages were in those days a major subject area in the high school curriculum. One was that academicians rather than professional administrators controlled school policy. For example, Charles Eliot, then President of Harvard University, was highly active in the affairs of the National Education Association, which was influential in setting curricular standards. Local school administrators tended to be academic teachers first, administrators second. It was the judgment of such people that academic subjects like foreign languages, mathematics, history, and science were basic to

---

[1] Frank M. Grittner, *Teaching Foreign Languages* (New York: Haper and Row, 1969), p. 8.

the needs of all those young people who chose to attend high school. In reality, this was a select group consisting of students who had the desire, the ability, and the family financial support to complete twelve years of public education. In any case, the educators of the day felt that academic courses were the best possible preparation for coping with the complexities of the emerging industrial society.

Well before the turn of the century there were also articulation problems with that tiny minority of students who went on to college. Classicists, for example, would sometimes complain that the new crop of high school graduates had a watered-down background because "soft" subjects such as German, French or English had replaced Latin, Greek, and Hebrew. Unfortunately, the classicists were slow to perceive the fact that the American public high school was a different institution than the older academies and grammar schools. They were now dealing with an egalitarian institution in which elitist attitudes and elitist purposes could not long survive. Although there were some heroic individual attempts to stem the tide, by and large the classics have been unable to maintain their image as a subject worth learning by large numbers of students in secondary and higher education. In the early Sputnik era classicists were unable to maintain adequate programs for training teachers specifically for high school programs. This has resulted in a lack of replacements for those Latin teachers who have retired or have left the profession for other reasons. A similar fate could easily overtake German Studies should the colleges and universities of the nation fail to take seriously the task of preparing future teachers. I mention this here because the question of articulation has meaning only if higher education succeeds in supplying a large number of certifiable people who come into the schools equipped with linguistic capabilities and who, at the same time, have the professional and personal qualities to enable them to function within the secondary school as it actually exists and is likely to exist in the forseeable future. Thus, one kind of identifiable articulation problem relates to the responsibility of higher education to supply competent professional teachers who can function in the high schools.[2]

The other kind of articulation has received much more attention in recent years. I refer to the upward movement of students from the high school into the colleges and universities.[3] Recent changes in attitudes and in patterns of school attendance have intensified the articulation problem between secondary and higher education. The problem from the standpoint of the high school has to do with the shift in attitude over the past half century which has caused languages

[2] California Foreign Language Liaison Committee, *Foreign Language Articulation in California Schools and Colleges* (Sacramento: California State Department of Education, 1966), p. 7.

[3] Micheline Dufau, "From School to College; The Problem of Continuity," G. Reginald Bishop, ed., *Foreign Language Teaching: Challenges to the Profession* (Middlebury, VT: Northeast Conference), 1965.

to be viewed as "peripheral" rather than as "basic" subjects. In some cases language study is presented as nothing more than an entrance ticket to higher education. This has resulted in the unfortunate tendency of school people to answer the question "Why foreign languages?" with the response "You need it for college." The older attitude had been that anyone could profit from the study of German (or other languages) and that the few who were going on to college would also find it useful. In this regard, a very legitimate question has been raised, namely, "Should the high school program in any sense attempt to be sequential with the college program?" In some cases high school teachers have no choice whatever but to respond in the negative. That is, they must either forget about meeting college-prep standards or risk elimination from the curriculum. Such teachers can, perhaps, be forgiven if they choose to conform to new school-wide scheduling patterns and to local demand for such things as mini-courses, cultural units, and individualized programs in the interests of professional survival, and without regard for college curricula. In any case, college foreign language requirements have been severely eroded in recent years. In addition, the alleged socio-economic values of a college education itself have also been called into question, thus further weakening the argumentative force of the statement "You need it for college." People are now claiming that college itself is a waste of time.[4]

A further question which has been asked too infrequently and answered even less frequently is as follows: "Is there, in any event, a significant student population actually involved in program continuation between high school and college?" A study done over 30 years ago at Stanford University indicated that few of the students who went on to Stanford actually chose to continue with the language which they had begun in high school.[5] Klaus Mueller reported similar results in 1969.[6] If the facts from these studies still hold, it means that the articulation problem involves only about 10% of those students currently enrolled in languages at the high school level. That is, of all those students who have studied a foreign language in high school and who have then opted to go into higher education, approximately 90% do not continue with the language which they started in high school. A number of implications could be drawn from such facts. For example, since studies of German are terminal at the secondary level for the big majority of students, high school teachers could conclude that they should have no concern about articulation between high school and college. However, I believe this would be a mistake.

For high school teachers to accept a policy of negativism toward higher

[4] Caroline Bird, *The Case Against College* (New York: David McKay, 1975).

[5] Vera E. Wittmann and Walter V. Kaulfers, "Continuance in College of High-School Foreign Language," *The School Review,* 48 (1940), 606ff.

[6] Klaus Mueller, "Keynote Statement" in the panel discussion, "Articulation from the High School to College and the Problem of Placement," *Die Unterrichtspraxis,* 2:1 (Spring 1969), 74–76.

education in the area of articulation on the grounds mentioned above would be to fall victim to that brand of misplaced empiricism which says that, because a situation does exist, it therefore *ought to* exist. Empirical data can be used to *support* value judgments; however, such data cannot *substitute* for value judgments. Hence, decisions to seek articulated programs must be based not on measureable data but on a conviction that it is good practice to do so in terms of the discipline and the interest of the students whom the discipline serves. In this regard, there is evidence that achievement in foreign languages is directly related to the number of years of study.[7] To use the language of the psycho-linguistic investigator, it might be said that language acquisition is "a function of time." In everyday parlance this means that people who study a given language for a long period of time will learn that language better on the average than those whose contact with the language is brief. In my opinion it is essential that the profession make a value judgment in this regard which would state: "It is good for students to begin the study of German in the junior or senior high school and, for those who go into higher education, to continue to study it for as long as their abilities, talents and desires permit." Once we accept the fact that German is worth studying as a means of individual humanistic development—and the longer the better—then the articulation problem becomes definable in terms of one question: "How can the German Studies program be modified to encourage an increasing number of students to remain in sustained contact with the study of German?"

Nature of the Articulation Problem

As a former chairman of a national AATG committee on articulation, I have seen the problem from many sides. As I mentioned above, on the one extreme there are the high school people who say, in effect, "Forget the colleges. If we are to survive, we have to do what will draw students not what the colleges have decided that students ought to learn." At the other extreme we have people in higher education who, in effect, are saying, "We are the scholars. We know what is best. This is what students entering our institutions ought to know." The communications gap here stems from the fact that the college professor tends to look at German in terms of career specialization while the high school teacher tends to look at it from the pedagogical standpoint. The high school teacher is under economic pressure to maintain class size at a level which his school board considers to be fiscally sound. This means that to survive he has to present the language at a level of sophistication which his students understand. The college teacher, on the other hand, is under pressures (either overt or covert or both) to

[7] John B. Carroll, "Foreign Language Proficiency Levels Attained by Language Majors Near Graduation from College," *Foreign Language Annals,* 1 (1967), 131–151.

select out students who can perform respectably at the graduate level. The graduate school is oriented toward specialization in literature or linguistics while the high school is part of the tradition of popular humanistic education. The key to the articulation problem lies in reconciling the differences between these two traditions. With the possible exception of a few affluent suburban schools, teachers in the American high school cannot use as a basis for articulation the literature-based achievement standards such as those which have sometimes been advocated for advanced placement. The high school teacher is confronted with too vast a range of differences in such areas as student maturity, cultural sophistication, socio-economic background, and motivational drive for this to be practicable. The best the high school teacher can do is to attempt to meet students where they are and to move them, insofar as possible, toward a reasonable level of progress in the mastery of the discipline. It is for this reason that attempts at individualization keep recurring in American education.[8] High school teachers often dream of a system which will allow each student to move at his or her own best pace, using one's own best learning style through material which the individual finds aesthetically satisfying and pedagogically motivating. However, the individualization movement has remained an idealistic fantasy which is well beyond the resources of the typical school program. Therefore the problem remains how German can continue to function as a popular elective within the general education segment of the high school program while still maintaining its integrity as a discipline. Failure to resolve this problem is likely to result in low enrollments at all levels and, eventually, in total exclusion from high school curricula. And, as Sol Gittleman has noted elsewhere in this volume (pp. 207–210), the loss of high school programs ultimately has a direct negative effect on the college program. Thus, the colleges have a two-fold interest in the high school program: (1) The survival of German in higher education is ultimately connected with the success of the high school program; and (2) college programs have much to gain by further developing the skills of the best students from the high school German programs when those students opt for higher education.

Modes of Articulation

As has been noted above, the extremes in approaching the articulation problem have certain disadvantages. That is, the high school curriculum cannot become merely a miniaturized university program nor, on the other hand, can it afford to ignore the college German departments. In the 1960's there was some talk of a middle ground approach in which the AATG would establish a model

---

[8] Frank Grittner, "Individualized Instruction: An Historical Perspective," *Modern Language Journal,* 59 (1975), 323–333.

curriculum for national adoption.[9] It soon became apparent, however, that the national curriculum approach was not feasible. There were simply too many differences between states and within states to enable the profession to achieve any reasonable expectation of success.

A more manageable alternative involves a system of rewards to the individual rather than a mandated curriculum aimed at thousands of institutions. As a matter of fact, such a system appears to be working well in many of Wisconsin's colleges at the present time. I refer to the practice of awarding transcript credits for successful performance in intermediate and advanced courses for students who had engaged in many years of study at the high school level prior to entering college. We have instances of students being awarded as many as 16 additional semester hours after the successful completion of one fifth-semester university course (see pp. 70–71). This approach does not tell the high school teacher how to teach or what to teach. Instead, it is based upon the practice of making the high school student aware of the fact that it is to his or her advantage to be able to perform successfully in the advanced courses offered in college. The process of implementing this kind of articulation is simple, functional and inexpensive. Working through the appropriate persons and agencies (such as the State Foreign Language Consultant, the State Association of Foreign Language Teachers and state guidance organizations) the colleges within a given state can make the policy known to high school German teachers and school counselors. Knowing they can earn up to a semester's credit on the basis of their high school performance, students are inclined to go on in the language which they began in high school rather than to abandon it for another language. Further, since so many credits are potentially riding on their achievement, students are motivated to work hard in their college German courses. A further advantage of this system is its flexibility. If the student finds himself misplaced in college he can simply drop down (for example) from an advanced to an intermediate course, until he finds a level at which he can achieve success. The "retroactive" credit can still be awarded for the courses which he has bypassed.

Articulation College to High School

A spin-off value of the policy mentioned above is the good public relations which can be engendered in the high schools. Many parents in the local communities are elated to find that their college-age students have been able to complete a portion of their college work based upon previous achievement in high school. A number of Wisconsin's German departments have initiated the practice of writing a congratulatory letter to the local school superintendent and to the student's parents informing them of good student performance and of

[9] Klaus Mueller, p. 75.

the advanced placement for credit. This is a highly recommended procedure in that it strengthens the position of the local German teacher, contributes to a better public image for German Studies, and helps improve the image of higher education by the very act of showing an interest in the individual student and in the everyday affairs of education. And, in view of the present fiscal crunch, humanities programs at both the high school and college levels can well use any public support which is available.

Ultimately, the success of an articulation plan lies in the professional capabilities of the teachers involved. If the colleges fail to prepare a sufficient number of competent teachers to meet the demands of the junior and senior high schools, then it is axiomatic that a certain number of students coming from the secondary programs will be unable, for sheer lack of language skill, to articulate with the programs in higher education. I have heard complaints from university people from time to time about the quality of German teaching in the public schools. I cannot attest to the truth or falsity of their claims which are often merely an expression of personal bias or philosophical disagreement. However, to the extent that charges of poor teaching are true, where does the fault lie? Is it not the people in higher education who trained the high school teachers and who recommended them for certification? If any significant number of German teachers are not functioning properly in the local school situation is this not at least partly due to the lack of realistic articulation with the local schools on the part of college and university German departments? Or, to put the question another way, if German departments do not have a responsibility for maintaining and improving the quality of German instruction at all levels, then who does? My own bias is that there is still room for improvement here. For example, German departments could allocate more of their resources to teacher education and could modify their promotion and tenure procedures to give more status and support to the people who are involved in foreign language education. Education is an old and respected field which over the years has received the attention of scholars such as Plato, Rousseau, Kant, Dewey, Conant, and many others. Thus, it would seem that the pedagogical aspects of language learning could well receive a somewhat more prominent place in the departmental sun than has been allotted in the past without compromising the academic respectability of the department.[10]

There have been signs of increased willingness on the part of language professors to relate more directly to their colleagues in secondary education. For example, at our last two foreign language conferences in Wisconsin up to 20% of the participants were from colleges and universities of the state. By contrast, several years ago it often occurred that the only college people present were

[10] Frank M. Grittner, ed., "Course Content, Articulation and Materials: A Committee Report to the National Symposium on the Advancement of German Teaching," *Die Unterrichtspraxis,* 2:1 (Spring 1969), 53–72.

those who were invited to speak. Despite such signs of improved articulation, much remains to be done, particularly in the area of teacher education. More specifically, German departments must insist upon high standards of performance for any student who wishes to be certified as a teacher. In the overcrowded labor market of today there is no longer any excuse for recommending for certification anyone whose credentials are at all doubtful. However, even this is not enough. For in addition to using their influence to be more selective, German departments could also establish closer liaison with schools of education in their respective institutions for the purpose of improving the quality of the teacher training process itself. In this regard, the recommendations of James Conant and others might well be used as exploratory models.[11]

[11] James Bryant Conant, *The Education of American Teachers* (New York: McGraw-Hill Book Company, 1964), pp. 140–144; 233–238. Also worthy of note is the article by W.F. Twaddell, "Departmental Responsibilities for Foreign Language Teacher Education," *ADFL Bulletin*, 7:1 (September 1975), 21–25.

FROM JUNIOR HIGH SCHOOL TO GRADUATE PROGRAM: THE CRISIS OF COORDINATION

SOL GITTLEMAN
Tufts University

At a recent meeting of the Massachusetts Foreign Language Association, the normal, almost routine configuration of attendance was evident: ninety-five percent of the participants were junior high school and high school teachers, three percent were book salesmen and publishers' representatives, and the remaining trace came from colleges and universities. The hallway discussions in hushed tones centered on recent developments resulting from school committee meetings which were taking place all over the state: full-time positions in Latin were being cut back to half-time; half-time programs in German were being phased out as public school administrators searched through their curricula for "soft spots." Inevitably, it seemed that a foreign language program was designated as "soft." Priorities gave preference to an ice machine for the hockey team and new hats for the golf club over a half-time program in German at one high school! At the end of the day's discussions, one dedicated and still energetic German teacher approached me and, shaking her head, said with an edge of sadness and conviction, "You know, if we go under, you go under, too." At that moment, John Donne's metaphysics became clearer to me than ever before. In the business of *Germanistik* or German Studies, surely no man is an island.

Unless the profession as a whole comes to a full understanding of this fact, we are indeed destined to share the fate of the dodo bird. Right now, the signs are clear, this shared fate is obvious to anyone with the courage to study the facts. While school committees are attacking our pre-college programs as "irrelevant" and dispensable, graduate programs in German are facing a similar attack. Deans, provosts, trustees, regents, study committees of universities and colleges all over the country are taking a hard look at the graduate programs in our institutions of higher learning and are hacking away at the Ph.D. in German. Currently in the Boston metropolitan area, "the Athens of America" with its forty-six colleges and universities, there survives merely one doctorate program in German, at Harvard.

Meanwhile, as the attendance at the Massachusetts meeting suggests, we continue along in our splendid isolation, indifferent to the fact that every time a junior high school program is terminated, a nail is driven into the coffin of a graduate program in German. Of course, no one will disagree that we have overproduced in the area of graduate programs in German; we have too many mediocre ones which grew during the halcyon days of expansionist euphoria. There is room for a general house-cleaning, and the resulting attrition is desirable and will only make the remaining programs stronger. But it is essential that the profession itself oversee the cutbacks and orchestrate the reorganization, with some order and with an eye to the future form and content of our graduate programs for the next generation.

At no other time in the history of our discipline in this country has there been a greater need for the definition of *Germanistik* in its American context. Right now we are overcome by a sense of isolation. The "school teachers" talk to themselves and ask for help; the *"Germanisten"* dedicate themselves to the higher forms of scholarship; and we are in danger of falling on our faces because we do not come to each other's assistance. From junior high to graduate school, there is a need for cohesiveness, coordination, and the total mobilization of every teacher of German in the country. The key is organization on the specific local level, and the colleges and universities must provide the resources. We must be prepared to enter into the massive public relations/education program that calls for the participation of people who until now have in no way involved themselves. We must develop a sense of the collective continuity of the teaching of German in this country.

When was the last time that any German department at the college or university level was represented at an AATG or FLA meeting by more than a token member or two? How many faculty members have ever attended a school committee meeting at which foreign language programs were threatened? Indeed, how many university teachers ever hear about such meetings? These are all rhetorical questions, alas. But, one might ask: how would a suburban school committee in the Greater Boston area have reacted, if instead of none, twenty university and college faculty had appeared at the meeting when the German program was cancelled?

What is required is the time and energy of a university based faculty person, with the authority to organize his own department and the authorization to work in conjunction with opposite numbers at neighbor institutions to coordinate efforts for the promotion of German and German Studies. What this means is that there will be maximum use made of all the human resources in a given geographical area, for the purpose of bringing to bear all possible influence for the fostering and advocacy of "the business of German." Ideally, each institution of higher learning would have such a person designated as Coordinator of Programs. For my own part, I would suggest that this be a position off the traditional tenure ladder, for a person with a part-time teaching load, and with a primary administrative responsibility. My reasons stem from extended experience with university tenure and promotion committees, which are becoming increasingly rigid in their requirements and standards. The Coordinator's activities will, most likely, not result in the type of scholarship which tenure and promotion committees would recognize as "advancing the frontiers of knowledge." On the other hand, if senior faculty already tenured would be willing to rotate this position through the department, it would have, most likely, an even more salutary effect.

The job is enormous. First of all, the Coordinator would serve as an official resource person and lobbyist with all the local pre-college institutions, school committees, guidance counsellors, and principals. In this capacity, the Coordinator would have the authority to muster the collective resources of the total departmental roster, and in the event that there could be a common agreement on using one Coordinator in a consortium arrangement for any number of colleges or universities, this person could conceivably draw on the resources of *all* the departments in a region. For example, in the case of the suburban Boston school which lost its German program, if the isolated teacher in the high school could have contacted a resource person at the university or college so identified, and if this person could have orchestrated the proper response from the professional German community, including the Goethe Institute, I have no doubt that the program could have been saved. Furthermore, in conjunction with the high school programs, the Coordinator would provide linkage with the pre-college student as he/she prepares for the college experience, in order to maximize the articulation of the high school-to-college transition. In this capacity, the Coordinator is both a language teacher and proselytizer. As a language coordinator, he provides the high school and junior high school German teachers with an idea of the materials and texts used at the post-high school level. This provides for a more sensible integration of the high school-to-college language program. As a proselytizer, the Coordinator would move into the junior high and high schools with an arsenal of workshops, seminars, films, symposia on methodology and common problems which would define for the teachers as well as the prospective students the potential of German as a subject for study. In return, we would hopefully find our college campuses being visited by increasing numbers of pre-freshmen who are interested in sitting in on a college-level German class or participating in a meeting of a college German Club.

There is great advantage if our Coordinator could teach one course at the college level, ideally, the advanced-intermediate language and composition course at the third year. This would provide him with the opportunity to see the development of a student from the high school right through the year when we might send him/her off to a Junior Year Abroad.

What I am suggesting, then, is a final effort at regional or local coordination and allocation of resources, focusing on the particular problem of relations of the pre-college institutions with the college and university. This liaison is essential for the survival of the teaching of German in the United States. Some may say that our situation is not clearly so dramatic, but unless a machinery is established which can draw the various components of the profession together, unless we come to understand that the teacher of graduate students, in his most prized isolation, is just as threatened with extinction as the desperate half-timer in junior high school, we may all fall victim to this crisis of economic exigency. Perhaps a college-level Coordinator, with the proper focus on the high, mighty, as well as nitty, gritty aspects of our profession, can bring some integration into our diverse interests. We are all in this together.

THE FOREIGN STUDY ELEMENT IN GERMAN STUDIES

JOE FUGATE
Kalamazoo College

DIETHER HAENICKE
Wayne State University

KENNETH J. NORTHCOTT
University of Chicago

This paper addresses itself to some of the major issues which confront a student or foreign study advisor in trying to integrate a period of study abroad into a college curriculum whether of a language major or of a student whose primary interest is not in language or literature. Fundamentally, of course, we should all like to see a period of study abroad as a *sine qua non* for all language majors, but we are at the same time aware of the difficulties, and in part at least it is these difficulties with which this paper will deal.

A number of questions immediately present themselves when we think of the problems facing student and foreign study faculty alike. What should the student study? How long should he stay abroad? What sort of academic credit should he receive and for what? How can he finance his stay abroad? These are but some of the questions which arise and there is clearly no simple or immediate answer to any of them for they will, by their nature, vary from person to person and from institution to institution: nevertheless they still have to be faced.

For the student majoring in German (and we shall in this paper be talking of study in Germany, though most of what we say is, *mutatis mutandis,* applicable to other modern languages commonly taught in colleges) there are two major linked aspects to his[1] stay in Germany.

The one is the obvious one that he is there to perfect his language skills. We emphasize "perfection" and not "acquisition" for there has to be on the one hand a maximization of the advantage of the sojourn in Germany (and this can only be achieved on the basis of the prior knowledge of the language) and, on the other hand, if the student is enrolled in a University-affiliated program he

---

[1] We are sufficiently old-fashioned, or sexist, to regard the pronoun "he" in its various inflections as being a common gender.

will have to have had at least two years of college German, or the equivalent, with no less than a "B" average in order to take University courses—this is a standard requirement imposed by the universities. The nature of the language instruction for the would-be foreign study student will vary, but we feel very strongly that it should include a considerable element of conversational German. Much of the "literary" German taught in second-year college courses, though admirable in itself, will not always prepare the student for dealing with recalcitrant taxi-drivers or over-bureaucratized *Beamte.* A proficiency in the spoken language can also help to mitigate "culture-shock."

The second aspect which is closely related to what has just been said is that he is there to become familiar with that cultural environment of which the language he is learning is the verbal expression. He wants to become familiar with that environment and to integrate himself as quickly and as deeply as possible into the everyday life of the country. This is a difficult process and indeed often more difficult than we are prone to think, but not for what might seem the obvious reason. It is not that "culture-shock" in the cliché sense of that overused term is so great or so traumatic, but rather that the differences in Western cultures are today of a much more subtle nature, but lack of extent of differences should not blind us to the fact that they remain quantitatively great and are potential pitfalls for the unwary. It is indeed often harder to sense and appreciate the smaller nuances of behavioral and cultural differences than it is to come to terms with much more dramatic and obvious ones. It may be an exaggeration to suggest that the primary function of study abroad, the perfection of language skills, may be seriously or even completely thwarted if the student by some egregious, though seemingly minor form of social solecism excludes himself from the company of his peers or their families. There is then a reciprocal relationship between our two objectives, and the second is not necessarily subservient to the first if regarded in terms of true communication. There is much that can be done both in the United States and in Germany to help the student, particularly in the initial stages of his stay. Of course, if his stay is only to be a short one, then more detailed preparation becomes imperative. Before departing for Germany, the student should be made repeatedly aware that, though Western culture is of apparent uniformity, this seeming homogeneity cloaks many discrete cultures and the customs which are as different as the languages and the dialects which make up those languages.

The student, if he is enrolled in an integrated program, should be encouraged to take as many courses as possible at the German university, preferably with some sort of tutorial supervision in addition to his experience in the lecture hall. Some German professors, eminent scholars though they be, are notoriously poor teachers. Whenever possible the student should also try to undertake serious independent study in an area with which he is familiar from this country. This might perhaps take the form of a comparative study of an aspect of American and German life—trade unions, newspapers, media of all sorts etc., etc.

An American student usually has enough expertise in one or another aspect of daily life in this country to be able to profit from a project of this sort.

It is hard to determine the ideal length of time for the student to spend abroad, beyond saying "as long as possible," but even this is not a real answer, for the production of expatriates is clearly *counter*-productive to our true interests. For the student who is going to participate in an integrated program the term of stay has, effectively, to be a whole year and we are agreed that, generally speaking, the junior year is the best time for this, though in some disciplines a case for the sophomore year can be argued. However, because of the German universities' stipulation that a student studying at a German university must have "junior" status, sophomore study would have to take place in a non-affiliated program. If the student is spending less than a year and going to a non-integrated program, he must exercise the greatest care in the selection of his program. The program must be efficiently organized both academically and practically. A student with only six months to spend in Germany should not have to waste hours finding accommodations or dealing with similar non-productive frustrations.

If a German major is unable to spend a full year in Germany, then at least one semester would seem to be an absolute minimum for a real advantage. Shorter periods may turn out merely to be a waste of money. Foreign study advisors can be of tremendous help in advising the student that for the expenditure of perhaps very little extra money he can have a longer and much more fruitful stay. It could be added at this point that though we have talked much about integrated programs this does not mean that there are not several excellent non-integrated programs. The problem is the garnering of accurate data about them and indeed about any program, affiliated or non-affiliated. In every case the student should start off by seeking, with the aid of a qualified advisor, a well-run, well-structured, reputable program of the highest integrity. There are many, too many, catchpenny commercial operations anxious to lure the last cent from the unwary student and the uninformed faculty member. Indeed, one of the serious problems which study-abroad programs face is precisely this confidence trickery which blights so large an area of the enterprise.

Accreditation of foreign study programs is long overdue and though a start is being made in this direction, financial considerations will militate against anything substantial in this area. It remains the task of the advisor to gain intelligence of operations abroad in any legal way possible if he is to be successful in steering his students away from exploitation. The time has probably arrived when serious consideration should be given to the establishment of a national committee, consisting of faculty from a wide range of disciplines and institutions, to try to exercise some form of supervision over activities in the field of foreign study. Such a committee could provide at least a critical check-list of programs.

For the non-major, of whom more later, a one month stay (as part of, say, a

4-1-4 program) may whet his appetite for more: this is to be hoped for, but at the least it should awaken in him an awareness of the problems of communication in a foreign language. An excellent program of this sort has been developed at the University of Nebraska/Lincoln, through which students are taken to Munich and thrust into contact with everyday life in Germany. At least twenty percent of the participants have returned to Europe within a year of their initial exposure.

However long the length of the stay, the problem of the integration of the American student into German society remains a cardinal one and requires particular attention on the part of those who are running the program. Students simply have to be exposed to people and places if their language skills are to be developed. This point brings up another and difficult question, namely that of program-directorship. The choice of the director of a foreign study program is a delicate one whether that director be an American or a local German one. The directorship of a foreign study program should neither be a reward for long and faithful service, nor should it be a sort of Ovidian exile for those who have proved themselves a nuisance or ineffective (or to continue the analogy further, even been over-amorous!) on a home campus. The appointment of either sort of person has potentially very harmful effects upon the students in the program: the former will not wish to spend his time in the *minutiae* of administration but will seek his reward in leisure and travel, the latter will be unlikely to change his spots merely because he has been removed five thousand or more miles from the scene of past triumphant failures.

The director must first and foremost be familiar with both the local and the American academic scene. If a German, he must be able to comprehend an American transcript and understand the vagaries and whims of registrars. He must also be, for integrated programs, of such academic stature as to be acceptable to his local colleagues, who on occasion may appear patronizing on this point. Colleges and universities on this side of the Atlantic should not expect that any faculty member they choose to send to Germany will automatically be granted *Gastprofessor* status—much ill-feeling has been caused in at least one German university of our acquaintance through this very point. The American director must be equally assured of his knowledge of the German university system (and the language!) before advising students on courses, pro-seminars etc., etc.

However the ultimate selection is made, and whether the director of the program is a member of the German department or not (and by no means a majority are), the German department still has a vested interest in seeing that the best available person is chosen—the German department is after all the focus of things Germanic on its campus. Ideally the person chosen should be given the chance of spending more than one year as a program-director, but this is rarely possible or politic if the director is American. If there is a constant change in directors a situation may arise in which the power of the local secretary or administrative assistant becomes abnormally great and he or she in fact eventually turns out, effectively, to be running the program. A good program needs an enthusiastic teacher-administrator who is willing to spend a considerable amount of time with his students, much more than he would under similar circumstances do on the home campus. Moreover the American director must show sympathy towards German culture, "an obvious requirement," one may think, but too often the American abroad will merely use the opportunity of his sojourn abroad to exercise his wit and sarcasm on the differences between the cultures of the two countries.

The American director must be able to turn to his home campus for full support and there must at the same time be a realization on the part of the home campus that this is not some sort of vacation trip which a faculty-member is taking, but that it will probably represent one of the most hard-working and responsible years of his career, if he has been chosen wisely.

Departments should also recognize that successful programs will redound to their credit, will attract majors and also interest other disciplines in the study of German. Many small colleges find that enrollment is substantially increased if there are foreign study opportunities built into the curriculum, so that everyone involved in foreign study has a personal stake in seeing that the resources and support of the institution are firmly committed to the venture, and that it is not just regarded as a personal eccentricity on the part of the person concerned.

We now come to the vexing question of academic credit. Our tendency is towards a degree of leniency as long as the student is actually working and using his time, as much of it as humanly possible, in learning German and perfecting his language skills, in other words, as long as he is trying to communicate with Germans in German. We say "with Germans" because useful as the idea of having students talk German among themselves may seem to be and may be, it is simply not the same thing as having them talk with Germans, and we should not delude ourselves into thinking that it is. The point can be made that the sheer concentration required even by quite a competent speaker to carry on the business of daily living in a foreign language is a true and arduous learning experience and should be rewarded. Students should not, on the other hand, get credit haphazardly for trips down the Rhine or similar ventures, for apart from the inherent lack of ethics in granting credit for such activities, it will also inevitably rouse the suspicion of registrars and other faculty, and this suspicion will then spread to and contaminate genuine academic ventures. Foreign study advisors must watch this most carefully.

The important thing is that the student should reach an agreement, if at all possible, with his advisors *before* leaving for study abroad as to what is or is not to be credited to him when he returns, and most colleges expect about thirty credit hours. Of course, this cannot always be carried out to the last crossing of the "t" or dotting the "i," because courses will change or be dropped or new ones will be offered which are more germane to the overall academic interests of the student, but there should be a broad basis of agreement between student and advisor, so that when the student returns he will not be disappointed or find that he is being held for another semester of study because the advisor downplays some of the courses which he has taken abroad. In this connection attention might be drawn to the joint program developed by the University of Connecticut and the Goethe Institut, where credit arrangements are formalized in an agreement between the two institutions. This sort of protection is invaluable for students and has the added flexibility that students at all levels can take the course, which lasts for seven weeks and gives them an intensive language training. The effects of their sojourn in Germany have been similar to those observed in the case of the University of Nebraska students.

The cost of foreign study is, regrettably, in many cases a bar to participation, especially for a student at a State University or one who is living at home and commuting; the additional two or three thousand dollars are simply not to be found overnight. For this reason it is important, if not in many cases essential, that the idea of spending a period abroad be introduced to a student as early as possible in his academic career, so that he can begin to make provision for the funds he will need for the realization of the project. Closely connected with this—in order to encourage students to make the maximum effort whether by saving or by additional part-time work—is a program which will maintain interest in study abroad. This interest can be stimulated in a number of ways. Perhaps the first and most important resource are students who have studied abroad, who have returned pleased and enriched by the experience, and who have been able to relate academic success on the home campus directly to the learning and experience of their stay in Germany; informal gatherings and discussions with them and with visiting German students can be of great help in orientation as well. Films, visits by German scholars and artists, all play their part, but the important thing is to maintain a dynamic and constant interest in German so that the appetite and curiosity of the student will be whetted.

So far we have been talking in the main about students who are German *majors* and who can be expected to see readily the benefits that can be derived from study in Germany. But we are also interested in maintaining and increasing the study of German in high schools and colleges. What can we do then to attract *others* into the study of German and what role can foreign study play in this process? We believe that the attraction of study abroad can serve as a drawing card for students in other disciplines. Here again it is important to emphasize early in the student's career the possibility of study abroad and its relationship to the student's particular field of study. This should be done not simply out of financial considerations this time, but also because the student will have to integrate his time abroad into a totally different set of academic requirements and conditions. What can the professor of German say in defense of the need to learn his language and learn about the culture of another country? Briefly, we believe that there is a growing realization that in an age of seeming homogeneity, the sense and knowledge of heterogenity is gradually assuming a greater importance. People are seeking more and more to differentiate the roots of their existence in modern society. One methodological path towards differentiation is the learning of a foreign language and making the effort to communicate with another person in his language and realizing the problems which are inherent in this whole question of human communication. We believe that it is not an exaggeration to say that anyone who is unwilling to learn another language is fundamentally uninterested in communicating with any other people.

There are practical considerations which can also be advanced, for many students will not be swayed by arguments such as the one just made—there is an increasing concern with practicality to be discerned in many students. Moreover, if a student's high-school experience with foreign languages has been an unfortunate one and he has been "turned off" long before he comes to college, it will take more than fine talk to overcome his prejudices. The potential businessman, the lawyer, the civil servant (who knows how much closer relations with the EEC will become in the next decade?) the scholar in history, anthropology, political science, archaelogy, the list goes on and on, must be brought to see that the acquisition of German is not frosting on a cake but an essential part of his education for the practicalities of his chosen profession.

It is of course likely to be true that the non-major will not have the time to achieve the language skill sufficient for him to be able to pass the *Zulassungsprüfung* and permit him to study at an integrated program of a German university, and in many areas, for instance medicine or the physical sciences, the *numerus clausus* would preclude an American student's being admitted to the university; nevertheless alternatives can be found.[2] Kalamazoo College has an arrangement for natural science majors to study at the *Kernforschungsanlage* in Jülich; a joint concentration in German and Chemistry has been organized by Brown University in conjunction with a large German concern, and we are sure that there are other such possibilities; *Pädagogische Hochschulen,* for example, are an almost untapped and excellent resource. American educators should not be misled by the often derisive attitude of German university colleagues to the *PH*. The University of Wisconsin's practice of having courses outside the German department taught in German (see p. 73) seems an excellent introduction to the idea of foreign study. It is to be most highly recommended that there should always be a minimal requirement of language skill before leaving.

Incidentally, we should not overlook the value of having students on campus who have studied abroad and who can bring cultural breadth to a campus which may be quite isolated intellectually or geographically or both. It is

---

[2] It was pointed out in discussion at the German Studies Conference at the University of Wisconsin—Madison that a letter from a colleague on the home campus to a colleague in a *numerus-clausus-Fach* in Germany will often do wonders! (Incidentally, another reason for continuity of directorship, for this permits the director to establish and *maintain* contacts.)

important to use them if possible and to occupy them, for frequently there is a serious and prolonged sense of let-down on returning to Cedar Rapids or Boise after a year among the delights of Munich. Moreover, the University of Connecticut, for example, has found that students returning from the stay abroad have proved effective missionaries for the study of German.

Our concern is in great part for the revival of the study of German, not, presumably, because German teachers are merely concerned with keeping their jobs, but because of a belief that the study of a foreign language should continue to be part of the education of an American in the latter part of the twentieth century. The study of foreign languages can, however, only really revive when there is a revival of interest in the public high schools or, if we are more optimistic, in the public elementary schools of this country. That interest will come when a new generation of parents sees and understands the value of the study of foreign languages and a knowledge of a foreign culture. Study abroad is an important, if not crucial, element in rousing this interest in our students, who are after all, the parents and, if we have done our job properly, the *influential* parents of tomorrow.

It would be wrong not to point out the debit side of this balance sheet. One of the most serious problems which we face if students are to study abroad during their junior year is the drop in third year enrollments and a sense among the faculty that just at the moment when their students were becoming interesting they are whisked away to Germany; perhaps not even to get such good instruction in literature as they would have had had they stayed at home. Frankly, there seems to be no counter to this argument, beyond the belief, which is in many situations a demonstrated fact, that in the senior year there will have been such an improvement in language skills that far more sophisticated work can be carried on, for example real stylistic exercises, real attention to differences in language whether on the level of dialect or style. There will, too, be a reluctance on the part of some institutions to lose student fees for a year; our only hope can be that educational concerns will prevail over purely fiscal ones. We should be aware too of the possible disappointment felt by a student when the academic dishes which he has been served in Germany do not measure up to the quality of the ones which he might have received had he stayed at home. Here we can mitigate the disappointment by pointing out the advantages which he has gained and which he could not have possibly received had he stayed at home, but again this will depend on the advisor's having guided him wisely towards a high quality program.

We have considered very seriously the disadvantages outlined above, but we remain firmly of the opinion that, with the safeguards suggested in this paper, there is simply no substitute for a foreign study element in the education of a German major, and that this element will prove, for the majority of those who are non-majors but who care to take the plunge, an educational experience of the first magnitude.

THE TEXTBOOK: A PRINTED TEACHING DEVICE

W. FREEMAN TWADDELL
Brown University

For centuries the formal study of foreign languages as part of an education has had its focus on a book with several functions, related but distinguishable. It is a substantial book, rather carefully manufactured to survive hard use for many months. It provides a program of study and classroom performance by providing assignments to be studied in preparation for classroom activities. In so doing, it introduces new material to be learned, organized according to linguistic topics or situational relevance. It is a reference book of sorts. It can serve as a reminder and clarifier of what happened in the classroom. It is an emergency surrogate for classroom activities for a student who has been absent. It is the body of lore to be reviewed in preparation for a quiz or longer-range examination. In the totality of its uses, it offers an implied syllabus for the organization of a course, to be followed faithfully, modified intelligently or capriciously, or rejected by the teacher in charge. It is known as the textbook.

Within the past generation, the traditional textbook has been supplemented by records, tapes and language labs, sound-film skits, and the like. Usually the audio presentations are incorporated in part into the textbook in script form—sometimes totally, sometimes with judicious omissions to give practice in listening as listening. Also available in many textbooks are directions for assembling and exploiting visual materials. Teacher's manuals cover many kinds of hints and instructions, and often provide additional materials for use in the classroom at the teacher's discretion. We find tests and testing programs, workbooks with tear-out sheets to minimize one of the teacher's burdens.

Some teachers have elected to dispense entirely with textbook-like learning devices. Such experiments seem in general to be short-lived; the responsibility for continual total creation and management becomes too onerous.

As of the later 1970's, the adjuncts to language teaching and learning are so numerous and varied that the traditional name "textbook" does not describe the variety of teaching materials and devices and the combination of them that are to be found in many classrooms. The current quest for the ideal of "individualization" demands in theory a multiplicity of materials and procedures which in practice have to be supplied by strenuous classroom teaching management and ingenious hair-trigger innovations on the part of the teacher.

Lacking any convenient short designation for the various kinds of possible printed materials, let us use the old term "textbook" but understand it as covering considerable ranges of flexibility and diversification.

Where, and how, does the textbook have a major role in a program of learning German?

Clearly a textbook has no function in the advanced stages of study in a German curriculum. In courses dealing with the conventional cultural aspects—belletristic, philosophical, historical, critical—the student's reading is the study of the documents themselves under the guidance of the instructor's course plan in the form of lectures and discussions.

Just as clearly, the textbook has a decisive role on the elementary and intermediate levels. This is the stage where the learner's task is primarily linguistic, the task of becoming capable of participating in communication in the foreign language, as listener, speaker, reader, and (in a very limited way) as writer. A textbook is a printed device which aids in the development of the linguistic skills and resources; secondarily it can be a guide to some features of cultural contrasts between the learner's and the other community's ways of life, through factual notes on the history, geography, social structures, prestige symbols, etc., familiar and taken for granted by members of the foreign community but unfamiliar, even strange and startling, to the learner.

One limitation of the usefulness of textbooks is that they are books. A book is something to be read, and a textbook is a book to be read carefully; only a reader can read and only a proficient reader can read carefully. Many secondary school pupils and even some of the college students our colleagues must expect to encounter in foreign-language classrooms in the later 70's and the 80's, are uncomfortable about paying attention to a static black-and-white page, unaccompanied by the sight of gesturing and acting television advertising and other actors. But let us be candidly somewhat elitist (=snobbish) and tell ourselves that learners of German are by and large somewhat more competent and less resentful about using books than many of their fellow-students.

Admittedly, nearly all pupils and many teachers nowadays welcome efforts toward "individualization." That desire can be satisfied only very partially by even the most judiciously constructed textbook. Despite all efforts to offer individual learning materials to everybody, the textbook is the least adaptable component, and the one which must be constructed so as to accommodate omissions, modifications, complementations.

For a textbook, after it is once committed to type and printed, is distributed to a population of great variability. The learners vary in many dimensions (parameters, if you will). They bring with them experiences of all kinds. Some have home environments which are favorable to academic achievement; others do not. Some attach values of various kinds to competence in a foreign language; others do not. The home environment may be reinforced or counteracted by the attitudes of the learner's contemporaries and friends. Further, those learners have had widely different kinds of previous educational experiences: predominantly permissive or predominantly structured. Their academic and other school behavior patterns may have encountered neglect or discipline, either intelligent or unenlightened. They may take for granted the enforcement of standards, or they may be contemptuous of standards. They may have acquired a sense for their future, or they may judge all encounters with reality in terms of their often immature and aimless immediate interest, pleasure, and energy or laziness. Above all, the most telling difference is that although all human beings may be equal before the law, they are not equal in situations that call for intellectual action: some people learn more quickly and more eagerly than others.

All the foregoing heterogeneities are met in any class of more than minimal size. An experienced teacher can make adjustments and compensations, and to some extent adapt a textbook to the capacities and needs of an individual student and to those of the class as a whole. Such a teacher is accustomed to classes of the size of the one being taught. And that teacher knows how to make allowances for the various goals of the learners.

Their goals may range from the hope that the current German course will be terminal, to an expectation that this course is the preparation for further study of German. The motivation may be the reluctant satisfying of an unwelcome requirement; the classic manifestation is the pathetic complaint about a teacher: "All I wanted was to pass the course, and she wanted me to learn some German!" A more forward-looking learner may regard the current course as offering an opportunity to develop a needed skill or become able to communicate with members of another community—in face-to-face interaction or through their highly esteemed achievements of intellect and art. The variety of goals is reflected in the covert or overt semester-end farewells: a sigh of relief, "Thank God that's over!" or a more or less satisfied murmur, "I am learning to cope." Either way, the teacher's task has been a difficult one. And any attempt to devise a textbook that will be helpful to all learners is doomed to partial success at best.

What no textbook should try to do is what no teacher would dream of doing: ignore the sovereign factors of age and educational level. Even the most cursory knowledge of the nature of language and the related problems of foreign language acquisition dictates the major ingredients of both course and textbook: they must provide some rational balance between the exercise of memory and understanding; they must distribute coverage and intensity of repetition, very specifically in terms of maturity and the educational preparation of the learners. Detail by detail, as well as section by section, the textbook has to support an appropriate program for use in each class hour, each week, each month of a course—and it must do so with judicious flexibility.

Mastery of a language, native or foreign, is control of two kinds: one is based on the unquestioned, unanalyzed stock of unitary signals, the arbitrary meanings of words and some habitually familiar utterances and utterance fractions. The other is a skill, conscious or unconscious, in adapting the forms of words and the structures of utterances to a specific given communicatory need. The first is a product of habit produced by saturation hearing and imitation; the second may originate in awareness and then develop into habits of constructing and recognizing unmemorized wholes consisting of remembered parts—what is somewhat pretentiously called the creative use of language for communication. In the jargon of computer technology, the first is a process of look-up, the second is a program of algorithms. The first kind of control is arbitrary and involves word-stems and special idioms, which have to be "looked up" in memory. The second is an interlocking network of grammatical patterns which can rather poetically be called "rules."—Both kinds of resource are indispensable. Without the stock of words and idioms, linguistic experience would be like that of the student of Latin who can recite a list of verbs taking the ablative but cannot understand a paragraph of a Ciceronian oration without laborious puzzle-solving. Without the ability to manipulate and adapt grammatical patterns, a learner's use of language would remain at the "Me Tarzan, you Jane" level.

There is no question as to the sequence of acquiring these components of language mastery. A stage of memorizing, even by a crude reinforcement of a stimulus-reaction behavior, has its place in an initial stage. It is equally obvious that cognitive processes must organize the naively acquired elements, organizing the idioms into grammatical patterns. (Be it remembered that every grammatical pattern, the first time it is met, appears as an integral unanalyzable idiom; grammatical "rules" are only descriptions of idioms which occur very frequently and with very few counter-exceptions.)

How can a textbook help a learner acquire these resources? The proportion of memorizing and analyzing cannot be the same for different ages: what would be tedious mechanical over-practice for an adult learner is pleasurable and profitable for a child; the cognitive learning which the adult accepts and appreciates is baffling and repellent to a child. The textbook has to be judicious in providing material for over-practice and for cognition, in proportions depending on the answer to the question "For whom?"

Dorothy L. Sayers, in a chapter on "The Lost Tools of Learning" in her brilliant *The Poetry of Search and the Poetry of Statement*,[1] writes cleverly and wisely about the stages of intellectual development. She labels the stages "the Poll-parrot, the Pert, and the Poetic."

> The Poll-parrot stage is the one in which learning by heart is easy and, on the whole, pleasurable; whereas reasoning is difficult and, on the whole, little relished. At this age, one readily memorizes . . . one likes to recite the number-plates of cars; one rejoices in the chanting of

---

[1] Dorothy L. Sayers, *The Poetry of Search and the Poetry of Statement* (London: Victor Gollancz Ltd., 1963), p. 165.

rhymes and thunder of unintelligible polysyllables; one enjoys the mere accumulation of things. The Pert Age, which follows upon this (and, naturally, overlaps it to some extent) . . . is characterized by contradicting, answering-back . . . Its nuisance-value is extremely high . . . . The Poetic Age is . . . . self-centered; it yearns to express itself; . . . it is restless and tries to achieve independence; and, with good luck and good guidance, it should show the beginnings of creativeness, a reaching-out toward a synthesis of what it already knows . . . .

It follows that the textbook (that is, everything subsumed on page 219 under the cover-term "textbook") which is suitable for use in schools is different from one designed for college use. A team of textbook writers which ignores the difference does the profession and itself a disservice. A school textbook necessarily provides for more distraction and entertainment, and for a longer period of intensive habit-forming memorizing; but that distribution of time does not alter the fact that this is still only an initial phase. It is worth many hours of singsong poll-parroting for a child to learn the sequence of letters in the alphabet and the multiplication table; an adult or even an adolescent may be able to understand and enjoy formulating the "rules" of multiplication; but a foundation which includes "six times seven is forty-two" is indispensable.

The phase of conscious understanding, of overt discovery or formulation of "rules"—this is the stage when knowledge of the *theory* of a language, its structure, its structures, serves to supplement and synthesizes the previously learned (="internalized") *samples* of the language; it is the stage of "rules of grammar" as a focus of learning. It comes relatively early in an adult's study of a foreign language, later in a child's learning. It and its timing pose hard decisions for teacher and textbook, and hence for a realistic curricular syllabus.

A foreign language teacher with a real bent for the teaching task is almost by definition deeply interested in grammar. (The person who is assigned a foreign language class *merely* because he or she is a native speaker of the language can be excluded from consideration.) But precisely this enthusiasm and zeal for grammar may be a dangerous trap. For that enthusiasm and zeal will be shared by only a small minority of a class—an important minority to be sure, but still only a minority. Most of the class will be as anti-grammar as any teacher could be pro-grammar.

A "direct method" which exalted sheer practice and absorption was an unwise concession to an uncritical anti-grammar rebellion and merely threw out the baby with the bathwater. It amounted to a prolongation of a poll-parrot stage. That stage has its place, of course, adapted in length and intensity, for both the young and the mature learner. But all learners must be trained in the use of the labor-saving tool of valid grammatical generalization, and it is primarily the business of the textbook to provide judiciously both the material for learning samples and the "rules" for organizing previously learned samples. ("Judicious" here means "appropriate to the age group involved.") The balance and pacing of the transitions can be guided in a textbook, determined by the realization that grammar is a means and not an end. For of course our students do not study German in order to learn German grammar; they study German grammar in order to learn German.

There have been swings in the pendulum during the past century, in textbooks and hence in teaching and curricula. The tradition of exalting grammatical sophistication as the proper goal of foreign language study was understandable when Latin was the foreign language par excellence. And learning a language via studying the grammar made a certain amount of sense when a modern language was studied by students who had already learned a considerable amount of Latin. The great textbooks of Whitney (1870), von Jagemann (1892), Calvin Thomas (1896), Bierwirth (1900) are monumental works.

Student populations changed after World War II, even that part of the student population involved in the study of German. No longer could college or high school teachers count on a class with a fairly homogeneous background of liberal arts education. It was not surprising that students included grammatical discipline among the other kinds of discipline with which they were impatient. That impatience was supported in high places of the educational establishment. But the German-teaching profession, as reflected in its elementary textbooks, continued to worship the golden calf of grammar for its own sake. The concessions were in the form of less technical descriptions, greater wealth of grammatical practice materials, and wider spacing of topics according to difficulty, real difficulty, or what guild tradition had declared to be difficult. This spacing reached an ultimate when the modal auxiliaries were deferred to the second semester. The kind of German learned for an entire semester without modal auxiliaries can just barely be imagined. This was not throwing out the baby with the bathwater; this was throwing out the bathwater before bathing the baby.

Various textbooks displayed various forms of compromise between the lingering reverence for grammar as such and concessions to anti-grammar populations of learners and teachers. And there were various degrees of growing sophistication in the profession, which permitted a critical examination of some of the traditional terminologies and formulations. The Latin tradition of the sequence of cases in declensional tables (Nominative, Genitive, Dative, Accusative) is clearly unsuitable in a description of a Germanic language. As early as 1923, Leonard Bloomfield, in his book *First Year German,* used the sensible order (Nominative, Accusative, Dative, Genitive). But when, in 1944, more than two decades later, Rehder and I used the same order of cases, there was a considerable fluttering in the dovecotes about this sequence which, we were told by some of our colleagues, made it more difficult for students to learn noun endings. (Parenthetically it may be noted that in declensional tables the sequence of genders "Feminine, Neuter, Masculine" is more appropriate for modern German than the traditional "Masculine, Feminine, Neuter."—But this may be, as Dr. Watson put it, a story for which the world is not yet ready.)

Another example: The names "present and past subjunctive" conflict maddeningly with the semantic and syntactic facts and complicate a real difficulty by interposing a needless hindrance to understanding and use. Such efforts as "first and second subjunctive" were not falsifications, but were meaningless and unhelpful.—Some writers, as a general policy, abandoned Latin terminology and introduced terms from contemporary German grammatical theory or devised strikingly new terms.—Some textbooks to be used in grammar review work, or in courses drolly advertised as "Composition and Conversation," display the same trends.

The textbook is one component of the teaching/learning enterprise. It is a tool for the teacher; for the learner it is a corpus of material to be studied and learned (and be tested on). The many kinds of heterogeneity mentioned earlier make it certain that no textbook will be wholly appropriate for any given class or wholly satisfy any teacher but its writer. Hence all other teachers will find any textbook a more or less inadequate or redundant tool. The teacher and the textbook are condemned to an uneasy marriage; the teacher cannot function without the textbook, and at the same time the teacher cannot be entirely happy with it. Textbooks impose a fixed structure on the classroom program; teachers would rather work with their own structurings. The experienced teacher quietly adapts and modifies; the inexperienced teacher betrays insecurity and lack of experience by calling attention to real or fancied shortcomings of the textbook, trying to demonstrate superiority and succeeding only in shaking the student's confidence in the textbook.

Can a textbook author team anticipate and help a teacher adapt? How? The unavoidable dilemma is summarized in the question whether the textbook is to be the sovereign structuring of a course, or a reference source. As a structure, it can aid a teacher as a kind of foundation garment which enhances facade and symmetries; but in achieving these boons it incurs a rebellion against its similarity to a straitjacket. (This conflict between helpfulness and constraint is particularly acute in a Teacher's Manual when one is provided. But it is implicit in any book put into the hands of teachers. The clash is aggravated when the structuring is revealed to learners as well as teachers: what is in a Teacher's Manual is optional, but what is in a Students' Book is obligatory.)

The total tone of a curriculum is reflected in the build of textbooks, elementary or intermediate. In the elementary book, is the material to be organized into topics of social interaction, or of linguistic categories? Put crudely: Is it a curricular goal that students, at the end of a section of the course, should feel happy that they can now accept invitations, and participate in an outing, or are they to rejoice in their newly acquired command of the cases used with the common prepositions?

A related dilemma is a product of the total curricular strategy of a department or a school system: Is the course which a textbook serves regarded as a self-contained unit, or is it its function to prepare for the following course? Should it present a wide range of selections with their inherent interest and values as specimens of culture and language, or should its primary aim be to establish vocabulary and grammatical skills which can be presupposed in the following course? For example: Is the complete grammar of conditional sentences treated as a major learning objective in the first college semester or the first year of high school German? If so, then the grammar of conditions requires only review and some refresher practice in the next course. Or can examples of conditional sentences appear whenever a conversation or exposition makes a conditional sentence natural and useful? In that case, it can be treated as an idiom, and only after a number of such "temporary idioms" have been planted is it economical to present a generalizing synthesis, with a battery of exercises and set of "rules" for understanding in conscious awareness.

Within the curricular structure in formal academic language learning, a textbook shares responsibility with a human teacher and other teaching aids. In various proportions, it may consist of straightforward adjuncts to the classroom or as an accompaniment to work with tapes and records—and that work may be done in fixed schedules by the students as a class, or as individuals, by assignment or optionally.

A minor factor to be considered by textbook authors is the possibility that the book may be used informally, outside the usual classroom situation. It may be used by a tutor and a single learner or a very small group of learners. In such cases, obviously, the teacher can adapt ad libitum; the teacher dominates the structuring and scheduling of instruction. A textbook may even be used as a guide in self-instruction—preferably along with tapes and records. Here the usefulness of the textbook as a teaching device depends crucially on the general intelligence and training of the learner: is that learner sophisticated, with experience in language learning and a clear understanding of the nature of language and the nature of language learning? Is the book being used as a refresher by some one with a previous study of the language or a previous period of actual use of the language years or decades ago? Is the learner blindly hoping that by reading a textbook he will "learn" a language, unaware that "learning a language" means developing habits and acquiring control of resources of vocabulary and patterns of grammar? The textbook author cannot be blamed for disappointing *that* kind of hopeful reader.

Textbooks for intermediate courses have the purpose of providing reading practice and some oral practice, with the aim of vocabulary expansion and increased assurance in dealing with sentence structure. German study is at a disadvantage here, as compared with the other West European languages. It is not hard to find belletristic and technical writing in French, for example, which is both intellectually respectable and linguistically within the competence of an English-speaking learner with a few hundred hours of preparation. But in German it is anything but easy to find reading practice materials which are feasible and inherently worthwhile.

Hence German curricula face a major problem in providing material for reading practice in the third and fourth college semesters or high school years. (Indeed, few secondary schools provide third and fourth year German courses, probably at least in part because of the scarcity of suitable material for learners in the later adolescent years.)

One uncomfortable solution is the use of "cooked" readings—the literary output of professors, or drastically modified simplified paraphrases of real German, prepared with reverent attention to frequency lists. That kind of German is a vexation to a teacher with a sensitive *Sprachgefühl,* and is also transparently fake German in the judgment of students, who are legitimately impatient at a seemingly interminable treadmill of apron-string preparation for the real use of real German.

The alternative is the use of real German (or at worst a very slightly emasculated German). The grim fact is that a second-year college student, confronted with real German, has wholly inadequate resources of vocabulary and usually a still shaky control of the patterns of grammar needed for quick comprehension of the structure of phrases, clauses, and sentences. The vocabulary shortcoming used to be managed by a brutal insistence on the students' resort to an end-vocabulary—a wildly time-consuming operation. More recently, glossings of the so-called difficult or rare words are provided in margins, in footnotes, or on a facing page. This saves time as compared with hunting through an end-vocabulary, but it suffers by suggesting one English translation as the equivalent or clue to the semantic spread of the German word. Also, these techniques of glossing complicate book manufacture and require more paper, and they unavoidably prolong an apron-string guidance. None of the glossing devices is wholly satisfactory, but some systematic procedure has to be provided; and the worst is still better than nothing.

The selection of a content for reading practice has been various and represents efforts to accomplish various goals. Before the 1930's the goal of preparation for literary study was taken for granted; and *Immensee* was the implement of choice. Then, in an effort to make German studies more attractive, the goal of entertainment was smuggled into the canon, and *Emil und die Detektive* was its manifestation. Since that far-off time authors have been hunting and occasionally finding materials they hope students will accept as "relevant" (in the jargon sense of that term). This purpose dictates the use of contemporary and often overtly propagandistic selections of various degrees of literary style and linguistic utility: some elegant and some crude, some valid preparation for the reading of other documents, others essentially wasteful. The work may be an entire novella or selections from tracts. The sovereign criterion for selection of this kind of reading matter is that it be the work of a contemporary or quite recent author, famous or notorious, and/or that it treat social controversies, as advocate or critic.

By no means all authors of textbooks aim at this kind of material; many choose materials of cultural, usually literary, prestige. Just now, there seems to be a preference for an anthological format of textbooks for intermediate German courses. Authors and publishers appear to feel the desirability of a connecting theme. The profession is offered reading texts based on a topic or a specialized genre, usually consisting of short narratives or discussions culled from a literary corpus or popularizations of samples of expositions. The quest for originality and hoped-for wide appeal of topic and title has produced collections of various degrees of plausibility and significance, ranging across the gamut from the ingenious through the banal to the grotesque.

One feature that is frequently found in all kinds of reading texts is a Question Section to check comprehension. This serves as a self-testing device for the user and a guide which directs attention to points the reader may have overlooked or misinterpreted. Less common is an apparatus for grammar review and reinforcement, using the vocabulary and samples of grammatical structure in the reading passages. It requires skill and experience to construct this kind of apparatus, and it puts demands on the teacher to manage the exercises.

Here as always it is the joint responsibility of textbook writer teams and teachers to keep practice and testing quite separate. Errors in the practice have to be corrected and counter-practice provided, to be sure. But the students must be quite secure in the knowledge that their performance in the practice does not play a part in determining their final grades.

Auxiliary devices are often supplied with elementary textbooks, sometimes with intermediate course books.

A workbook with tear-out and hand-in sheets certainly spares a teacher the task of constructing homework or study-period assignments—a significant lightening of the burden. In the nature of the case, workbook assignments are prepared by authors who are familiar with the entire textbook and hence will normally be better than assignments constructed by a teacher who has to work under the pressure of time and competing obligations. A further sheer mechanical advantage is the uniformity of paper size and the location of answers on the sheet, which simplifies significantly the task of correction.—The disadvantages are the factor of additional cost (but this may be outweighed by the expenses of dittoing or mimeographing and the value of the teacher's time), and also the fact that in every teacher's opinion the workbook over-emphasizes some aspects of the course and neglects others.

If the total program of elementary German incorporates a tightly structured audio-visual curriculum, the textbook can be the printed part of that program, serving among other things as a selective or total script of the audio component. That script may be a separate pamphlet or a bound-in part of the textbook, either as an appendix or dispersed throughout the book to parallel the audio schedule. The advantage of a separate script pamphlet is that it can be changed and issued as a revision as the audio program is revised; a disadvantage is that it is extremely vulnerable to being mislaid and lost.

It was noted above that textbooks play a minor role or none at all in courses beyond the intermediate level: that is, roughly, from the fifth semester onward. There is one important exception: the course or courses dealing systematically with German grammar. The earlier courses quite properly deal only with the major structures and present them to the learner as the grammatical information needed for the comprehension of what the learner hears and reads, or as a model for an intelligible production of what he has to say and (to a very limited extent) write. But at some time during the transition between guided study about the German language and the secure use of the language, German grammar as such is a proper and necessary object of learning. A knowledge of that grammar must be a part of the preparation for truly advanced study, enabling the student to react easily and correctly to the less commonly met structures. A textbook providing information and practice exercises to give the learner such resources must be both linguistically sound and pedagogically sensible. It must organize and synthesize the bits and pieces of grammar which the learner has encountered and in part mastered in connection with earlier study. It must also deal with such minor structures as a weak ending of an adjective modifying a preceding personal pronoun, "Da wären wir!", "Hat Inge doch längst gewußt, daß . . . " and such unpredictable noun plurals as "Ratschläge, Mordtaten, Friedensschlüsse." It must also expound, illustrate, and provide practice in the subtler semantics of the crucial "little words"—the prepositions and the sentence adverbs like "schon, erst, noch, bis, ja, doch, nämlich, wohl, denn."

Such a textbook has to be more than a minor adjunct of a so-called "Composition" course, although it may well contain theme topics for simple compositions and may even, with all due caution, contain assignments in the very complex skill of translation.

The 1970's are a difficult time for the writing of such a systematic textbook of German grammar. Many practicing teachers and teacher trainers have heard of turmoils in theoretical and speculative linguistics, but few can be expected to discriminate between noises and insights. If an author writes a straightforward comprehensible book using the standard established technical terminology, some of his colleagues and reviewers will dismiss his presentation as benighted and out-of-date. If he tries to treat German grammar in the manner of one of the recent or current doctrines of linguistic theory and its terminology, he is likely to be overtaken by shifts in fashion between the time he begins to write and the time his book is published. Further, his book is likely to be incomprehensible to many of his intended readers.

As of today, it seems probable that teachers put in charge of courses of Grammar Review, Systematic Grammar, or Composition, will be experienced and well-informed, and will have their own preferences and convictions as to methodology and content. Those teachers are well advised to prepare their own materials, diagrams, and tables, make use of the major standard reference grammars, and contrive exercises appropriate to the doctrine on which they base the course.

It is usual to think of the textbook as part of the team which includes also the teacher and whatever mechanical aids are used, all functioning within the framework of a curriculum. In the past decade a new factor has been added: the changed role of the publisher.

Until fairly recently textbooks have been written by teachers and contracted for by publishers. It was the responsibility of the publisher to provide the editorial, manufacturing, and distribution technologies. Decisions on the publisher's side were usually made by editors who were themselves experienced teachers, aided by advisors who were expert in the various languages.

In the 1960's and 1970's the structure of foreign language textbook publishing has changed. Many of the most respected foreign language textbook publishing companies are now parts of conglomerates whose top officials lack intimate understanding of publishing as such, let alone textbook publishing, let alone foreign language textbook publishing. Where once a foreign language editor was likely to become a vice-president, his successor today may be quite low in the hierarchy of one of the many satrapies of the conglomerate. Formerly, decisions were made on the basis of informed judgment and knowledge of the professional standing of the authors; indeed, it was often the publisher who approached a potential author and solicited a textbook. Nowadays, questions of quality and innovation and lasting power are subordinate to guesses or haphazard surveys about current marketing conditions. An uninformed manager may or may not know how to evaluate the accuracy or importance of the marketing reports.

Thus publishers are vulnerable to noisy faddists and may put out books that reflect the fashion of the moment. There may be calls to rectify ancient traditional social imbalances of one sort or another, and instead of making a legitimate appropriate correction a publisher may go overboard and subordinate other aspects of a textbook to a self-righteous flaunting of a fashionable virtue.

A corollary of the influence exerted by the image of the market is the activity of the advertiser and the importance attached to packaging. The packager has to decide between the sober and the gaudy: an aggressive art editor—who more often than not has no pedagogical sense—adorns a book with ornamental designs and photographs, often expensive color photographs, that are decorations rather than illustrations.

One practice which is occasionally encountered is the preliminary tryout of the materials. This seems to have some of the magic of market research for the publisher, and it can readily become a sales gimmick for salesmen. If the tryout was conducted by an author in the author's class or classes, caution is in order to determine whether that author-teacher is or is not a crank and whether the classes were typical of the school or college level, whether the classes were numerous or few and idiosyncratic, and what the size of the classes was. If many schools or colleges participated in the tryout, what kind of feedback did the author receive and what did he do about it? Obviously, changing or omitting every feature to which objections (by teachers and/or learners) were reported would result in a pretty bland document. There is also a moral question: Is an author, acting as teacher, and is his publisher justified in using learners as experimental animals, quite possibly at the expense of their language learning?

Despite all the pitfalls and difficulties of textbook writing, the textbook is retaining its importance as a major component in elementary and intermediate foreign language study. Textbooks reflect changes in methodology and goals of foreign language teaching. But since a textbook is designed for use in many different locations and in many different educational frames, it must have some measure of wholesome eclecticism and neutrality among various theories of foreign language teaching. Textbooks are written by teachers, and to a considerable degree are selected by teachers. Hence, a textbook must keep reasonably close to the hard realities of the classroom, or many classrooms.

Earlier I referred to the relationship between teachers and textbooks as an uneasy marriage. Uneasy or not, the relationship is decidedly one of mutual influencing and restraining. A textbook that is freakish is disposed of by being ignored by teachers. In the other direction, what teachers can use will be used; and textbooks can gently do things to and for teachers. Teachers of course display a great range of temperament, training, and experience. Some are impervious to innovations; others are vulnerable to shifts of fashion, not to say fads. But even the first kind of teacher cannot persist wholly unchanged in every detail of teaching procedure. The second kind can be reassured that lack of success in understanding and echoing the latest pronouncements of The New Truth is not a sign of total failure. The great majority of experienced teachers, of course, will demand to be shown why they should change this or that, and they will adopt intelligently whatever can be convincingly shown to be an improvement.

The curricular framework within which a textbook is used is of two kinds.

An externally imposed curriculum assigns to foreign language study a role (or no role) in the total educational enterprise for a pupil population. This kind of curricular structure is likely to be the product of educational experts or theoreticians, often themselves monolingual. For the profession, overall curricular priorities affecting the role of foreign language study are likely to seem uninformed or hostile. Coping with them calls for patience and a willingness to inform the public and the makers of decisions about education.

The internal curricular structure has to do with sequence, with goals and techniques for attaining them. Curriculum, in this meaning, usually has validity for a specific administrative organization—one school, the school system of one city or district, at most of one state. Decisions and prescriptions are the work of people who are familiar with foreign language teaching: knowledge of several languages is usually represented in such a decision-making body.

Internal curriculum building may be influenced or biased by a strong member of the board. The temptation to be messianic is not unknown. An official supervisor is professionally obligated to keep up with publications in the field of methodological theory (often publications that show signs of being responses to a "publish or perish" compulsion), and immersion in such reading involves the risk of being captivated by slogans and self-assured proclamations of a New Truth. On the college level, the staff member in charge of a multi-section course has the task of setting up a mini-curriculum; his colleagues' habits of scholarly skepticism and open-mindedness protect him and the teachers and the learners against excesses.

Thus the textbook as an institution has its indispensable role in both preserving established values and developing new values. Among the teacher population, the textbook stirs up the hidebound and restrains the flighty. In various curricular frameworks, a textbook designed for general use introduces a wholesome force for the common purpose without imposing a dangerous uniformity. The judicious, accurate, imaginative textbook, in short, is an instrument of sensible unity within sensible pluralism.

CAREER ALTERNATIVES FOR STUDENTS OF GERMAN

BARBARA ELLING
SUNY-Stony Brook

When we address ourselves to the future of German Studies in the United States, we are forced to examine our contributions to the intellectual, emotional, and economic future of those students who graduate from our programs. Despite the professional self-flagellation which we have witnessed in recent years, we can safely say that we have been fairly effective in fulfilling our role and function as regards the intellectual and emotional future of our students. But when we examine our attitude toward aspects related to their economic future, we must conclude that we have been remiss in many respects. The following discussion focuses on this problem in an attempt to establish some theoretical and practical guidelines which might aid Germanists in educating Americans who use German as a primary or secondary skill in their careers—as citizens of the 21st century.

Before looking into future possibilities, let us briefly examine the problems of the present without an attempt to look for a cause-effect relationship. German departments share the following problems with many other departments:
—declining enrollments;
—reductions in staff allotments;
—resistance of some faculty members to diversify;
—difficulties in establishing interdepartmental programs;
—students who are poorly prepared in all areas of the humanities;
—uncooperative administrations who force us, in many instances, to justify our very existence on campus;
—lack of comprehensive guidance and career placement systems;
—lack of teaching positions for graduating students (B.A., M.A., and Ph.D. levels).
In addition, we share with the entire foreign language profession the following problems:
—public disinterest, frequently outright hostility toward foreign languages on all levels;
—lack of political power in legislative bodies, Boards of Regents, Boards of Education, etc.;
—high attrition rate of students who enroll in foreign languages;
—incorrect notions regarding the degree of difficulty of the various languages;

—uninformed guidance personnel;
—lack of willingness or ability to "sell our product";
—lack of unity within our own ranks;
—lack of clear objectives;
—confusion in areas of curricular reform and methodological considerations;
—disinterest of those segments of society which could serve as possible employers of our students, foremost in the areas of business, science and governmental services.

Obviously, solutions to many of these problems, which might vary in intensity, from region to region, cannot be offered in this type of discussion. However, once we view the problems from the perspective of possible career options for students with a degree in or a knowledge of German (or another foreign language), we might arrive at some possible solutions. To offer more career options would mean an acceptance of "career education"—a term I use reluctantly and only in its broadest sense. It might provide a basis for curricular reform, a basis for converting the "non-believers" in our society and a platform for providing leadership. No one has proposed a definition of career education which satisfies everybody. Frequently attempts at definition are made by stating what it is not: it is not synonymous with vocational or technical education, although both may be parts of career education; it is not training all students to have salable skills at the time of graduation, although that may be one goal of career education; it need not, in fact must not, conflict with or replace the liberal and aesthetic traditions inherent in Western models of education. Stated in the simplest terms, career education is a form of education for which curricula are designed in such a way that all subjects taught have some connection with the ways in which people earn a living. Such a broad interpretation is useful in approaching the necessary reforms and at the same time prevents unnecessary and fruitless debates on the subject, conducted perennially on college campuses. We know only too well that any faculty member associated with career education in foreign languages, traditionally limited to teacher training, is considered at many universities a "second class citizen." I submit that it is irrelevant to even debate the merit or demerit of career education, but that instead we should consider it an obligation we have to the students and to society. The manner in which we fulfill this obligation is a decision that we must make as a profession. This decision should not be based on a value judgment reflecting our own philosophy of education—possibly a relic from the nineteenth century—but instead should be based on evidence that what we have to offer is of value to the students in the society in which they live and earn a living.

The general trend toward greater emphasis on career education can no longer be ignored. The concept and implications are discussed with ever increasing frequency in professional literature, the press, government publications, and educational materials distributed by publishers. State and federal monies are made available for faculty retraining, large scale projects and information dissemination. Guidelines and mandates are issued by State Departments of Education. We should not wait until reforms are mandated but instead take advantage of the obvious opportunity to assert leadership. It is essential that we act on four fronts simultaneously:

1. We must establish the existence of viable career alternatives.
2. We must create an awareness among employers on the local, state, and national levels that we do, in fact, provide students with a "marketable" skill by teaching them, as a primary or secondary skill, German language, literature, and culture.
3. We must inform students of career alternatives and of the fact that we can provide them with the necessary skills.
4. We must reform or enrich our departmental programs to include "enabling activities" for the acquisition of such skills.

Existing Career Options

A great deal of information is available to help us with step one. In order to structure our approach, it is useful to consider some charts provided by the United States Office of Education. The agency describes career education as a five-step developmental program including awareness, orientation, exploration, preparation, and specialization. Initially, career clusters (Figure 1) are identified to cover every field of occupation. Figure 2 shows possible foreign language careers within each cluster. The student begins with career awareness when he enters the university and begins in-depth exploration and career preparation during the sophomore year. Once the process of in-depth orientation has begun the student will single out those occupations which require a B.A. or B.S., M.A. or M.S., or Ph.D. degree. In broad terms the options that remain are:

A. Major areas which U.S. firms like to combine with a knowledge of a foreign language:
    1. Advertising
    2. Area Studies
    3. Civil Engineering
    4. Engineering
    5. Finance
    6. International Business Administration
    7. Law
    8. Marketing
    9. Political Science
    10. Statistics and Computer Science

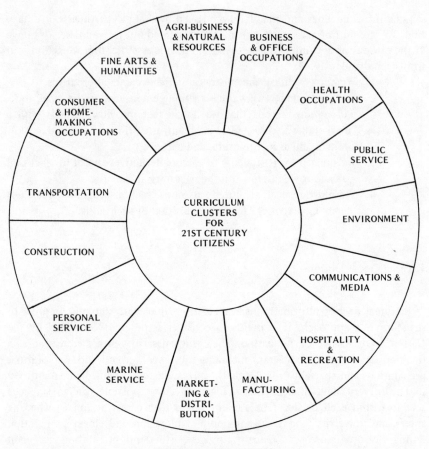

FIGURE I – CAREER CLUSTERS
United States Office of Education

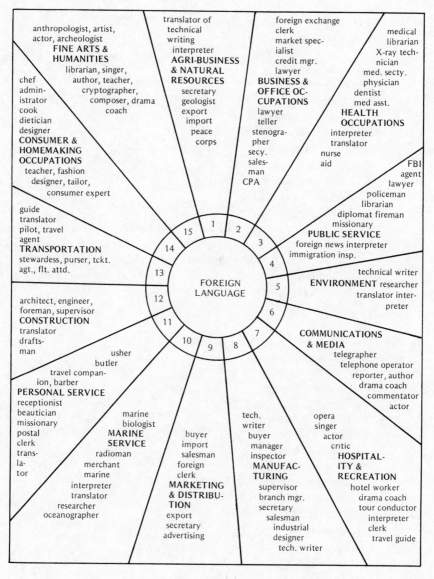

FIGURE 2. Foreign Language in Career Clusters.
United States Office of Education

B.   Careers in the field of *Communication*:
    1. Broadcaster[1]
        a.   Announcer
        b.   Writer
    2. Foreign Service
    3. Journalism[2]
        a.   Correspondent
        b.   Researcher
        c.   Reporter
    4. Librarian
    5. Pan American Union
    6. Publishing and editing
    7. Travel agency
    8. Science Information and Research Specialist
        a.   NASA
        b.   Bureau of Standards of the United States Government
    9. United Nations
        a.   Interpreter
        b.   Translator

C.   Careers in the field of *Service*:
    1. Agronomist
    2. Airlines
    3. Curator
    4. Diplomat
    5. Hotel and management
    6. Lawyer
    7. Personal service
    8. Social worker
    9. Teaching—college, high school

D.   Careers in the field of *Business*:
    1. Accountant
    2. Advertising
    3. Arts and crafts
    4. Banking
    5. Branch Manager
    6. Commercial Attaché
    7. Couture

---

[1] There are 389 radio stations in the U.S. with foreign language broadcasting: 57 in French, 60 in German, 90 in Italian, 182 in Spanish.
[2] *Directory of Newspapers, Periodicals* (N.W. Ayer and Sons, 1965).

8. Economist
9. Export-Import
10. Foreign Market Analyst

E. Careers in the *Arts and Entertainment*:
 1. Actor
 2. Critic
 3. Opera singer

F. Careers in *Science and Technology*:
 1. Archeologist
 2. Architect
 3. Chemist
 4. Entomologist
 5. Engineer
 6. Geologist
 7. Nurse
 8. Pharmacist
 9. Physician
 10. Translator of technical writings

G. Careers in *Linguistics*:
 1. Center for Applied Linguistics
 2. Smithsonian Institute
 3. Teaching

Some of the most important employers of foreign language graduates are:
 1. Agency of International Development
 2. American Express Agency
 3. Charles E. Merrill Publishing Company
 4. Colleges and universities
 5. Department of Agriculture
 6. Department of Commerce
 7. Department of Defense
 8. Department of State, Division of Language Service
 9. Immigration Service
 10. Institute of International Education
 11. Inter-American Schools Service
 12. International Atomic Energy Agency
 13. International banking & finance
 14. International Civil Aviation Organization
 15. International import, export
 16. International marketing

17. Junior colleges
18. National Education Association
19. National Security Agency
20. National Student Association
21. Pan American Airlines
22. Pan American Union—Division of Education
23. Peace Corps
24. Public schools
25. Students Abroad
26. UNESCO
27. United Nations
28. United States Department of State
29. United States Information Agency

For more specific information the student should be aware of the *Dictionary of Occupational Titles*, usually available in the library.

From this list of careers in which the foreign language skill is needed or helpful, it becomes evident that the number of career options for our students are numerous. In a survey of American industry, business, and service organizations conducted by the Modern Language Association of America in 1972, nearly 70% of the respondents said they do use, could use, or expect to use people with foreign language skills. These results are most encouraging.[3]

Specific information on job opportunities for students with German language skills is available from a survey by Rita Terras, Connecticut College, of 100 business establishments and government agencies.[4] Among the organizations surveyed were airlines, automobile rental agencies, broadcasting, manufacturing companies (automobile, chemical, pharmaceutical, machine, tool), marketing research, news services, public libraries, publishers, and U.S. agencies. 58% of the organizations contacted supplied the requested information. 39% of the 58% which employ personnel using German on the job offer more than 8,539 such occupational opportunities. The remaining organizations responded that the foreign language related positions were "considerable" or "numerous."

The survey did make clear that a German major without acquisition of additional skills has little occupational usefulness outside of teaching. The fields of knowledge in which German is combined with another skill were listed in the following order of importance: business, engineering, economics, chemistry, liberal arts, journalism, library science, marketing, political science, accounting, fine arts, computer science, law, psychology, and textiles.

[3] Richard I. Brod and Lucille Honig, *Foreign Languages and Careers* (New York: Modern Language Association, 1974), p. 1. Also as an article under the same title in the *Modern Language Journal*, 58:4 (April 1974), 157–185.
[4] Rita Terras, "The 'Market' for German-Speaking Employees: A Survey," *ADFL Bulletin*, 6:3 (March 1975), 26–28.

Concerning the choice of degree, the following were listed in order of importance: B.S., B.A., M.S., M.A., Ph.D. and M.B.A. When compared with the previously mentioned MLA survey, this survey yielded some interesting information: more organizations offer positions (63%) to applicants with German language skill than positions (47%) to applicants with foreign language skills in general, all foreign languages combined. These results were corroborated by another survey (conducted by Barbara Elling, SUNY, Stony Brook) in 1975.[5] This survey yielded information in two additional areas: (1) the number of positions in Germany for Americans with the German language skill is twice the number of those hired to work in the United States; (2) the skills most needed by the employee to obtain a position are in order of importance: reading comprehension, writing, oral comprehension, speaking. In designing our curricula, this has to be kept in mind. Disturbing was the reply given to the question of where the employees obtained their German language skill. The largest number had learned the language in a German speaking country. Only 1/3 of those employed by the companies had learned the language at the university level. The conclusion we must draw from this is that we do not fulfill our role as training institutions as well as we could or should, and that future employees of such companies and agencies are unaware that the university departments offer them the necessary skills.

It must also be borne in mind that the number of immigrants, which until now has provided companies and government agencies with a pool of native speakers from which they could draw employees, is expected to be drastically reduced. Fewer Germans emigrate to the U.S., and labor organizations on both sides of the ocean do not encourage the hiring of non-citizens.

Communication with the Public

Much is being written and said about career alternatives for our students. But most of these communications do not reach the public, since they are expressed in journals and during conferences designed for the "insiders."

We must reach the public at large. The national professional foreign language associations have to assume leadership in this area. The founding of the Joint National Committee on Foreign Languages and the AATG Placement Information Center, which relies on a national network of volunteers, are moves in the right direction. It is to be hoped that the efforts of such groups are not only directed toward careers in teaching but also toward career alternatives.

While these efforts are commendable, they may easily be too narrow in scope and effect. The membership of the various associations must exert pressure on the national offices in order to bring about a concentrated and large

---

[5] This survey has not been published.

scale public relations effort involving television, radio, and widely read newspapers and magazines. Other professions, e.g. art and music teachers, have done
it—we too can do it, particularly because the need for employees with language
skills is an established fact.

Communication with Future Employers

Obviously not all future employers (some 32,000 U.S. firms have branches
or representatives abroad; over 15,000 foreign businesses have interests in the
U.S.) can be reached or even identified. But multinational corporations can be
singled out and letters sent to the Directors of Personnel. The letters should be
written by the appropriate person(s) in the National Office of the AATG and
should indicate that it is no longer necessary for them to spend valuable time
and money teaching German to people who need a knowledge of the language,
but that high schools and universities can provide them with prepared applicants.

It might also be helpful to write to alumni of the various universities and to
organizations such as the Goethe Institutes. In states where numerous universities are concentrated in a small geographical area the effort should be
coordinated by one person in charge for the entire area.

In the area of business this is particularly important since this sector has
ignored the training universities can provide and has frequently relied on "on the
job training" and language schools for programs tailored to meet the needs of
businessmen. Among the latter are American University's Business Council for
International Understanding Institute, the School of International Management,
the International Business Option at the University of Cincinnati, a recently
opened school for tenants of the World Trade Center (120 companies in the
center use some German), the Language House in Chicago and the Berlitz
schools. Companies turn to these schools since the traditional distance between
business and foreign language departments is so great that they learned long ago
that employees trained in a business-related area who also had foreign language
skills were almost nonexistent.

On the local level much can be done by universities and professional
associations. In states such as Connecticut, Minnesota, New York, Ohio, South
Carolina, Texas, Utah, Washington, and Wisconsin, faculties of individual universities and high schools have conducted surveys, written letters, conducted
workshops and developed new programs. One particularly impressive effort
which involved the State Employment Service and the State Development Board
was reported by Edwin Arnold, Clemson University, published in the September,
1973 issue of *ADFL Bulletin*. This report can serve as a guideline to those who
would like to initiate a career information system on the local level. These
isolated efforts must be coordinated, expanded and given national recognition.

On campus we can begin our campaign with the University Office of

Placement Services. In looking through the files we can identify companies and agencies which traditionally recruit students from the institution. The University of Wisconsin-Eau Claire reports that this brought highly satisfying results.[6] Next, we can speak to recruiting officers when they visit the campus. Faculty and personnel of the employment service can write letters to local employers. Other colleges, within the university, then have to be involved, e.g. the deans of the colleges of business, engineering, law, and allied health services. Again the University of Wisconsin-Eau Claire reports good results after contacts with the departments of computer science, economics, journalism, political science, and sociology. These contacts yielded additional information on jobs with skills in the above areas combined with a foreign language skill. Furthermore, campus conferences and workshops for businessmen, community and political leaders should be conducted by foreign language departments and the career development offices. Executives and directors of personnel from local companies should be invited to the campus as speakers.

Informing the Students

The National Office of the AATG should distribute handbooks and articles which list available data, information, and addresses and identify career alternatives. This would also help the high school teachers, and it is without doubt the secondary schools where our work must begin in informing and convincing students, guidance departments, parents, and local school boards that German is a "useful" skill. Local chapters of the AATG can coordinate their efforts to organize career days, workshops, and lectures for students. A recent first, a career information session in the German Department at SUNY, Stony Brook, proved to be of great interest to the students and numerous requests for career information have come in since. Such lectures or informal sessions should be held by faculty members on a regular basis. On a larger scale, high schools and colleges might attempt an International Employment Day Fair.

Other often unused channels of communication are the guidance services of the undergraduate studies office and the student affairs office. Information packets on foreign language career alternatives should be prepared for the personnel in these offices. Information, such as provided on these pages can form the basis for such information packets. We must answer the students' justified question "What can I do with it?" with all the information we can obtain, with honesty and as much clarity as is possible at this time.

[6] Barbara Rolland, "Careers for our Foreign Language Graduates," *Careers, Communication and Culture in Foreign Language Teaching*, Report of the 1974 Central States Conference on Language Education, ed. Frank M. Grittner (Skokie, Ill.: National Textbook Company, 1974), pp. 41–50.

Implications for the Curriculum

The need for training students for career alternatives has been established. The areas in which alternative career goals can be pursued are fairly well identified. Creating an awareness on all levels and disseminating the necessary information is difficult, but not impossible. The most formidable task is to determine how we can best respond in restructuring our curricula to meet the need and the trend.

Most of our programs are designed for majors who use the language as a primary skill, either in teaching or, less frequently, in careers as interpreters and translators. Those students who enroll in the teacher training programs tell us that there is too much emphasis on literature, not enough on culture and language courses, such as advanced conversation/composition. Departments have responded by introducing German Studies programs, more *Landeskunde* and more courses dealing with curriculum development, pedagogy, and applied linguistics. Individualized instruction, tutorials and independent studies add to the flexibility of the programs. The emphasis on flexibility and diversification becomes obvious when one looks at the *MLA Job Information Lists*, giving evidence of the need for faculty to teach culture and civilization and pedagogy.

The area which has been neglected is the training of students who wish to use the language as a secondary skill either by obtaining a minor or simply minimal competence in German. Although most departments have always offered a course in scientific German, generally designed to enable the student to pass degree requirements in a foreign language, we have not offered enabling activities for students interested in the careers listed above on either the undergraduate or graduate level. How do we begin in designing these enabling activities within the existing departmental framework and constraints? The first step is to create general awareness and support among departmental faculty. Dissemination of information on this level is also important. The next step is to look at already existing interdepartmental or interdisciplinary programs at other universities such as Brown, Cincinnati, Indiana, Minnesota, Stanford, Texas, and Wisconsin. The programs range from an interdepartmental concentration in Chemistry and German to German Studies and Area Studies Programs to Executive German. These should be carefully reviewed and only those elements used which are possible and practical for a given department. The next step is self-assessment: what is our faculty equipped to handle, from which departments can we expect cooperation and what funds can be obtained either from campus or outside sources?

There are several approaches which seem viable for most institutions:
1. Programs designed to meet specific needs, e.g. Executive German, structured as follows:
   a. Solid undergraduate groundwork in basic grammar, vocabulary, and culture.

     b. Introduction to business terms, concepts, and practices as needed for translation, oral interpretation, document evaluation, and active company representation, e.g., at industrial fairs.

     c. Development of skills in the consultation of reference materials and current periodicals.

     d. Experiential learning (traineeship) with an international company at least during the semester interim.

2. German Studies programs which will incorporate the following topics on the German speaking countries:
     a. Anthropology
     b. Foreign Affairs
     c. History
     d. International Education
     e. Law
     f. Philosophy
     g. Political Science
     h. Sociology

Whatever lies within the competence of the departmental faculty should be taught in the German department. Where this is not possible, faculty from other departments should become involved in either the teaching of the courses or in aiding the German Department faculty in the design of independent study units.

3. Interdepartmental programs which could combine *one* other subject with German, e.g. Chemistry and German, or some of the areas specified in the preceding list of career options.

4. Design of (a) language courses to include such skills as writing a business letter, reading business journals and materials dealing with such areas as politics and *Bildungsreform*; (b) culture or *Landeskunde* courses which utilize the available information from the German Information Center, Goethe Institute and Inter Nationes, and which must include, like the German Studies programs, information on all German speaking areas.

5. Design of learning activity packages (LAPs) for self-paced and individualized study. The possibilities inherent in such LAPs are numerous; they can also be designed in conjunction with the agencies mentioned in 4b and exchanged among institutions. One such project in conjunction with the AATG and the Goethe Institute is presently under way. But once the information has been gathered and structured it can easily be adapted for student use. The use of packets of materials is efficient in terms of faculty time, once the initial development has been completed. These packages

can deal with:
    a.   a specific subject matter area.
    b.   aspects related to a specific occupation

6.   Expansion and/or restructuring of existing overseas studies or
     Junior Year Abroad programs to include academic areas in fields
     other than German. There are presently a number of such programs
     conducted by universities. Returning students should conduct in-
     formal sessions with students from other departments to dis-
     seminate information. The "publicity value" of such experiences
     must be fully utilized.

7.   Design of overseas programs for graduate students in fields other
     than German. Possibilities for funds available for this purpose must
     be explored and utilized.

8.   Design of competency-based programs which specifically state the
     competencies necessary for a given career and also state the "en-
     abling activities" of course clusters, offered in the German Depart-
     ment and other appropriate departments. (The fact that most
     departments are presently concerned about declining enrollments
     works in our favor and increases the probability that other depart-
     ments would agree to participate in this type of program design.)

9.   Design of German courses for businessmen, scientists and other
     interested members of the community under the auspices of Con-
     tinuing Education Programs.

Universities and secondary schools should be encouraged to establish a clearing
house for their programs, courses and packages designed to meet career needs at
individual institutions and schools.

The approaches suggested above constitute only some of the possibilities
open to us. Much of what has been said has been stated in the professional
literature since 1970. Yet the response we have seen has been minimal and
limited in concept and effect. Self-preservation now dictates that we *must*
respond immediately. The 1974 Bureau of Labor Statistics revised edition of
Occupational Manpower and Training Needs indicates that the oversupply of
secondary school teachers will have reached crisis proportions between the years
1980–85. The picture does not look better for positions on the college and
university levels. Obviously the universities will be directly effected by this and
can no longer assume the responsibility to train an oversupply of future teachers
and professors. At the same time, it can be predicted that there will be a great
need for professionals who combine a degree in their field with a degree in or
knowledge of a foreign language, and German specifically. As a result and in
order to remain a viable contributor to American education and society, and in
order to serve the economic future of our students, the German teaching
profession must be aware of these trends and train students for alternate career
options.

GERMAN STUDIES: THE WOMAN'S PERSPECTIVE*

RUTH K. ANGRESS
University of Virginia

The first question I need to ask before speaking of the woman's perspective on German Studies is whether the subject is at all legitimate. It is not like the New Left and the Comparative perspectives, for these are freely chosen intellectual points of view. And it is not like the American perspective which, as Sammons so forcefully points out (see pp. 17–23), involves the very function *of Auslandsgermanistik.* When we talk of *the* woman's perspective of the field, we are skirting prejudice, for is there not the danger of implying that women must necessarily turn out to be different literary scholars from men? To make the point clearer, I should like to offer an analogy from a realm of ethnic prejudice where our thinking has evolved to a higher degree of sophistication and self-consciousness than in matters pertaining to women: how would you feel about "The Jewish perspective on German Studies"? Are there not suggestions of antisemitic overtones and undercurrents in such a heading? Does it not suggest exclusion, an intellectual ghetto? In any case, one would hesitate to put the Jewish perspective in the same category as these others, even though among our numerous Jewish colleagues there can hardly be a single one who has not given some thought to what his Jewishness does to his perception of German culture.

Let me pursue this analogy a little. Sartre describes an antisemitic schoolboy's feeling that his Jewish classmate who receives higher grades in French literature still does not and cannot understand Racine with the same sort of intuitive grasp as the non-Jewish French boy. For it is not the Jew's birthright to understand this literature. It was not *his* ancestors who produced it. In such a view, the Jewish perspective is superficial, clever perhaps, but not drenched with the right emotions, perhaps corrosive, certainly uncreative.

This view of Jewish literary abilities is now unfashionable, but it is uncannily similar to the widespread feeling that relegates women's insights to the domain of the unsolid, clever perhaps, but also fluffy and ultimately lacking in a true understanding of the masculinity that is the motive force of works written by men. A woman's understanding is axiomatically taken to be more shallow

*This paper was delivered as a talk to the MLA Germanic Section in San Francisco, 28 December 1975.

than that of a less gifted colleague who has the advantage of a shared sex with the author under study.

Now if by "woman's perspective" any such exclusionary principle is implied, then the subject is indeed a non-subject and you could no more expect a woman to talk about it than you could expect a Jew to talk about his basic and inherent inability to deal with Christian symbolism. But neither Jews nor women nor, for that matter, blacks can be said to have a special view of literature automatically theirs because of their Jewishness, their womanhood, their négritude. One of the joys of reading books is precisely that we transcend our personal background and consent to take on the author's point of view. I believe it was Ralph Ellison who pointed out that when he read *Huckleberry Finn* as a boy it never occurred to him to identify with Nigger Jim who was quite remote from the blacks he knew: like all children, and this includes girls, he identified with Huck. Female children assume the male perspective which most books offer them, and they have no difficulty continuing to do so when they grow up. The difficulty lies rather in pulling away from that perspective. Similarly, Jewish readers have no trouble assuming the Christian or quasi-Christian view of most of Western literature.

Clearly, however, I would not have started on the subject if there was no more to be said on it. For having established that the understanding of a work of literature is not contingent on the similarity of the reader's and the author's background (one of those truisms that needs to be reiterated once in a while), we can now go on to say that a special group may indeed bring its special experiences to bear on literature and thereby contribute substantially to the understanding of some works and their background. Yet in all cases the added insights must be accessible to all readers, though the interpreter's background may have helped sensitize him to his discoveries. In this sense, as a contributory and not as an exclusive property, there is a woman's perspective as there is a Jewish perspective.

The simplest example of exercising it is to withdraw the consent of which I spoke. A Jew reading *Soll und Haben* will soon disagree with its author and end up disliking the book. That is easy enough. There are other, more complex cases where he may be in a good position to question certain specifically Christian assumptions which the author presents as universals. The analogy to women is obvious: our literature is permeated with unexamined premises regarding the relation of women to men, to society, even to God. Women *are* in a better position than men to ask questions about these assumptions though they have to learn to do so, since until recently they would not even have questioned the most questionable of Freudian assumptions.

Thus we may postulate that as female Germanists we are in a sense outsiders with the outsider's sensitivities, *if* we choose to use this particular perspective. For it is neither our exclusive birthright nor is it our only birthright. I believe that my Jewish background makes me particularly sensitive to *Blut and Boden* rhetoric, and I tend to find it where others tend to overlook it. But I am surely not the only teacher who has gleefully pointed out to a class that an apparently objective and technical book like Kayser's *Kleine Deutsche Versschule* may contain stylistically contaminated passages, such as: "Die vierhebige Zeile als Ordnungseinheit liegt uns seit germanischer Zeit im Blute."[1] Similarly, as a woman I am less inclined to overlook such passages as the following on Droste-Hülshoff from a standard work on nineteenth-century literature: "Sie war nach Albrecht Schaeffers schönem Wort, eine Pallas, jungfräulich und erfinderisch, eine jungfräuliche Frau, die alle Kunst der Welt und ewigen Ruhm ohne Laut hingegeben hätte für zwei Augenblicke, die ihr unbekannt blieben: den einen, wo sie Liebe empfing, den anderen wo sie Liebe gebar."[2] Irrelevant metaphor on the one hand, biography in the subjunctive on the other: both are objectionable by accepted standards, and sensitivity to prejudice may help us pinpoint them.

The mention of women authors brings up the inevitable question: who are they? Nowadays when we are often asked to do a course on women authors, we have to face up to the deplorable fact that in German we simply do not have as sizable a body of first-rate works by women as English or French does. A course on German women writers would presuppose on the part of the students an interest in such diverse and hermetic writers as Mechthild von Magdeburg and Ingeborg Bachmann. It *can* be done, sure, but it is not the same as getting up a course on Jane Austen, the Brontë sisters, George Eliot, and Virginia Woolf. And there is, let's face it, a limit to what can be done with *Die Judenbuche.* So far I have not seen my way to doing a course of this kind. Perhaps I can do a seminar on some *modern* women, such as Lasker-Schüler, Langgässer, Bachmann, and Aichinger. But again the Jewish analogy may provide a warning: who would want to teach Heine and Kafka together because of their shared faith (or non-faith) in Judaism? In other words, women authors do not automatically form an entity, least of all in our literature.

But if women's studies are not easily accomodated in the *Germanistik* curriculum, there are some other things that we should be ready to do. One is to clean up or at least object audibly to the sexist inanities which riddle our secondary literature and of which the quote on Droste was just one glaring example. The same goes for our language textbooks, which are a sink of sexism. If you have to use a grammar where the hostess pours coffee and the men talk politics, where the *Student* wants to become a scholar and the *Studentin* wants to get married, correct the picture, reverse the adjectives, treat the text as an object for study, as a source book of stereotypes. (The students will love it because it jolts them out of rote learning.)

Yet the main task, and what the near future will surely bring, is a body of

---

[1] Wolfgang Kayser, *Kleine deutsche Versschule,* 9th ed., Dalp Taschenbücher (Bern: Francke Verlag, 1962) p. 23.

[2] Ernst Alker, *Die deutsche Literatur im 19. Jahrhundert (1832–1914)* 2nd ed. (Stuttgart: Kröner, 1962) p. 386.

feminist criticism. This will not only involve a reevaluation of women writers and the social background that allowed them to be creative, but it should ultimately give us a consistent view of how the literary presentation of women reflects not the lives of women and not even their aspirations but rather the wish fulfillment and fear projections of their male creators, from Wolfram's Condwiramurs to Dürrenmatt's Claire Zachanassian. To do this will take subtlety, a great deal of knowledge, and a little more than general cries of outrage. For while feminist criticism is regarded with suspicion in many quarters, we should not make it so easy for ourselves as to ascribe this suspicion solely to the entrenched male chauvinism of the profession. The truth is that we haven't even begun to do the job.

Take a medieval example. Everyone knows that Siegfried beats his wife, and the pertinent lines in the *Nibelungenlied* usually get a facetious comment on how reality intrudes on the chivalric code. It is taken for granted that the code cannot accomodate wife beating, and that there is an inconsistency between the earlier and the later treatment which Kriemhild receives. But she herself does not think so, and I think it can be shown that there is no such inconsistency, just as the raping of peasant women was not contrary to the veneration of aristocratic women, as we know on the excellent authority of Andreas Capellanus. Exalting and abusing women are two sides of the same coin, something that medievalists like to forget, for the value of this particular coin changes considerably when we keep its two faces in mind. We have learned to do this when we read Victorian novels: the purity of middle-class womanhood appears to us in a different light when we think of the widespread acceptance of prostitution as part of the same package. But our sociological consciousness has not been sufficiently raised to perform an analogous task with the medieval *minne* concept. Incidentally, such a reevaluation might show that the poems of Neidhart are not so much a new departure and even less a debasement of the currency of chivalry but perhaps simply a different way of placing the chips.

Or, to take a problem from the eighteenth century: why does Schiller, who in some ways was as suspicious of women as agents as Nietzsche was, choose them as heroes for his tragedies? It was not an obvious thing to do, and it would be worthwhile to put together the various pronouncements on women in his work and try to make sense of the inconsistencies. Yet again, what about the sudden interest in matriarchy and related societal models which crops up in the nineteenth century, not only in Bachofen but in Kleist's *Penthesilea,* Grillparzer's *Libussa,* and Stifter's *Brigitta,* an admittedly unorthodox constellation of works which may yield interesting results? These are not problems where it helps to have an axe to grind: they are distinctly non-axe-grinding questions. They call for some courage but mostly for an ability to make literary, sociological, and psychological distinctions.

On the other hand, if you want to be aggressive, there is work to be done in contemporary literature. I suggest that one of our younger colleagues (since they tend to be better axe grinders than we who were brought up in the co-opting fifties and earlier) write an article entitled "The Machismo of Günter Grass," which should be easy, obvious, and publishable and should deal with the pathetic chicks which this eminent contemporary habitually inflicts on his readers, and which are nothing but Biedermeier stereotypes under a patina of pornography. And why not tackle one of our more recent sacred cows, Brecht's portrayal of women? While it is not unjust to admire the vividness of his female characters and the sympathy which he often shows for them, it would also do no harm to point out that Brecht began his career with the familiar and pernicious position that rapists and sadists have irresistible sex appeal (*Dreigroschenoper, Baal*) and that in his later work he showed women almost exclusively as creatures with a golden heart and little rationality (Kattrin in *Mutter Courage,* Grusche in *Kreidekreis*), which is incidentally precisely the combination of qualities that causes the Young Comrade to be sentenced to death in *Die Maßnahme.* In other words, the woman's perspective can be a way of breaking away from a criticism dominated by *Nachvollziehen,* that ultimate consent which a reader may, but which a critic should not completely give to his author.

Finally, I should like to return once more to the Jewish analogy. I have a hunch, which does not quite amount to a theory, that Jewish characters in German postwar fiction and drama are treated with the same condescension as women. Jews are often shown as passive and pathetic victims with no sense of their past and future and only a confused, if any, capacity for grief and anger. Such characters can be found in the work of Zuckmayer, Grass, Walser, Hochhuth (all of them quite well-meaning, I am sure) and the same works show a related lack of purpose and reduction of the humanity of the woman characters. I think it would be very useful to work out such a connection, if I am indeed correct and it exists. For it would tend to show that different prejudices against different groups of human beings are after all made of the same cloth.

If feminist criticism will address itself to genuinely and generally interesting questions, it will soon cease to be peripheral. A "woman's perspective" will then become one of the Germanist's indispensable tools, whether that Germanist be male or female.

ON LEAVING EXILE:
AMERICAN *GERMANISTIK* IN ITS SOCIAL CONTEXT*

DAVID BATHRICK
University of Wisconsin–Madison

Periodic self-flagellation and reform have long been features of foreign language and literature study in this country. The army language program of the 1940's, the sputnik renaissance of 1957, the response to challenges of the student movement in the late sixties—all emerged at times of political and economic urgency and were directed to meet the alleged pragmatic needs of the day. The present "retooling" effort within *Germanistik* is no exception. Like all historic soul searchings, it emanates as much from the *social* realities of the moment as from any intrinsic spiritual awakening. There are no jobs.

And yet for all its familiarity, there is to be noted in the present discussion a decidedly more desperate—and I would also submit—more fundamental questioning look at the long-range values and practices at the heart of our profession. It is in the spirit of such questioning that I offer the following remarks.

In a certain sense American *Germanistik* has always been in a state of intellectual isolation, and recent reform measures tacitly and explicitly confirm this fact even as they attempt to transcend it. Behind the call for a relevant, cross-cultural, comparative, interdisciplinary, *kulturwissenschaftliche*, contemporary, practical German Studies lies *ex negativo* its beleaguered opposite: the literature-and-language-centered, monocultural, tradition-bound, proudly apolitical orientation which has been at the basis of our outlook for so long. Perhaps before we cast it aside, we should explore for a moment the historical experiences and traditions which have sustained such attitudes—to look at the implicit values underlying its assumptions about literature, about society, about German and American culture and the relations between them.

If, as Michael Pehlke tells us, the history of *Germanistik* in Germany is the ideological history of the German bourgeoisie in the nineteenth and twentieth century, what about *Germanistik im Ausland*?[1] What about it in this country?

---

*This is a revised version of a talk to the MLA Germanic Section in San Francisco, 28 December 1975.
[1] Michael Pehlke, "Aufstieg und Fall der Germanistik—von der Agonie einer bürgerlichen Wissenschaft," *Ansichten einer künftigen Germanistik* (München, 1969), pp. 18–44.

What are the ideological premises which constitute the underpinnings and institutional functioning of American *Germanistik* and more generally of the whole oddball enclave known as foreign language departments? Keeping in mind that any typology simplifies and flattens as it attempts to organize, let me offer the following generalization. At the intellectual heart of American *Germanistik* lie two forms of exile: that of the German emigrant and that of the American expatriate. The German emigrant has come to us for a variety of reasons and at different historical times. In the 1930's as refugees from Fascism, in the 1950's and again in the 1960's for both political and economic reasons. In all cases we have intellectuals who have found it necessary to leave their society, yet who for the most part continue to define their cultural and scholarly framework in relation to a world left behind. This relationship to the native culture has defined itself in both a positive and negative way. On the one hand, there is a continued effort by many native Germanists to legitimatize their work by publishing exclusively abroad in order to be validated and recognized by the powers there, regardless of any impact upon the intellectual and political community in which they function. Or on the other hand, this relationship can be a negative one: a reaction against the methodologies and values prevailing in Germany at a given time in an effort to preserve what are perceived to be more valuable practices and traditions from the past. In the thirties, exile scholars sought to confront the Fascist culture with an alternative tradition. Certainly the prevailing disdain among many Germanists here toward current attempts in West Germany to develop a socially critical Marxist study of literature represents another negative, essentially preserving response. While both kinds of reactions, the negative and the positive, may have provided important impulses for the study of German here and abroad, rarely has it involved a critical perspective nourished by and directed toward the social and intellectual concerns of the American society.

But are the American-born Germanists any more indigenous? Sadly, they are not—and in many cases, care even less to be so. While the impetus to study and teach *Germanistik* might define itself as an attempt to understand and mediate a foreign culture from one's own perspective, the results of this study as manifested in scholarly publications and traditional course offerings often do not reflect such interchange and mediation. The insistence by Americans upon recapitulating the monocultural version of nineteenth-century *Germanistik* represents a parody of—if not a capitulation to—this now alien tradition. Moreover, like their German-born colleagues, they measure achievement and prestige and define the areas of scholarly study either by the worst aspects of prevailing academic conservativism in the FRG or by a Germany which no longer exists. Concerning contemporary developments, the Americans are often as resistant to the politicizing process in Germany as they are to similar developments and questioning within their own society. Thus this symbiosis of outer and inner emigration has produced a strange enclave—one which exists necessarily apart from the culture which spawned it and is at the same time quite often estranged from the one in which it is embedded. With all their differences, the American and German Germanist in this country share a number of cultural attitudes which make them anomalies both here and in Germany.

The result has been a monumental failure to develop both a self-critical and socially critical field of study rooted in the needs and conflicts of American society. American *Germanistik* is founded upon separations: the study of literature separated from dialogue and interchange with related disciplines and the community around it; a notion of literature separate from the social matrix in which it is written and, just as importantly, in which it is received. At the core of these separations resides an elitist notion of culture not so very distant from that of Emerson or Henry James. Like the American expatriates who fled to Paris at the beginning of the century, the American enclaves for foreign study often tend to view themselves as defenders of high culture against the wasteland of what James himself once called a "vast crude democracy of trade." For many, culture is something to emulate because one has none of one's own; it is something to be exposed to, as an object of possession and emblem of social authenticity. Thus the study of the German classics as transmitted through the high priest of "Aura" becomes a one-way trip to the altar. The student and the scholar perform a kind of lobotomy on their own social history; they divest themselves of their sex, of their race, of their class, of their experience, of their loves and hates and enter into the sacred realm of cultural "appreciation." The result is a parody of the humanities: literature students unwilling and afraid to make value judgments because they have only been taught to interpret, i.e., understand; curricula which continue to hold on to an archaic canon unrelated *even* to the archaic canons of the Anglo-American tradition. To return to Michael Pehlke, the history of American *Germanistik* is an ideological history of intellectual alienation.

It is against this background of attitudes—the concept of *Kultur* in the old European sense of the word—that efforts have been undertaken both abroad and in this country to develop a "synoptic" view of German culture, one which would subordinate knowledge of the past to knowledge of the present, one based on what Louis Helbig has called "an American concept of culture" (see pp. 47–55). While such attempts represent a laudable effort to provide a more contemporary, totalistic concept of German Studies as the basis for a new *Germanistik,* in some cases they recapitulate unknowingly in their generalizations the same world view as the object of their attack.

It seems to me that any reorientation of our field should not lose sight of the deeper issues implied in the call for such. What we need now is not a redoctored curriculum "tailored" to the needs of immediate consumption, but a new *sense of culture* and our roles as transmitters of it. This would entail developing a concept of culture not as artifact of the past, oblivious of spatial and temporal reality; not as a mere derivative factor in human development, but—in the words of Stanley Aronowitz—"as an active *functional* force in the way people create and recreate their modes of existence."[2]

Such a stress on the *function* of culture would in turn force us to view our activities in relation to the global changes of the present era. The crisis of *Germanistik* is but part of the admitted helplessness of all humanistic sciences at a time of social upheaval in this country. The struggle of blacks for civil and economic justice, the Vietnam—and now possibly Angolan—war of intervention, the women's movement, Watergate, economic dislocation—all have helped tear the veil of legitimacy from the would-be liberal order; all have opened our eyes to the real nature of American capitalism and the myths which have grown up to sustain it. Within the study of literature this has meant a sensed bankruptcy of the professional and pedagogic practices *and* the literary models which have been our givens for so long. It has meant a search for new methodological starting points, for new metaphors of experience, for new ideals which would link us more *meaningfully* with the experiences of the past ten years; a search for methodologies which would present a real alternative to the ahistorical variations of new criticism; a search for practices and goals which would place our professional lives in a supportive rather than privileged relationship to working and third world peoples both within and outside of this country. What we need now is not a streamlined, business-school oriented, neutrally comparative "updated" *Germanistik* geared to reintegrating us as intellectuals into a continued service of the few at the expense of the many. What we need now is a *Germanistik* which will take seriously its claim of humanism by realizing that its present notion of humanistic study is located in an elitist concept of culture; one which will devote itself to breaking down those separations in every sphere of our activities as cultural workers.

The insight that a study of foreign culture should be rooted in larger social interests has led among other things to assaults upon the literary canon, both as canon and as literature. Calls for a study of popular literature, women's literature, working class literature, media-study, or literature of the GDR give vent to the frustration with a course of study too long mired in the interests of established norms of literary excellence. While such developments have provided important revisions, both about what we consider good as well as what we consider literature, they have in some instances led to obscuring the real issues. The problem is not only or even primarily what is being taught, but still *how* we teach it. Merely a shift in subject matter, while providing a kind of holding action of interest, can also help obfuscate or even postpone the more fundamental task of methodological reconsideration.

With this focus upon method let us return to the problem of exile and alienated labor. The isolated nature of *Germanistik* is, of course, not peculiar to foreign language study. If anything it represents in exaggerated form the quintes-

---

[2] Stanley Aronowitz, *False Promises* (New York, 1973), p. 118.

sence of intellectual labor within the academy as a whole. It is also self-evident that any reordering of priorities will not be accomplished simply by reforms within language and literature programs. Nevertheless, there are a number of ways in which those concerned with working toward more egalitarian and democratic practices within the field might begin collaborative efforts both in teaching and in our institutional relationships to bring about changes. With this in mind I offer the following points for consideration.

> 1. The development of an approach to German Studies which would question and overcome the notion of disciplines having differing and essentially incompatible epistemological bases. Up to now the concept of "interdisciplinary" has come to mean a coexistence or panel-of-experts approach to learning. Each expert injects willy-nilly a closed package of knowledge or information which then adds up to a giant *Nebeneinander* of unassimilated material. I would offer as an alternative a dialectical materialist approach. By this I mean a method which sees the prevailing separation of our disciplines not as ontological givens but as another form of social fragmentation; one which would seek from within existing disciplines the methodological means by which to reintegrate one's understanding of a subject into a totalizing historical process. This method would reject any notion of a "super"-discipline (economics, sociology) providing the basis for the study of literature. Rather, the starting point of exploration would be within the field of literature and with the concrete work itself. The process of linking the work to the larger political, philosophical, or social questions would be guided by the historical realities of the object under consideration.

> 2. A commitment to engage oneself as teacher and scholar in the efforts of working people to eliminate the class, sex, and race-founded dominations upon which high culture rests and which have made us perforce purveyors of that culture. This in turn means grasping the high-low dichotomy as ultimately a social and class-antagonistic one and putting aside notions of neutral, value-free, disinterested scholarship to direct one's institutional and scholarly work against the affirmative legitimizing forces which seek to maintain and promote these separations. Whether we wish to admit it or not, our view of Germany tells us as much about our own predilections and biases as about the object of scrutiny. Consider for instance the following description of "the German" which appeared recently in *Unterrichtspraxis* as a suggested view of German culture:

>> The German unconsciously assumes that he and his fellow men are integral parts of the universal order which functions in accordance with universal laws of nature ... the German has a pronounced feeling of belonging to the whole; he derives gratification and satisfies his ambi-

tion from the fact that he is a small but indispensible cog in a functioning machine. Work in a limited area of production gives him as much satisfaction as a position of leadership and arouses no bitterness as it does among the Poles.[3]

Needless to say, what we have here is not *the* German at all, but rather a world view of the male middle class German projected as an entire societal phenomenon. While obviously meaningless in their generality, such depictions are not uncommon and themselves reflect a view of society as devoid of social differences. Given the social upheavals in this country during the past years, would questions about contemporary Germans asked from the perspective of an increasingly critical younger generation permit the kind of view expressed in the above citation? I submit that they would not and I urge that we begin to look historically at that country *and* explore its literature from such a perspective.

    3. More concretely, I would urge that existing journals and organizations in *Germanistik* open themselves up to discussions around fundamental alternatives to prevailing practices and that those interested join organizationally to present their views, share experiences, carry out collective scholarship, etc. I would also urge that within the MLA and AATG more Germanists look to such organizations as the Marxist Literary Group, the Radical Caucus, Women in *Germanistik,* and *New German Critique* as institutional forums for exploring democratic alternatives to present teaching and scholarly practices.

Overcoming the elitism of our discipline will not be achieved simply by organization or bureaucratic fiat. We as teachers must be willing to engage ourselves in the intellectual and social issues outside our immediate communities. It is indeed ironic that the major interests which have sprung up in this country around such thinkers as Marcuse, Adorno, Enzensberger, Habermas, Hesse and, more recently, Leni Riefenstahl have occurred peripherally—often in spite of debates and undertakings in our field. Of course, to deal seriously with such materials will entail an approach to culture which will break down the methodological and institutional barriers within which we presently operate. It will first of all involve an exploration of areas heretofore considered neighboring disciplines, such as history, philosophy, film, sociology, etc., which in turn will mean an end to literature-centered studies of culture. It will also entail making value judgments. The concern for an Adorno, or a Hesse, or a Riefenstahl has arisen from social and political interests within this society. In leaving exile, we must be able to confront such interests as contrary or consonant with our own—and to take sides.

[3] Royal L. Tinsley, jr. and David J. Woloshin, "Approaching German Culture: A Tentative Analysis," *Die Unterrichtspraxis* 7:1 (1974), pp. 126–7.

THE ORGANIZATIONAL STRUCTURE OF THE PROFESSION

FRANK G. RYDER
University of Virginia

Principles and goals, even if we agree upon them, do not automatically identify the specific steps we should take to serve them. They do narrow the range of choices for the responsible observer, eliminating some paths as digressions. Reminding ourselves of principles which age has withered or custom staled, we may become aware that we have been doing things we should not have done, or leaving undone certain things we should have been doing.

If this is a surfeit of maxims and clichés it is also a kind of necessary corrective to muddling, and the message that follows is couched in just such terms, that is, in generalities to which I hope the profession may reply with specifics. I do not imply that the answers I prefer are the only ones for a right-thinking Germanist; in some cases I see no cause to identify preferred courses of action.

Lest I be accused of feigning impartiality, I will admit candidly that I find our profession to differ even from its closest fraternity, the modern literature and language associations, in two seemingly contradictory respects, and in these respects to be in need of particular self-examination. The first way in which we are exceptional is in the complexity and magnitude of our organizational structures, budgets, services, activities. The second lies in what I see, perhaps mistakenly, as a degree of corporate malaise.

If the second point is subjective and open to disagreement, the first is a well-attested (if not simple) fact. Comparing the AATG with the MLA, on the basis of the last published reports of both organizations, reveals a striking disparity. The 1975 membership totals for the AATG as of August were 7,258; of MLA as of February, 30,399. For the year ending August 31, 1974 the two organizations reported actual expenditures (apart from contract grants) as follows: AATG $529,588; MLA $1,470,631. The AATG, with fewer than one-fourth the membership of the MLA, spends over one-third as much. This difference amounts to more than it sounds. If the AATG had had to get along on the same per capita basis as the MLA, it would have had barely $350,000 to spend, not almost $530,000. If the MLA could have spent as we do, it would have disbursed not $1,470,000 but almost $2,220,000 (and its financial troubles would be over). Most of the customary variables and indeterminacies only serve to exaggerate the difference. Noteworthy among them is the fact that MLA lists

$152,086 for rents, while the favorable relationship of the AATG to the National Park Service results in a total expense for "buildings" of only $28,609.

If we reduce the basic figures to expenditures per member, the disparity is even more obvious. Including rent and buildings, the MLA spends $48.39, per member per year, the AATG $72.94. Apart from rent and buildings, the figures are $42.07 and $69.00. In other words the AATG spends on each of us 150% (or 164%) of what the MLA spends on each of its members.

I can only conclude that in its organizational aspect our profession is relatively well endowed. Wealth, they say, doesn't produce happiness, but in a reasonably unified organizational context, where money and effort produce results and results usually satisfy people, any substantial distress would seem paradoxical. It is incumbent on every observer in such a moot domain to admit subjectivity and invite contradiction, but it is also fair—even necessary—to *make* a subjective assessment of the degree to which members, particularly those most "involved," are satisfied with our organizational structures. Because ultimately each member's attitude, as much as his reason, determines his vote. Le coeur a ses raisons. I don't know how to put my own judgment most constructively, but I do sense greater malaise, in quarters I respect, than would seem consonant with our *relative* fiscal health.

Assuming that readers are willing to contemplate at least the possibility of a paradox here, or are simply interested in a reexamination of principles and goals as an activity useful from time to time, I should like to list certain propositions I take to be axiomatic and suggest for some of them the range of choices indicated by the acceptance of such axioms.

1. *The organizational structure of a teaching and scholarly profession is an ancillary device and not an end in itself.* The only way to decide whether at any given moment we have transgressed this delicate boundary is to examine the magnitude of the operation at the various "headquarters" (chapters, state associations, AAT's, etc.) compared to the services rendered and the clientele served. At one extreme is homely austerity, the shirt-sleeved campus office with part of a secretary. It costs less and is worth it. At its best it condemns us to amiable formalities and Chipsian gentility. Paradoxically, it may also represent a subtle form of personality cult, anxious and isolated, apprehensive of change, a narrow bastion of lean and hungry egos. Even in its impoverishment, it is an eccentric luxury we can ill afford. At the other extreme, the professional association can become so elaborate as to transcend its natural mission, turning into a kind of more or less benign tumor with little functional attachment and no benefit to the body of which it was once a part, multiplying itself pointlessly and independently, constituting its own purpose and seeing its own continuity and welfare as a self-evident, not a contingent goal. The phenomenon is familiar enough in the college or high school administration. Poorly functioning or alienated administrations tend in the former direction, efficiently functioning and aggressive ones in the latter. Both cease to serve and become self-serving.

2. *Benefits to the membership must be proportionate to the effort ex-pended and the financial support generated.* Corollary to the foregoing this implies an organizational structure which serves as a funnel, not as a reservoir, whose aim is to get the largest proportion of accruing income out into specific services in the fastest way and with the least attrition en route. Obviously, some of this process can only be served by augmentation of staff, but the danger is familiar: most healthy organisms like to grow. Yet the health of the larger organism must limit the size of any of its parts.

In this sense, one must inevitably ask, and ask regularly, questions concerning the magnitude of administrative structures and costs. Such questions may well be uncomfortable, as we all know from college faculty sessions examining college administrations. I remember a colleague at an institution of mine who, extrapolating from the five year period just passed, showed by line graphs that in the foreseeable future our institution would have three administrators for each faculty member. This did not happen—and the observation was regarded as latently hostile. I fear that in the groves of academe and their professional copses, we are singularly apt to take umbrage at any inquiry into our budgetary legitimacy, but we should be as prepared for such examinations as government agencies must be prepared for congressional committees of inquiry. In charitable organizations, after all, even the IRS has had to intervene when too much of the income was applied to headquarters operations and never turned into the right kind of "outgo."

3. *An academic community neither deserves nor should have imposed upon it a professional organization more complex than it can comprehend.* It is of course incumbent particularly upon the latter to make itself more comprehensible to the former and some professional hierarchies are relatively adept at this educational function. The natural tendency of any group is to generalize from its own familiarity with what it is doing—and its sense that this activity is a right and proper thing, sanctioned somewhere in Heaven—therefore to assume that the entire electorate has a pretty good picture of the mission and of course approves of it. That this is not so becomes apparent at many annual meetings.

4. *Members of any governing or policy-making board must have sufficient competence, time, information, and facilities to oversee intelligently the activities of the executive, without being rushed or swamped.* The more energetic the executive branch, the more this proposition holds, a statement which is made without animus. Strong presidents nationally need strong cabinets and strong legislatures. It takes less effort to keep a turtle on the right path than to do the same for a tiger. No one wants to hitch his star to a turtle; we would all prefer to have our show run by the metaphoric "tiger," but our representatives may have to be smarter than Honorio and more patient than Pankraz.

5. *The executive or administrative segment of a national society must have unmediated familiarity with the collective personality, the traditions and mode of operations, the accepted aims of the profession it serves.* This may not

constitute a preemptive reason for selecting as principal executive officer a member of the profession itself, though such a person apparently represents the most obvious choice for the MLA and related organizations. Probably a teacher or professor is able better and with surer instincts to apprehend the mood of the discipline, other things being equal. But other things are rarely equal and it is quite imaginable that the more deeply involved one is in teaching and scholarship, the less likely one is to abandon these and take up the administrative gauntlet. Or equally imaginable that a dedicated person from "outside" would see weaknesses and delusions with which almost all members of the profession have tacitly and innocently made a sort of peace by compromise. What is needed is a nice balance of administrative savoir faire, academic competence, and that jargon (but real) virtue, drive. What is to be eschewed is an executive echelon made up entirely of persons outside the field, or one built solely on *academic* abilities, whether in scholarship or in teaching.

6. *The executive staff has only one locus of loyalty: the professional organization it serves; entangling alliances are unthinkable.* All members of national staffs, academics or otherwise, enter into a position of trust and exclusive loyalty, a kind of temporary marriage which involves "forsaking all others," neither carrying into the job old connections nor cultivating new ones which foster undue advantage. The principle is not unique to associations of our kind; it is a general concept of legality, comprehended under its negative rubric, conflict of interest. This issue was raised, rightly or wrongly, by the AATG Management Study Committee years ago, in urging the utmost caution in the developing of plans for any private or profit-making organization.

7. *The executive officers and their staff should consistently be seekers of counsel more often than purveyors of it.* No teacher, no scholar, no school administrator is infallible, but the collective wisdom of our most thoughtful and experienced people at secondary and college level is the best guidance we now have or ever will have, and any professional organization will prosper to the degree that it embodies—or seeks out—this kind of wisdom and applies it for the advancement of the profession. In a negative but still vitally important sense: Any time the executive body begins to feel alienated from, irritated by, or impatient with respected members of the profession, it should examine carefully where the fault may lie and speedily seek to remedy the situation. This is *not* to say that all initiative must be taken or all fault shouldered by headquarters. Academic persons can be arbitrary and capricious, but they are essential to our task and a good headquarters is only desirable. We do not have room for any facsimile of those governing boards or administrators of colleges, for example, who regard the faculty with mild horror or with condescension or apprehension.

8. *Until and unless the Constitution is amended, those functions mandated by the Constitution deserve a certain priority of effort and budget,* or speaking in the defensive vocabulary of our particular season, a certain protection from budget cuts. This is not to say that the *German Quarterly,* the *Unterrichtspraxis,*

and other publications must remain in full flower even if all else falls to the ground, but it would seem on the one hand ironical if with greater and greater resources these activities should remain at a constant level of funding and thus be progressively dwarfed by others, however desirable in themselves. Nor on the other hand does it mean that all functions must grow at a forever proportionate rate. This could conceivably mean a monthly *GQ* complete with gossip column. No less untenable however is the opposite absurdity: in less affluent years a proportional reduction in expenditures across the board, say a 50 per cent cut in all activities, whether constitutionally mandated or not.

9. *Whenever there is a choice between stimulation from afar and physically present aid, between supporting the effort of individual members and local groups to do something and doing things* for *them, the administration of a professional society should choose the former.* Unquestionably this will engender a great deal of slippage, an at times dizzying variety of responses to what seems the same challenge, and much frustration. But it will keep the grass roots growing, and the resources and numbers "out there" are, compared to any conceivable or tolerable headquarters, inexhaustible. What is inexhaustible in a headquarters is the number of things an ingenious administrator can think up to do for people, and the corps of assistants and deputies he or she might need for this purpose. If we are willing to be imaginatively paranoid we can picture an AAT gradually centralizing the choice of readings, systematizing methodology, prescribing curricula and sending out model teachers from the HQ staff or broadcasting homogenized audio-visual courses. But each advance from this quarter risks a certain stultifying of effort and originality in the electorate, and ultimately not even God can help those who will not help themselves.

In this light our own special development, during the last decade, of chapter activities and initiative has been exemplary, while other aspects of national staffing and policies may well have erred toward debilitating centralization.

10. *The aggregate of the organizational aspects of our profession should be so comprehensive (which is not to say: massive) that every significant relationship we bear to our environment is covered by some entity or facility which expresses our influence and our legitimate aims.* In point of fact we are rather well off in most such domains, and it will not hurt to recapitulate. The full spectrum of teachers and instructional levels from elementary grades to graduate school is represented in the AATG. We *can* communicate with one another. Our total geographical setting and therefore our relationship each of his particular region is covered by chapters, and the structure of chapters is flexible enough so that new crystallizations of geographical focus can be dealt with by new entities. "Foreign relations," our ties with other languages, are dealt with by ACTFL and by the Joint National Committee. The special interests of students find expression—more than in other languages—in the NFSG, through the *Rundschau*, etc. Our ties with the government of the Federal Republic are manifested in and governed by the ACGS, which serves the important and delicate function of

securing benefit and cooperation without surrendering control. By its origin and special structure it may not be able to perform the same function vis-à-vis Austria and Switzerland but perhaps a way could and should be found to do so. The beginnings at least of a beneficial relationship with American business and industry may lie in the work of the ACGS and the NCSA, but this is an area that needs further development and more organizational effort.

Other avenues of logical relationships are largely unexplored, so much so that mentioning them may even come as a kind of cultural shock. As delicate yet as necessary to our interests as the tie with the FRG is the potential tie with our own government, both at the Federal level and in the states. With what specific voice do we speak on FL matters to the HEW? Who is our liaison with the State Boards of Education? More serious by far is the dearth of contact with those mysterious forces which could arrange the offering of our subject in high schools and two-year colleges (the only growing segment of American education—one where German is *not* growing)—or which could preclude or terminate it. In almost all cases the center of responsibility is probably local and thus variable: in boards, principals, PTA's, deans, chairmen, depending on the place and the institution. But where is *our* source of advice and experience in the care and fostering of administrative beneficence, *our* handy kit of proven persuaders? Specifically for German, it is painfully true that unless we expand our beachhead in the high schools and at least make a modest incursion into the junior and community college curriculum, the welfare of our college and university programs and of the degree holders who come from them will be permanently jeopardized.

Finally, in an area about which I am particularly sensitive: how are we in German (or French or any other FL) represented in the councils of our own institutions? Jeffrey Sammons writes elsewhere in this volume (pp. 17–23) of our invisibility in another context. For related reasons we also tend to be invisible in the arenas where local policy is fought out, and if the price of not figuring in the collective life of the American Scholar is that we are ignored or thought of little consequence, the price of not figuring in policy decisions at our own institution lies somewhere between second-class citizenship and slow death.

By coincidence we have reached the magic number of ten, and if these items are not commandments they are at least rubrics for self-examination. Any one of us who is alive and means to stay that way should consider our existing structures, to see how well they serve our purposes and how, in accordance with the results of that examination, to protect existing functions, or to support change, or to create anew.*

---

*This essay was written while organizational changes in our profession were under consideration or in progress. It does not purport to reflect or assess those developments.

Library of Congress Cataloging in Publication Data

Main entry under title:
German studies in the United States
    (Monatshefte occasional volume; no. 1)
    Includes bibliographical references.
    1. German philology–Study and teaching–United
States–Addresses, essays, lectures. I. Lohnes,
Walter F. W. II. Nollendorfs, Valters. III. Series.
PF3068.U6G4   430'.07'1073   76-13346
ISBN 0-299-97009-4
ISBN 0-299-97010-8 pbk.